IMAGES
of America

MADISON, NORRIDGEWOCK, AND SMITHFIELD

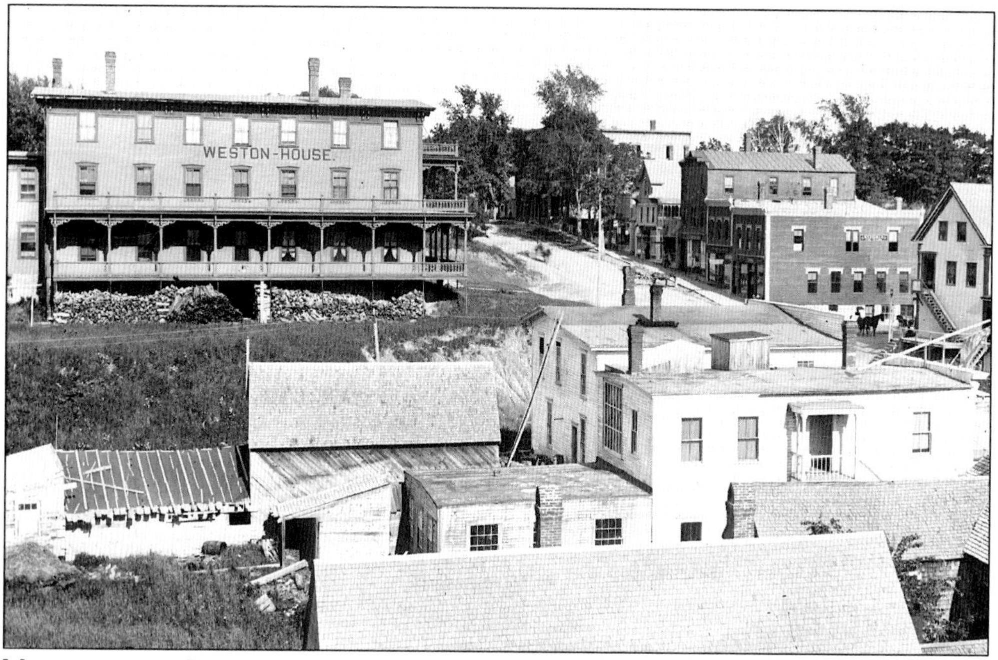

MADISON IN THE LATE 1800s AND EARLY 1900s. The town was a flourishing community. A woolen mill had started up in 1881, and a pulp and paper mill soon followed. The Weston House, rear left, was often full. Madison has been relatively prosperous ever since.

IMAGES
of America

MADISON, NORRIDGEWOCK, AND SMITHFIELD

Frank Sleeper

ARCADIA
PUBLISHING

ISBN 978-0-7385-6444-9

Published by Arcadia Publishing
Charleston SC, Chicago IL, Portsmouth NH, San Francisco CA

Printed in the United States of America

Library of Congress Catalog Card Number: 2008940201

For all general information contact Arcadia Publishing at:
Telephone 843-853-2070
Fax 843-853-0044
E-mail sales@arcadiapublishing.com
For customer service and orders:
Toll-Free 1-888-313-2665

Visit us on the Internet at www.arcadiapublishing.com

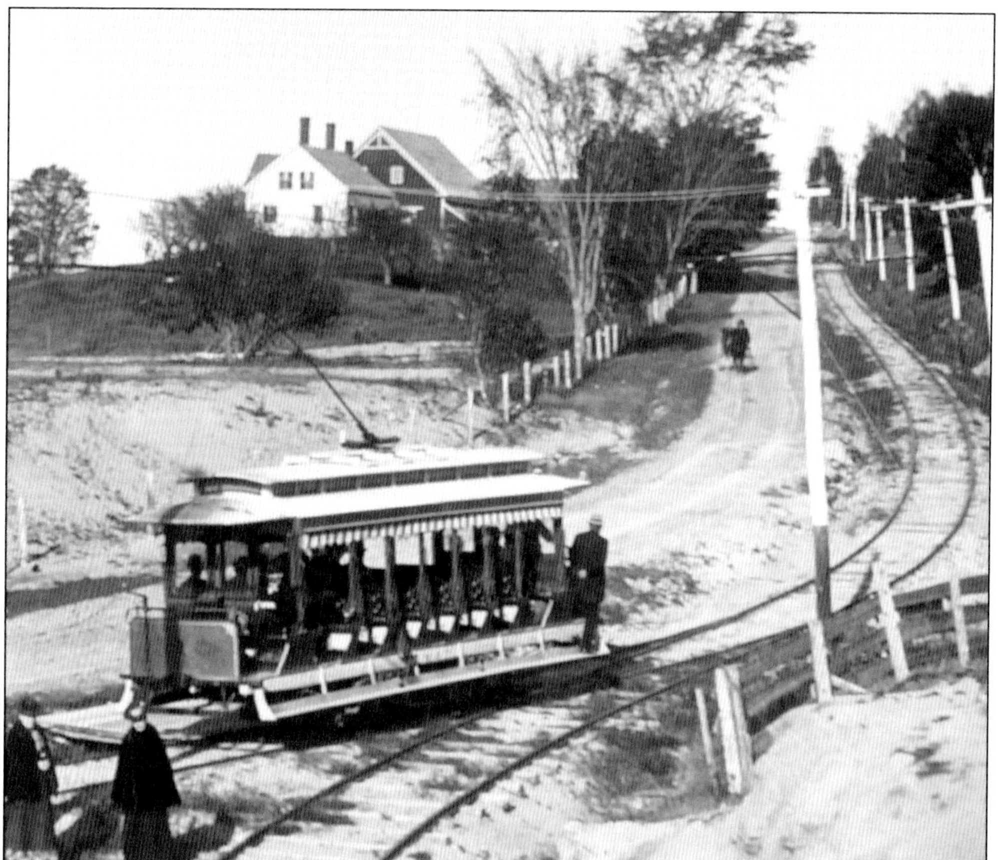

TROLLEY IN SOUTH NORRIDGEWOCK AROUND THE TURN OF THE CENTURY. The trolley is located at the bottom of the hill leading up to Isaac Morse's home. A horse and buggy comes down the hill. Two ladies stand at the left, while a man stands on the edge of the trolley.

Contents

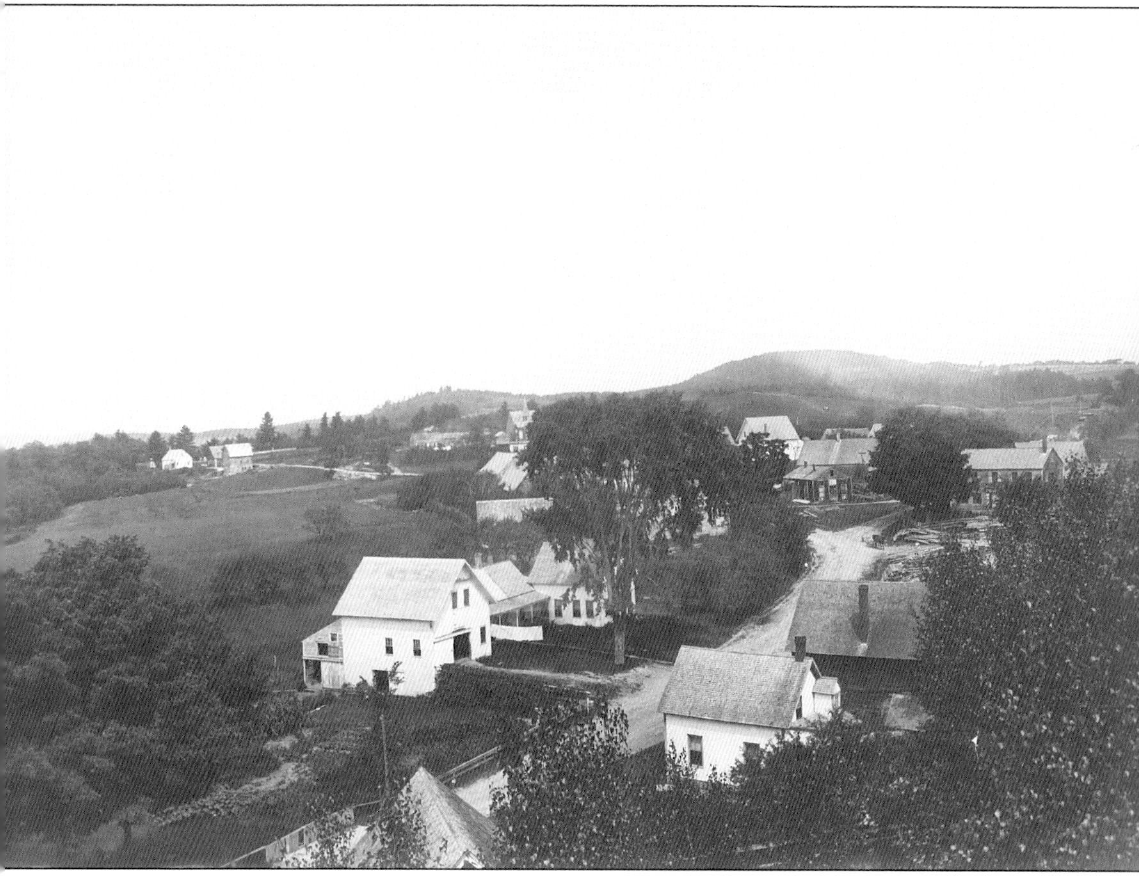

Smithfield Village About 1910. The logs on the right go with a sawmill that is not shown because it is located farther on the right (outside the view of the camera). Fred T. Stevens's blacksmith shop is the third building on the right. The village store is the large building behind the trees. The road, which is presently Route 8, was built in 1823. In the left rear is the village school, which is across from the cemetery's fence. The Hartford house is still there. Finally, the Smithfield Baptist Church was built in 1897.

Introduction

Just west of Skowhegan, in a scenic central Maine area, lies Madison, home of the pulp and paper mill that now makes, among other things, the paper used in the Sunday rotogravure section of the *New York Times*. It's perhaps not too strange that this mill, which over its 100 years plus of existence has known all sorts of ups and downs, is now half owned by the *Times* and half by a Finnish company, Myllykoski Oy. Look back at 1881. That's the year Madison became a manufacturing town, as a woolen company started operations there. The waterpower from the Kennebec River attracted the company. The town has flourished ever since. Recently announced was an $11.5 million chemical plant, which would be operated by a different company but tied in with the pulp and paper mill through the products made.

Eight miles south of Madison is Norridgewock, from the Native American words meaning the "quiet place" in the river, in this case, of course, the Kennebec. For Norridgewock, the date to remember is 1872. That's the year the community lost its position as county seat of Somerset County to Skowhegan. Many of the fine, old homes in Norridgewock are reminders of the days when Somerset County came to that town. Norridgewock lost some of its population after 1872 for a good number of years. Now, however, like Madison, it has been showing good growth. With its historical society, historical calendars, and several antique shops, this town lays an emphasis on history that is equaled by very few other Maine communities. Norridgewock really cares about its past.

Smithfield lies 6 miles south of Norridgewock. Smallest of the three communities, this town of less than 1,000 feels that it is "on the edge of things," as its bicentennial book says, or "out of things" as one of its residents told me. As long as the town contains beautiful North Pond, I don't think Smithfield has to worry about all that. This community is not left out. For years, North Pond has been the place where many of those from Madison and Norridgewock have their summer cottages. The village's location reminds me a bit of Monticello on Route 1 in Aroostook County with a hill on either side. And after losing population just as Norridgewock did over many years in the late nineteenth and early twentieth centuries, the town's population will have almost doubled between 1970 and 2000. Its famous waterslide no longer exists, but Smithfield remains the recreation center for the three communities covered. One big difference is that the Kennebec River does not pass through Smithfield as it does through Madison and Norridgewock. Thus, the town had no waterpower for mills and factories. But it did have North Pond with restful surroundings.

Family life is very important in the three towns. We focus on two of those families here. One is the Parker family of Norridgewock, who have been in the area since 1770 (except for a brief time during the Revolutionary War) and were owners of a large dairy farm most of those years. The dairy farm has closed, as have many others in the area. Norridgewock and the other two communities were once well known for their dairy farms and were considered one of Maine's centers for such farming. Now, only a few dairy farms remain. The other family is the Harris-Everett family with some of its offshoots. The Harrises and the Everetts were relatively late comers to these three communities and were centered in Norridgewock. Photos show us farm life in the case of both families, with a bit more emphasis on life in the town on the Harris-Everett side. Did you know that the Dole family of Hawaiian pineapple fame had direct ancestors in Norridgewock? I assume most know that the monument to Father Sebastian Rasle, Catholic missionary to the Native Americans and killed by the British in a massacre, is in Norridgewock.

This was frontier territory right up until after the Revolution. As a result, communities weren't incorporated until later than those farther south in Maine. When the great migrations from Maine to the West took many of this state's best people in the late nineteenth and early twentieth centuries, Norridgewock and Smithfield were hurt like many towns in the state. Madison, because of its woolen and paper mills, did not suffer as badly. These are quiet towns, where life is generally peaceful. Farming was the chief mode of life until the woolen mill opened in Madison in 1881. The sections on family life show how people adjusted to a relatively predictable existence on the farm. With the advent of the train and the automobile, life became less predictable. Now, Smithfield, for example, has become somewhat of a bedroom community for Waterville, Oakland, Skowhegan, Madison, and Norridgewock. The population advances recently in both Madison and Norridgewock show they may also be moving toward the bedroom community label, though Madison, with its paper mill, will always have a nucleus of people living in the town and also working there.

One would have to think of Maine rural towns like these three as communities where there was relative peace, hard work, and survival. They are probably representative of Maine rural life in the late nineteenth and early twentieth centuries. Take a look at them through the photographs in this book and you are taking a look at life in rural Maine in general.

Frank H. Sleeper

One

Madison

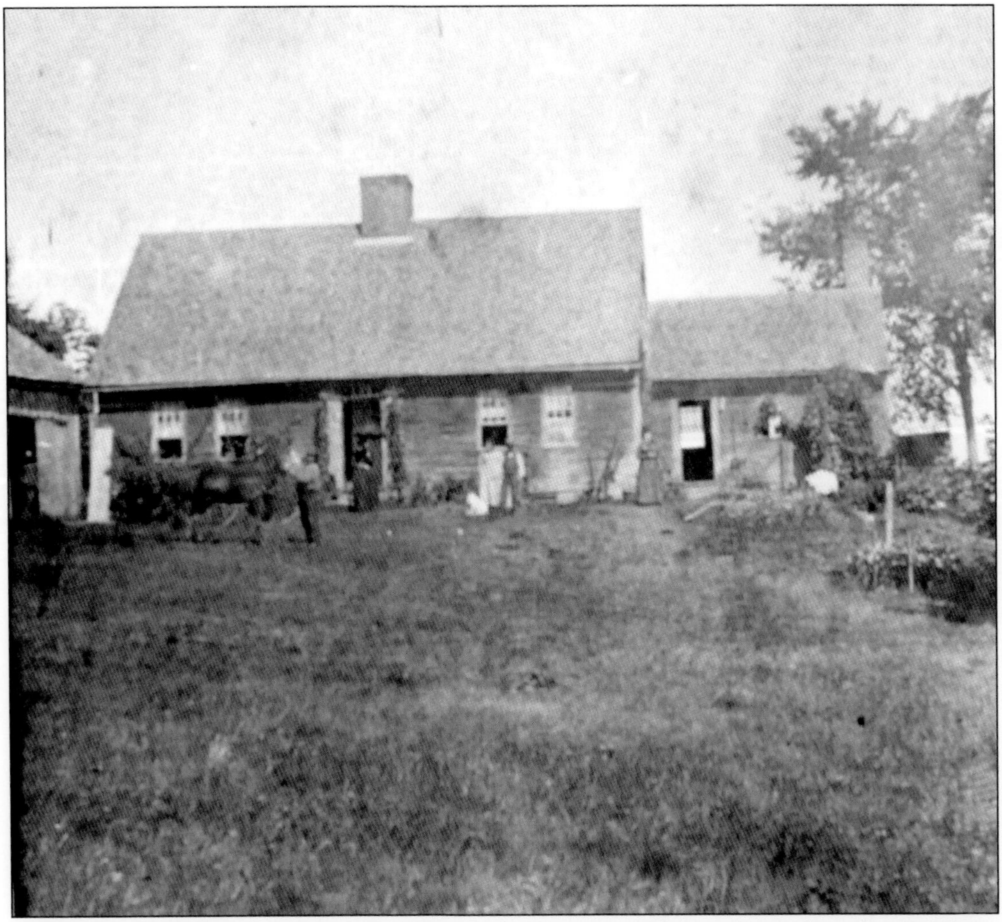

A Typical Farmhouse in the Area. This is the Isaac Rowell farm, located south of Madison Pond, in August 1880, which was the year before the first woolen mill opened in that town.

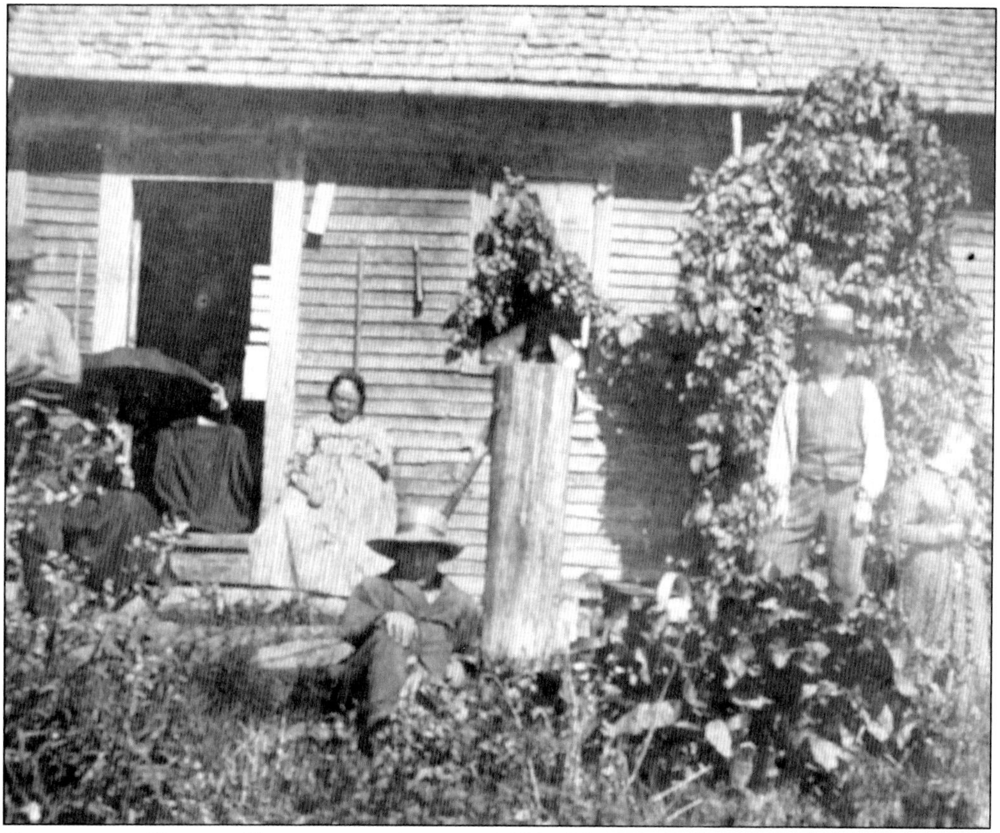

Close-up of Rowell Farmhouse, August 1880. There you find Grandpa Isaac Rowell, Grandma Rachel Rowell, Uncles Will and George Rowell, and Aunt Myra Rowell (not listed in order). The house was probably built around 1830.

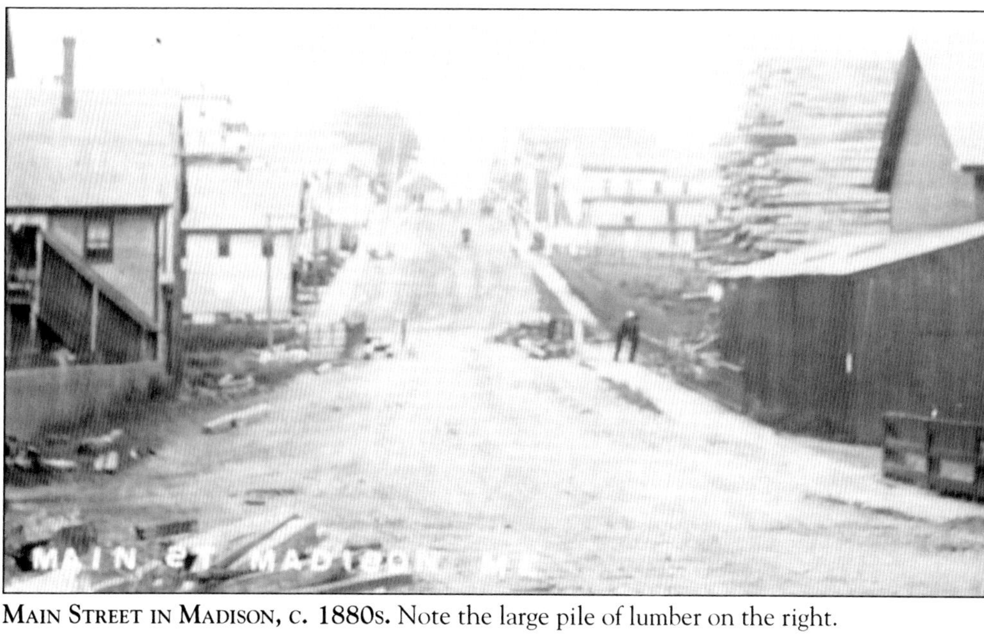

Main Street in Madison, c. 1880s. Note the large pile of lumber on the right.

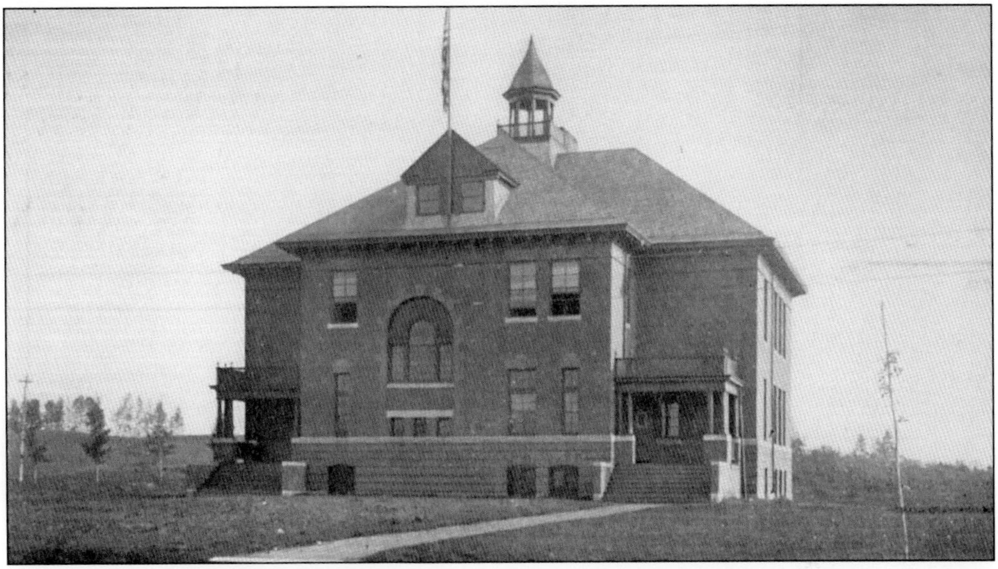

MADISON HIGH SCHOOL IN THE 1900S.

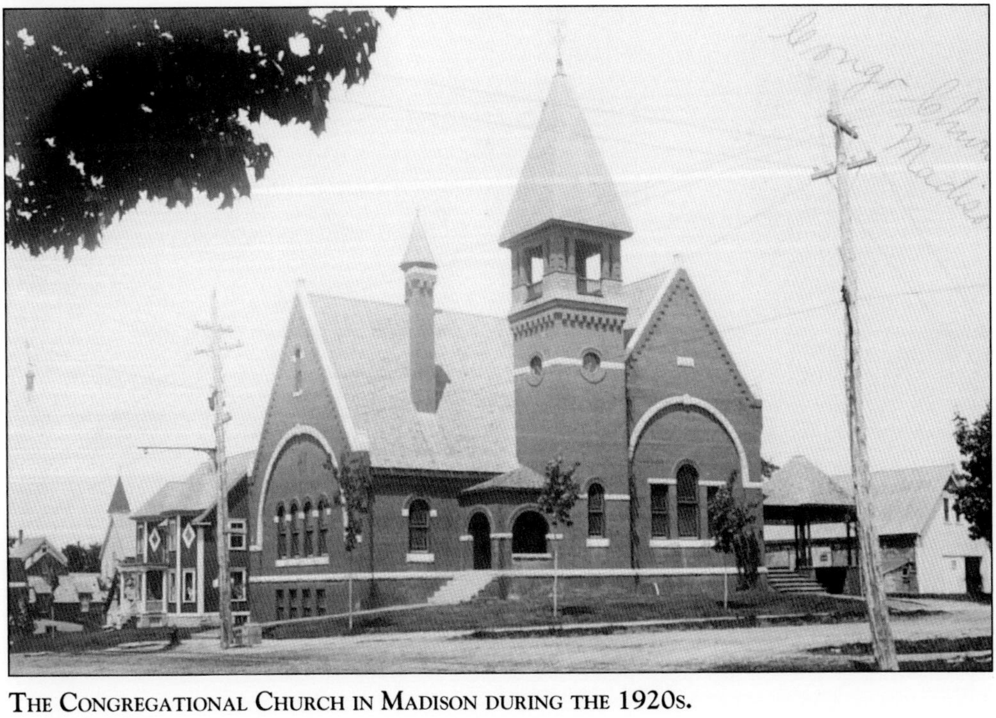

THE CONGREGATIONAL CHURCH IN MADISON DURING THE 1920S.

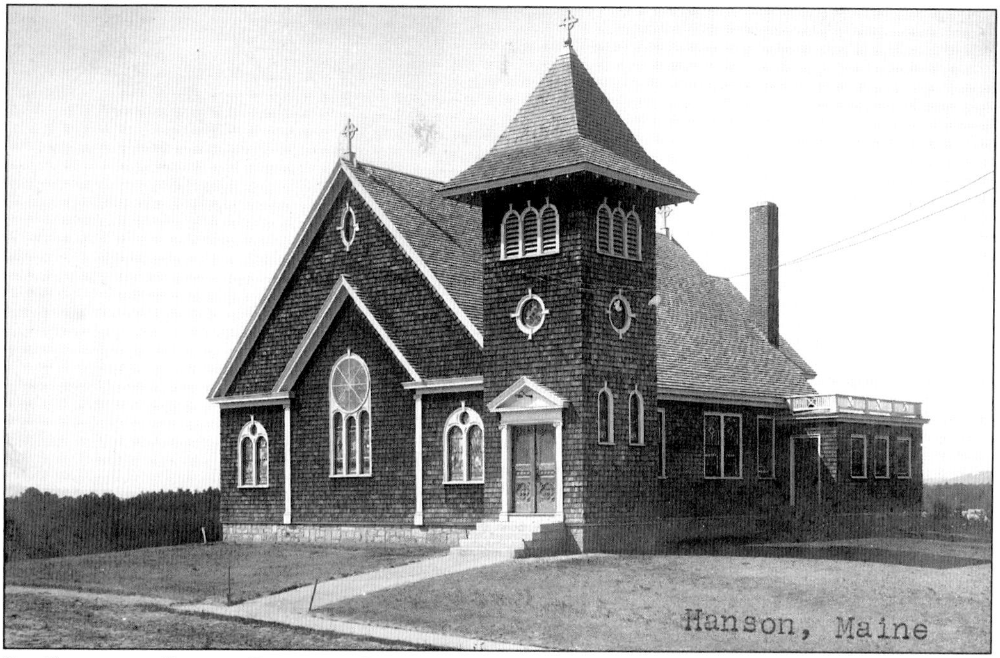

St. Sebastian Roman Catholic Church, Madison, in the 1920s.

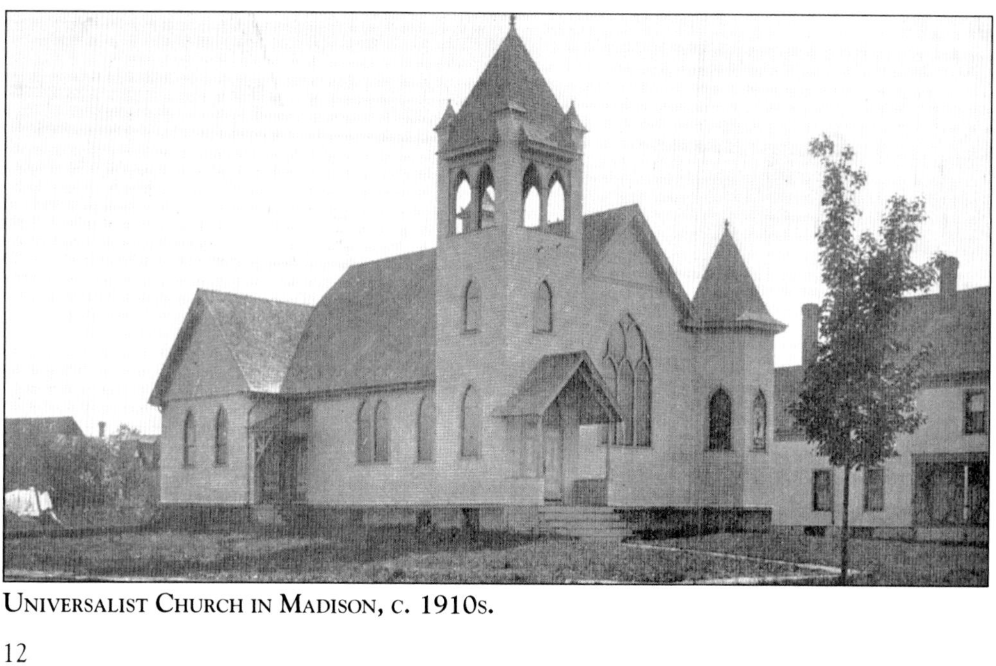

Universalist Church in Madison, c. 1910s.

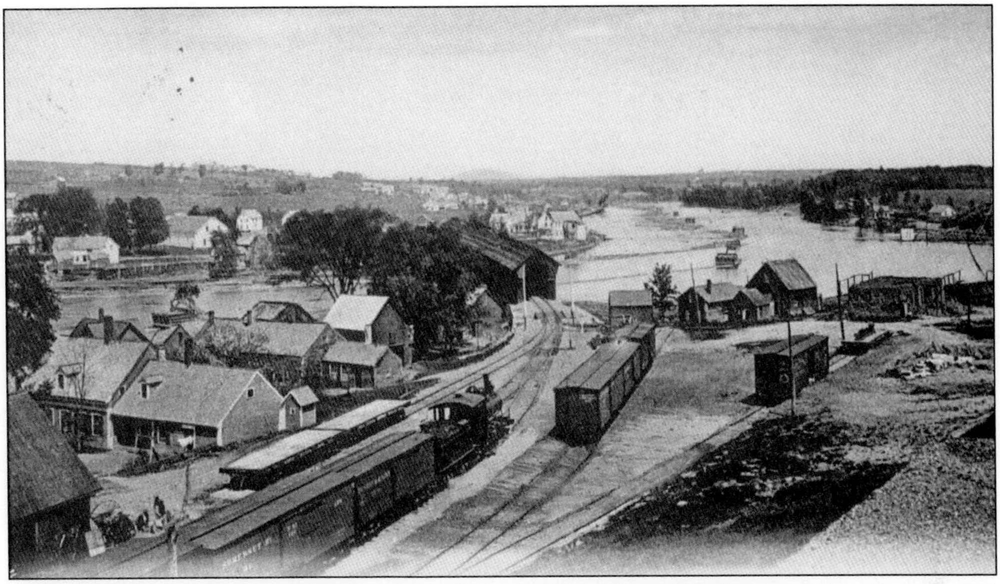

Up the Kennebec River from Madison, About 1900. The railroad cars, engines, houses, and river show the activity that was taking place in the town at this time.

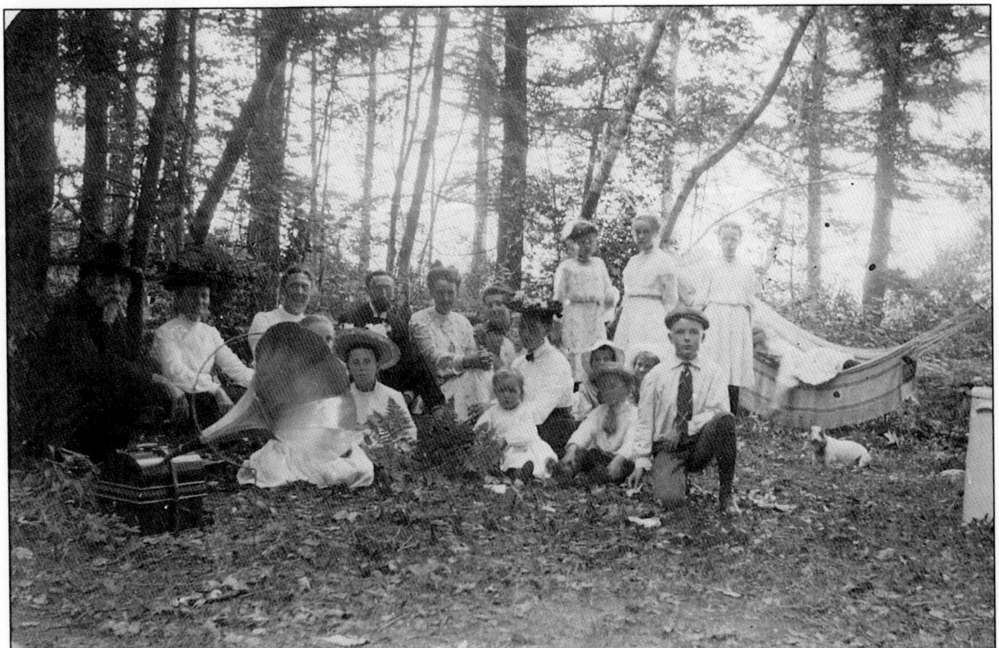

A Madison Postcard. Dated September 1, 1905, this postcard reads, "Where is this?" It is postmarked Madison, and that is probably where it was taken.

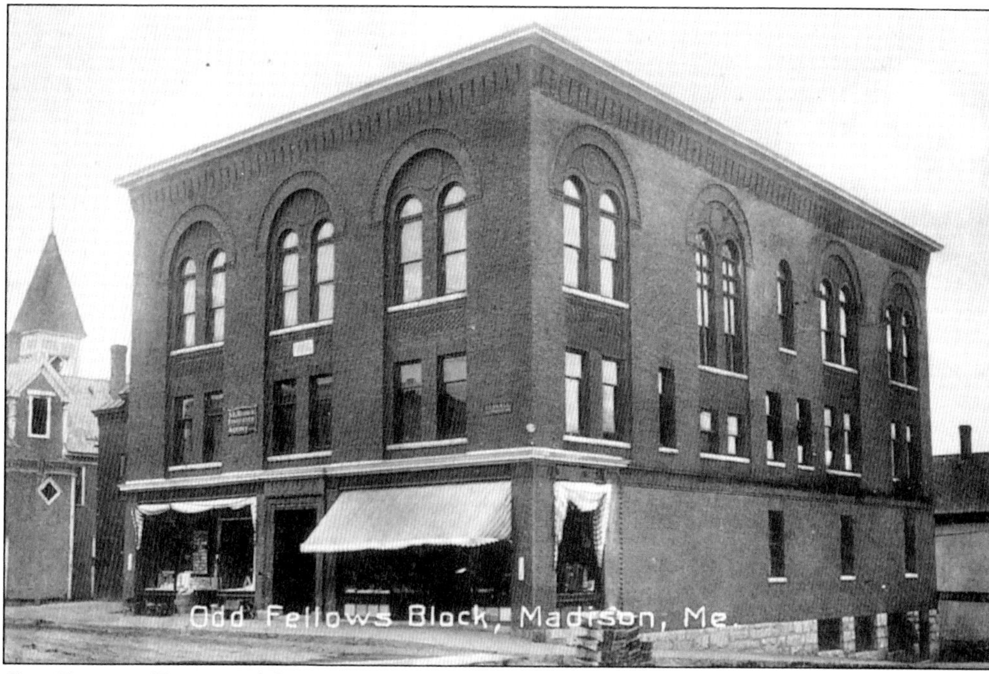

ODD FELLOWS BLOCK IN MADISON IN THE EARLY 1900S.

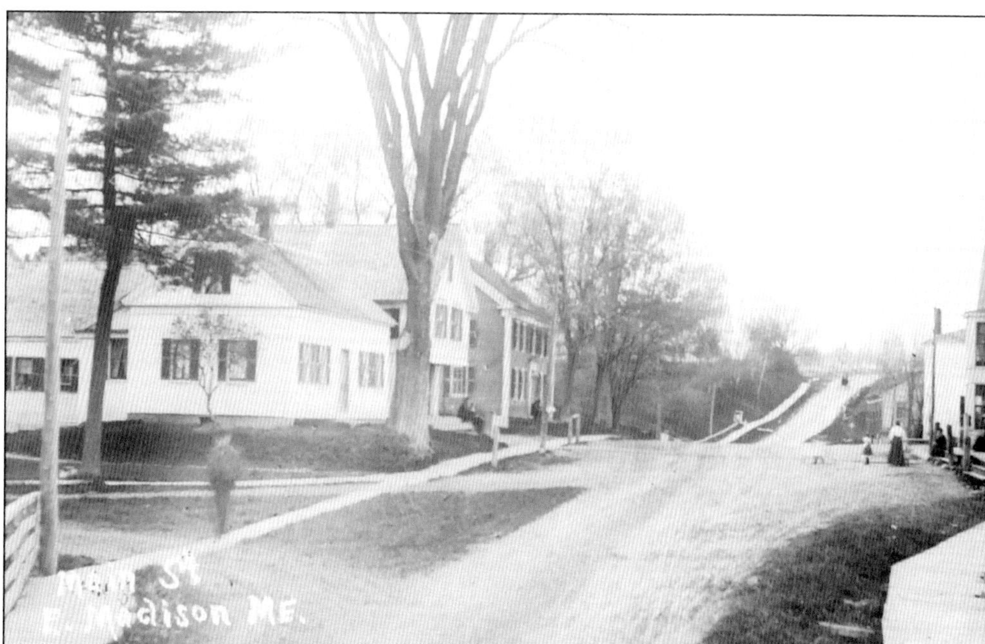

MAIN STREET IN EAST MADISON, EARLY 1900S. Feel the peace and serenity in this scene.

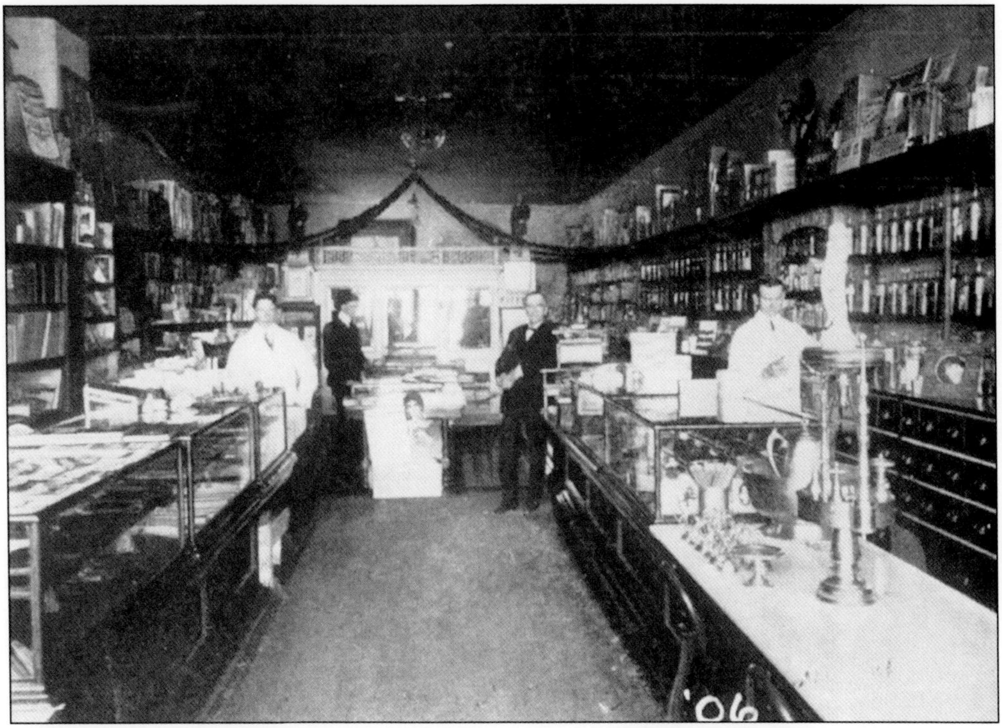

INTERIOR VIEW OF GEORGE CUSHING'S DRUG AND BOOKSTORE IN MADISON, FEBRUARY 24, 1906. The books appear to be on the left; the drugs are on the right.

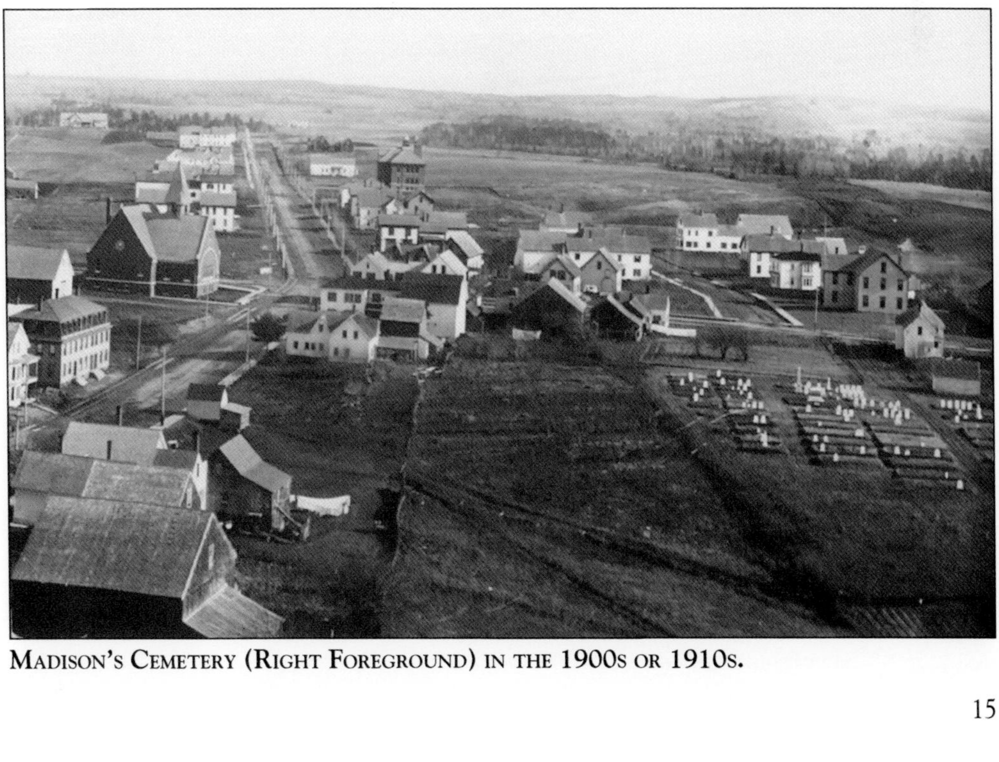

MADISON'S CEMETERY (RIGHT FOREGROUND) IN THE 1900S OR 1910S.

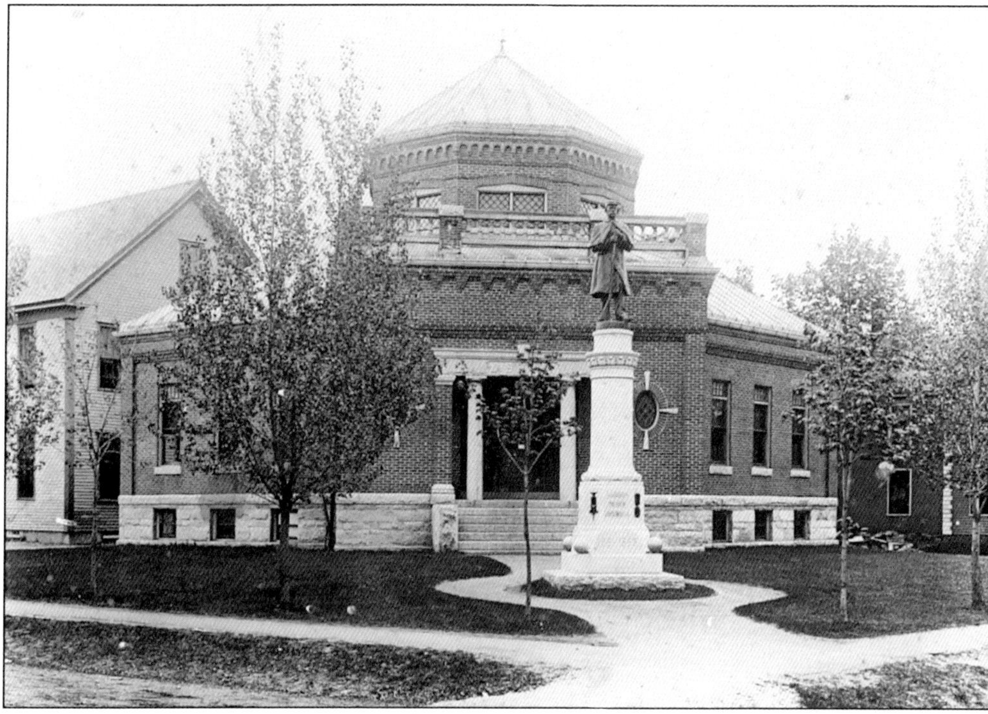

MADISON PUBLIC LIBRARY, C. 1920S. The library was built in 1905 with the help of an Andrew Carnegie grant.

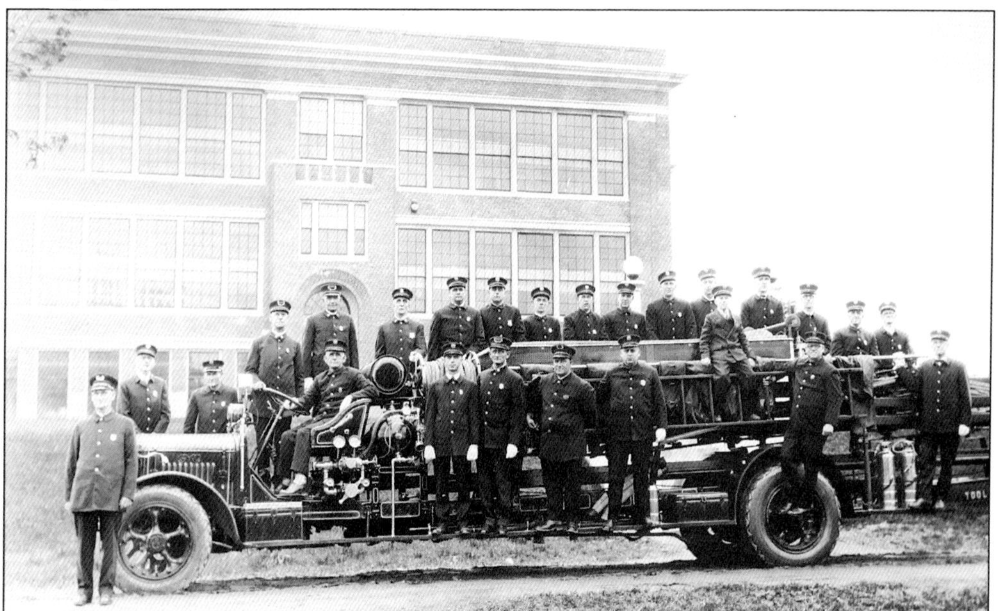

MADISON FIRE DEPARTMENT, C. 1924. From left to right are as follows: (first row) F. Brackett, A. Burwood, R. Gilbert, J. Brooks, George Willie, W. Warman, A. Strang, and H. Laisonecond; (last row) Duckworth, V. Williams, Caldwell, Nichols, Wescott, A. Williams, R. Heald, M. Cavanaugh, S. Golding, E. Moody, S. Wright, A. Daggett, E. Strickland, Duckworth, D. Warman, C. Sawyer, and G. Hill.

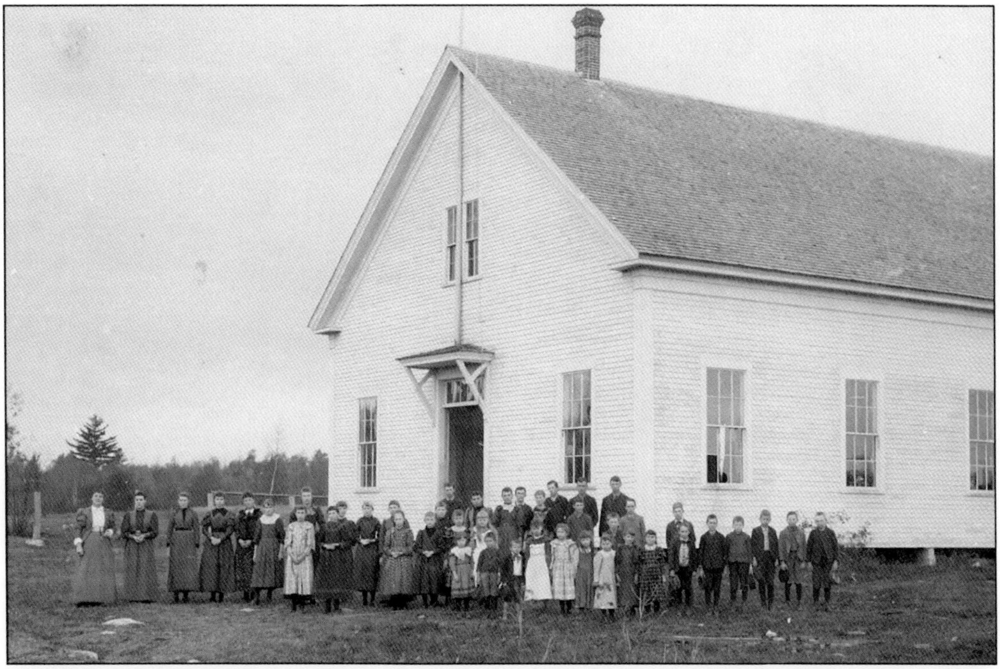

MADISON SCHOOLHOUSE. Once the town hall, this building was the school at Blackwell Corner, Madison, in 1896. Names of those shown, not in any order, are Mittie Batchelder and Mae Holway (teachers); and Edith Barron, Annie Turner, Nettie Holway, Lettie Rowe, Hazel Holway, Nettie Burnes, Grace Barron, G. Sawyer, Lottie Moore, Ethel French, Laura Moore, Mabel Clough, Mabel Davis, Daisy Holway, Nettie Moore, Elsie Jones, Beatrice Emery, Nellie Turner, Elsie Laurence, Guy Prince, Harold Danforth, Ethelyn Lawrence, Eileen Davis, Alice Knight, Maud Holway, Lula Holway, Agnes Emery, Mabilou Welch, Carl, Rog Danforth, Perley Adams, Gene Burnes, Don Welch, Everett Lilley, Allie Gilbert, David Holway, Elmer Sealey, Mabilou Whipple, Lester Holway, Davis, Johnnie Sawyer, and Linwood Nutting.

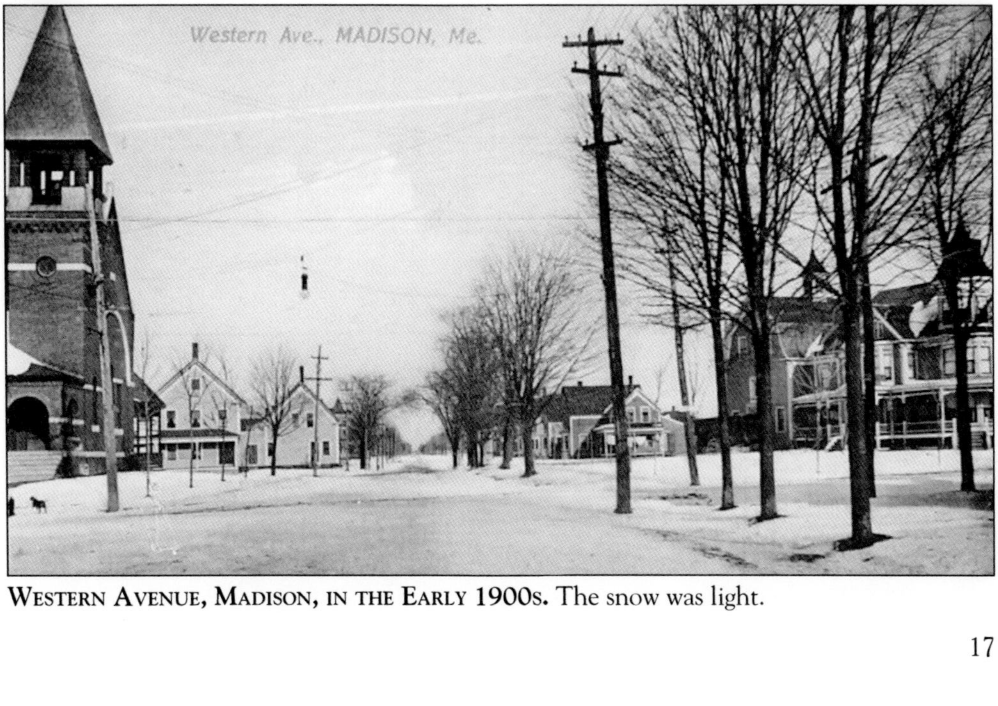

WESTERN AVENUE, MADISON, IN THE EARLY 1900S. The snow was light.

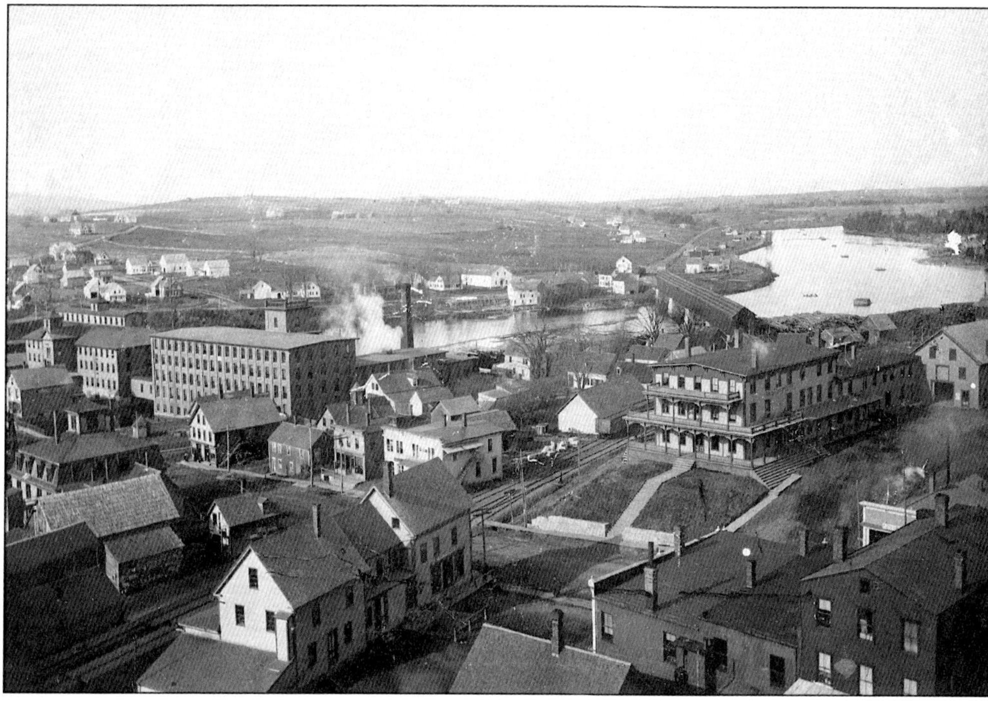

A View of Madison, c. 1888. This image shows the covered bridge, the Weston House, and the woolen mill.

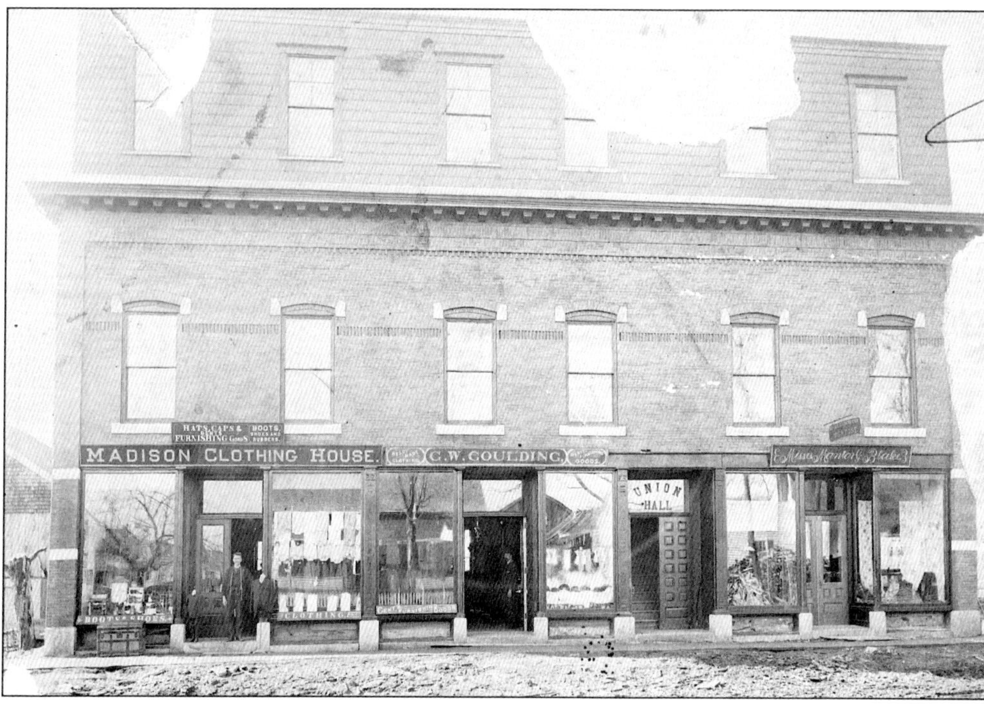

Main Street, Madison, in 1887 or 1888. Pictured from left to right are Madison Clothing House, G.W. Goulding, Union Hall, Miss Mantor, and J. Blake. There was a dentist on the second floor. The top of the building was burnt off and not rebuilt.

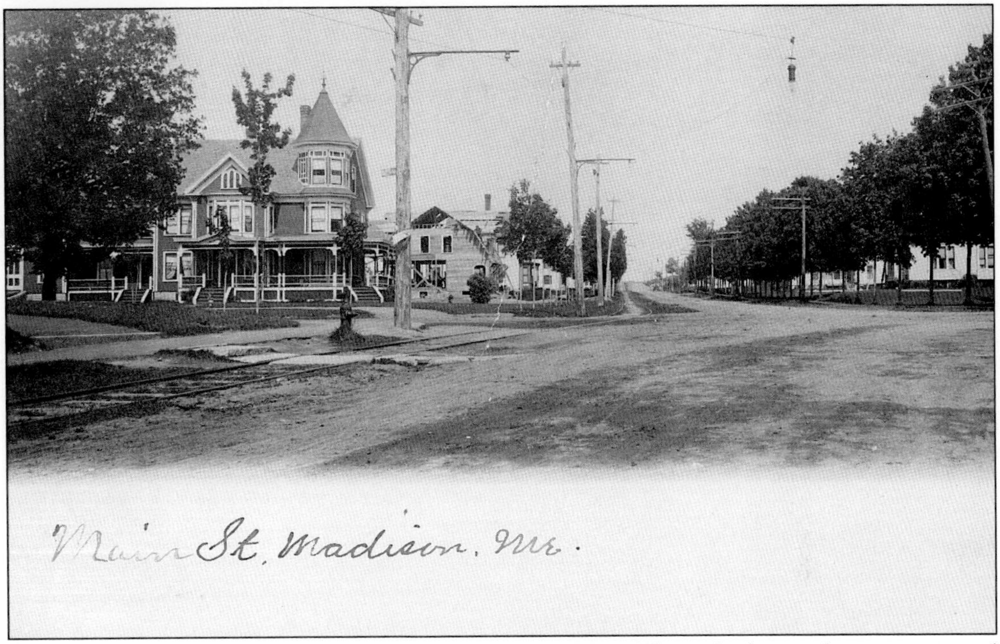

Another View of Main Street, Madison, in the 1900s. The wide dirt road appears in good shape and there are many houses visible along the street.

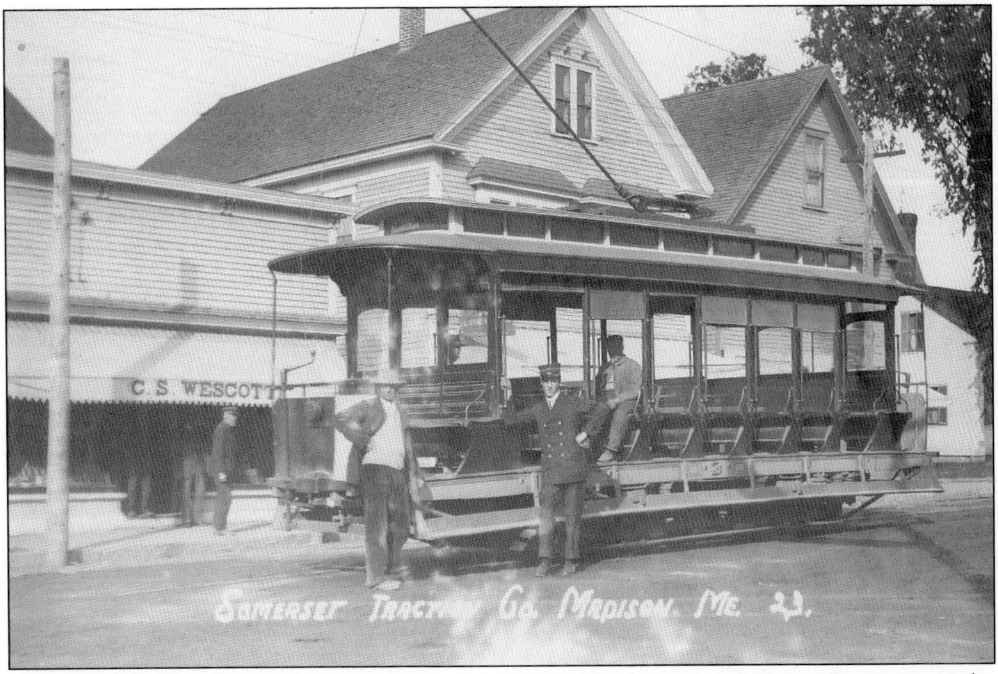

Madison's Street Railway. The railway was operated by Somerset Traction Company in the early part of 1900s.

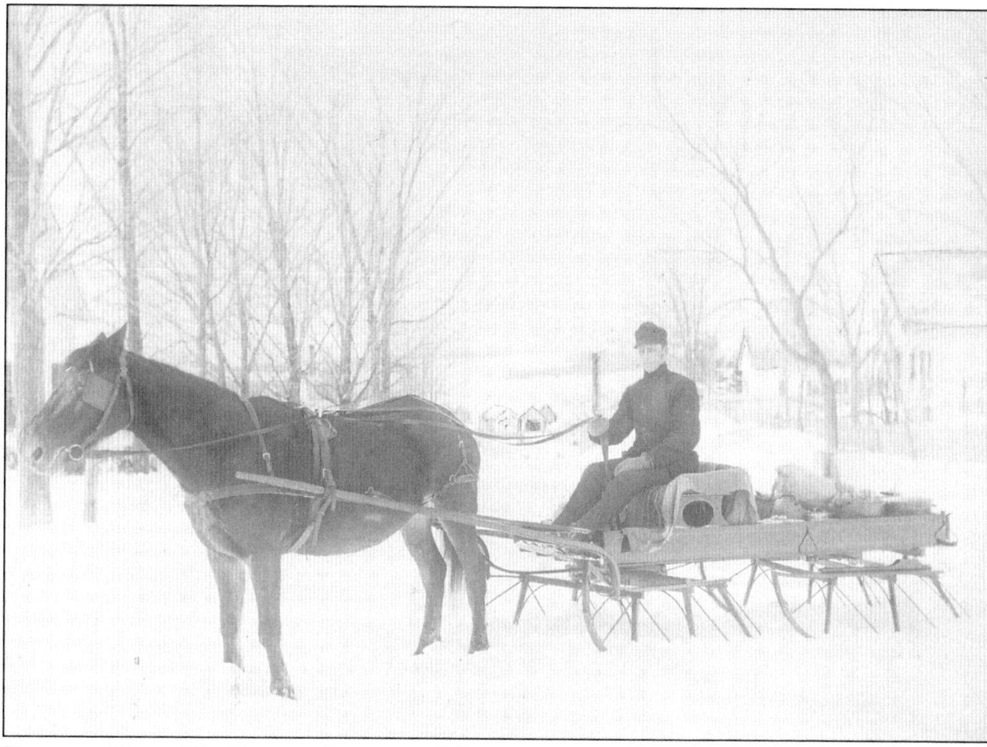

Delivery Team. The first regular winter delivery team put on in Madison in December 1882. K.C. Gray is pictured on the sled with his horse, Kitty Shaw.

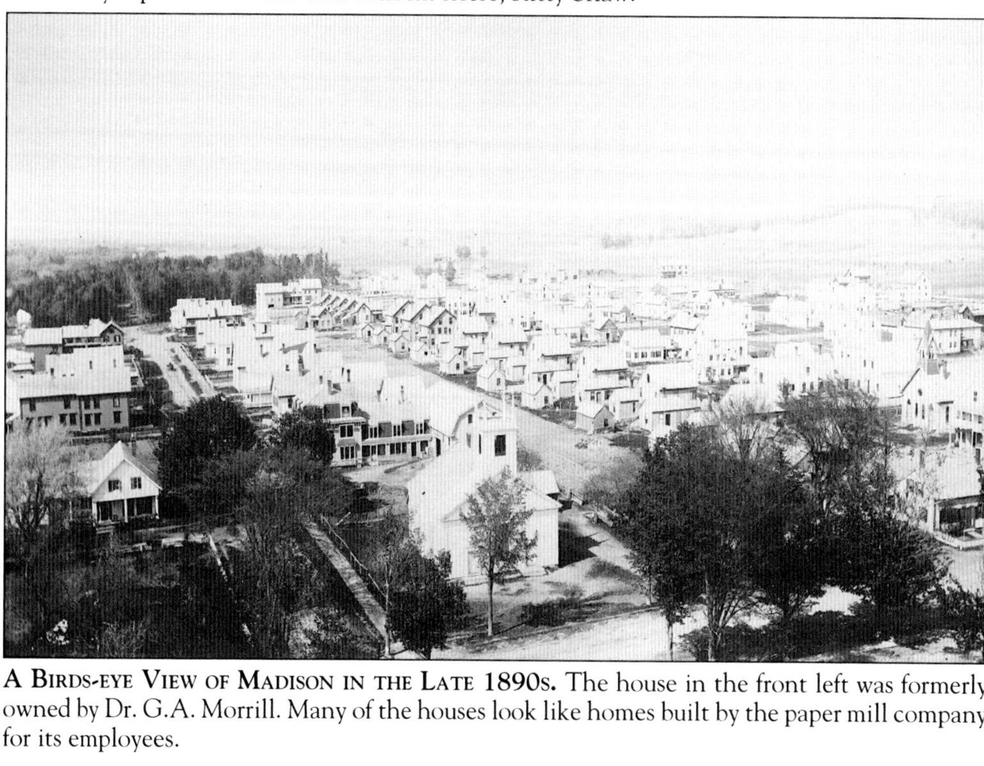

A Birds-eye View of Madison in the Late 1890s. The house in the front left was formerly owned by Dr. G.A. Morrill. Many of the houses look like homes built by the paper mill company for its employees.

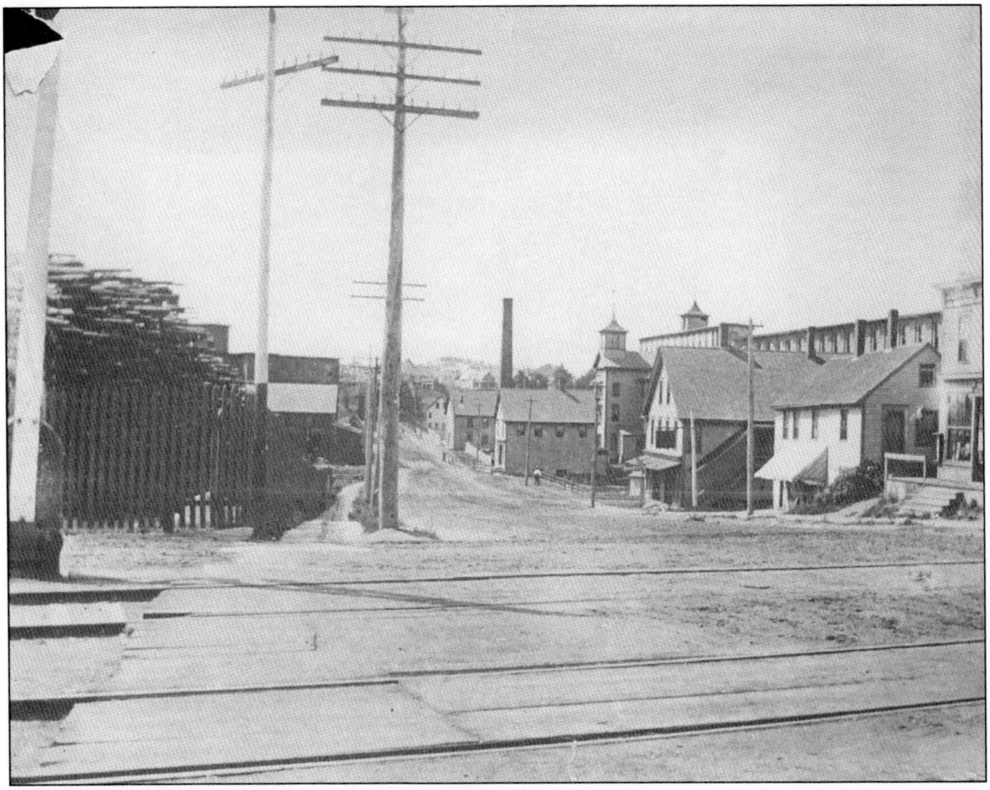

Lower Main Street, Madison, in the 1910s.

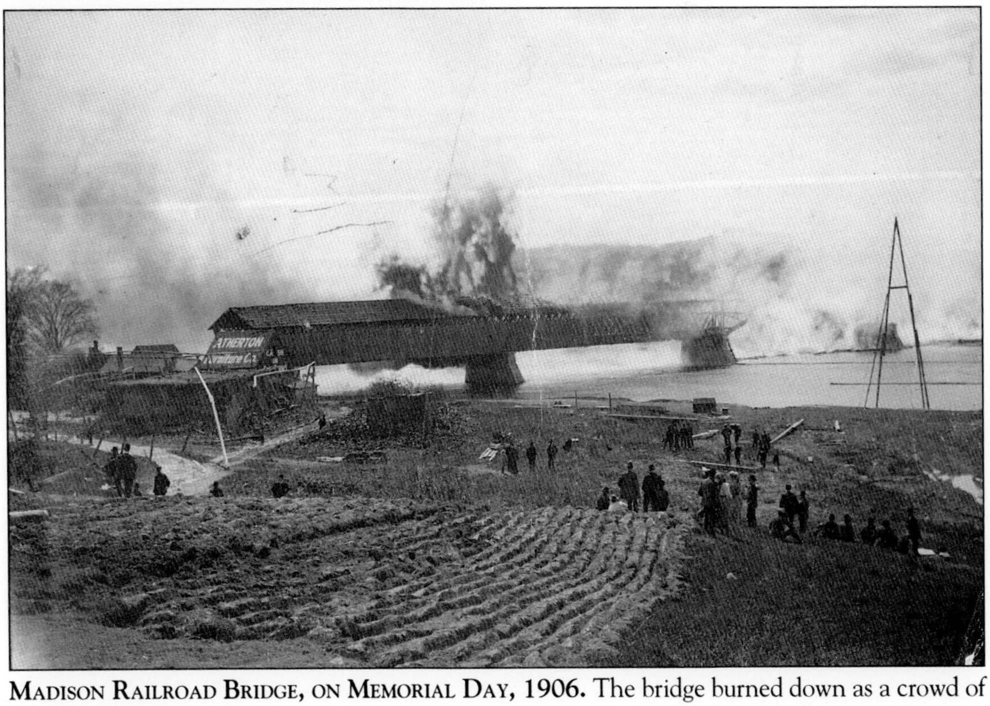

Madison Railroad Bridge, on Memorial Day, 1906. The bridge burned down as a crowd of people watched.

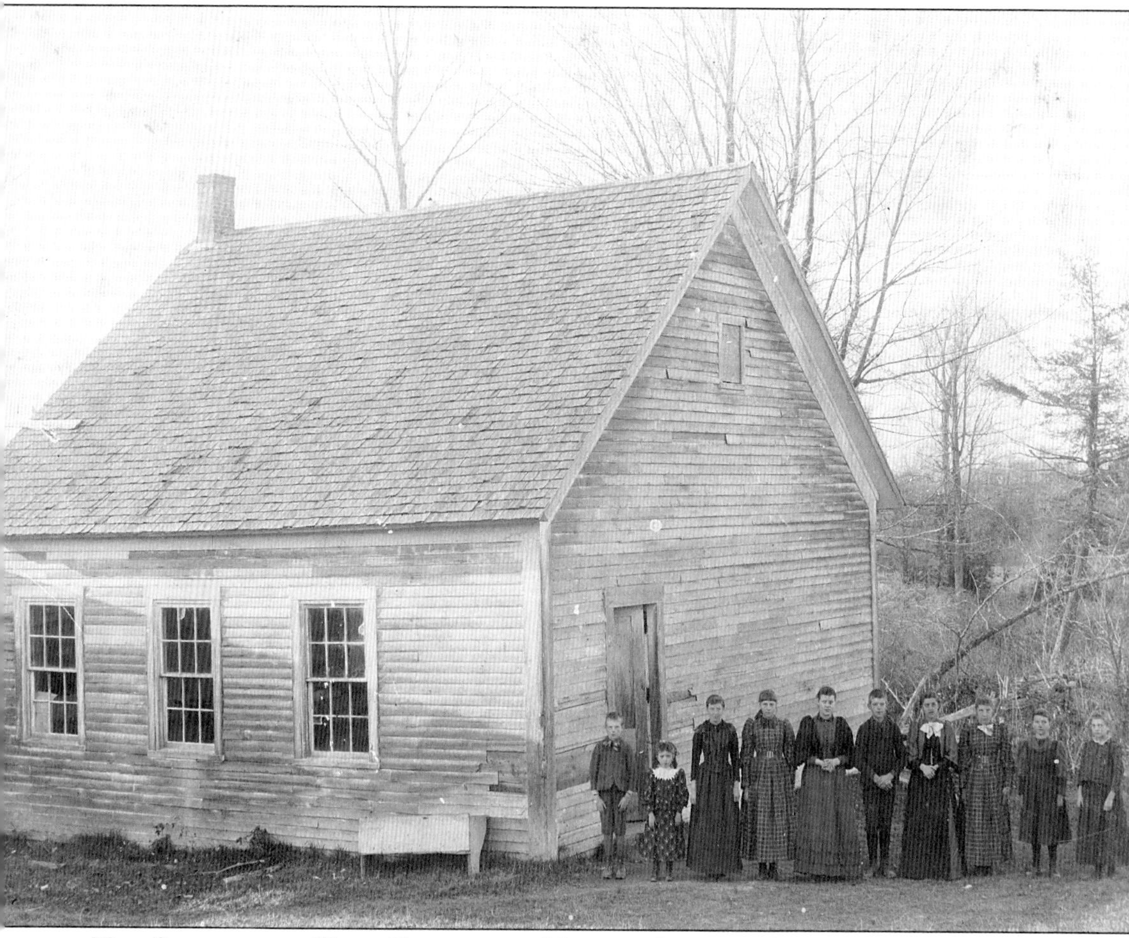

NINE STUDENTS AND THEIR TEACHER AT A MADISON ONE-ROOM SCHOOLHOUSE IN THE 1890S. For years, these towns had small schools with relatively few students. In more modern times, these schools were consolidated. The one-room schoolhouse now has pretty well disappeared from the Maine scene except on some of the state's islands and in tiny communities. While there were often few students in the one-room schools, they could range through all the grades and sometimes into the equivalent of present-day high schools.

Two

Mining and Manufacturing

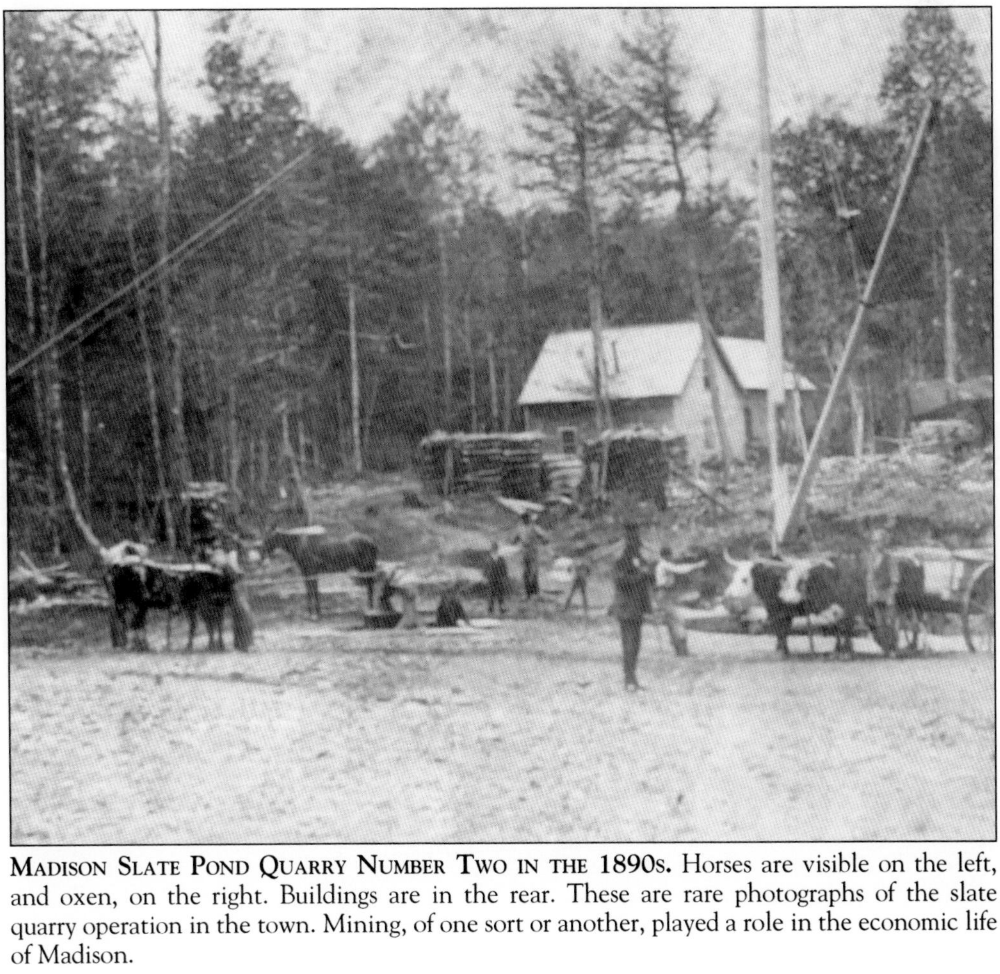

Madison Slate Pond Quarry Number Two in the 1890s. Horses are visible on the left, and oxen, on the right. Buildings are in the rear. These are rare photographs of the slate quarry operation in the town. Mining, of one sort or another, played a role in the economic life of Madison.

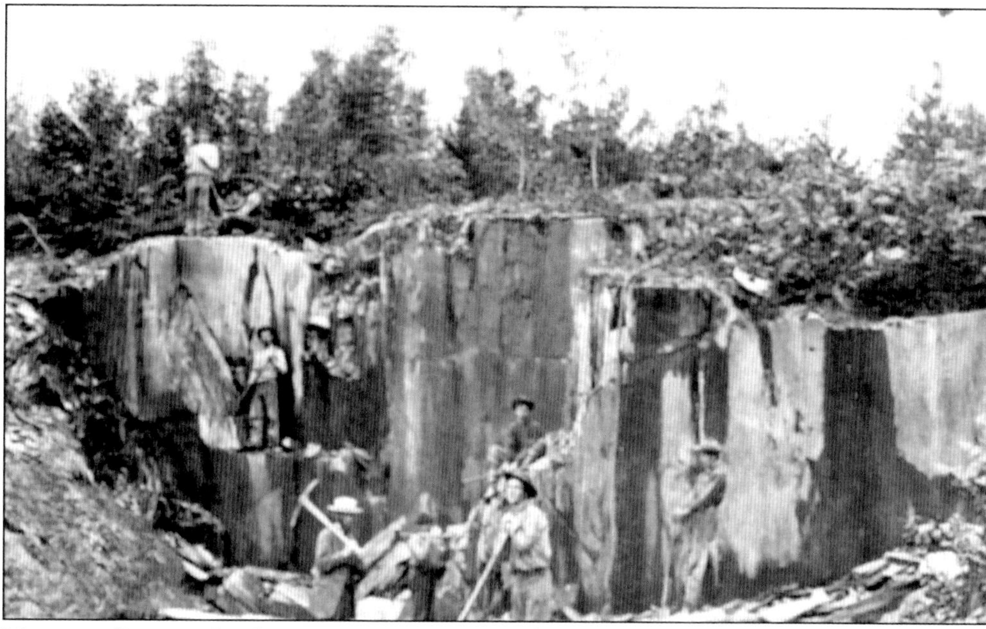

Madison Quarry. In this picture, men are standing with their tools at the slate quarry in Madison. Slabs of slate and the quarry show up well in this image.

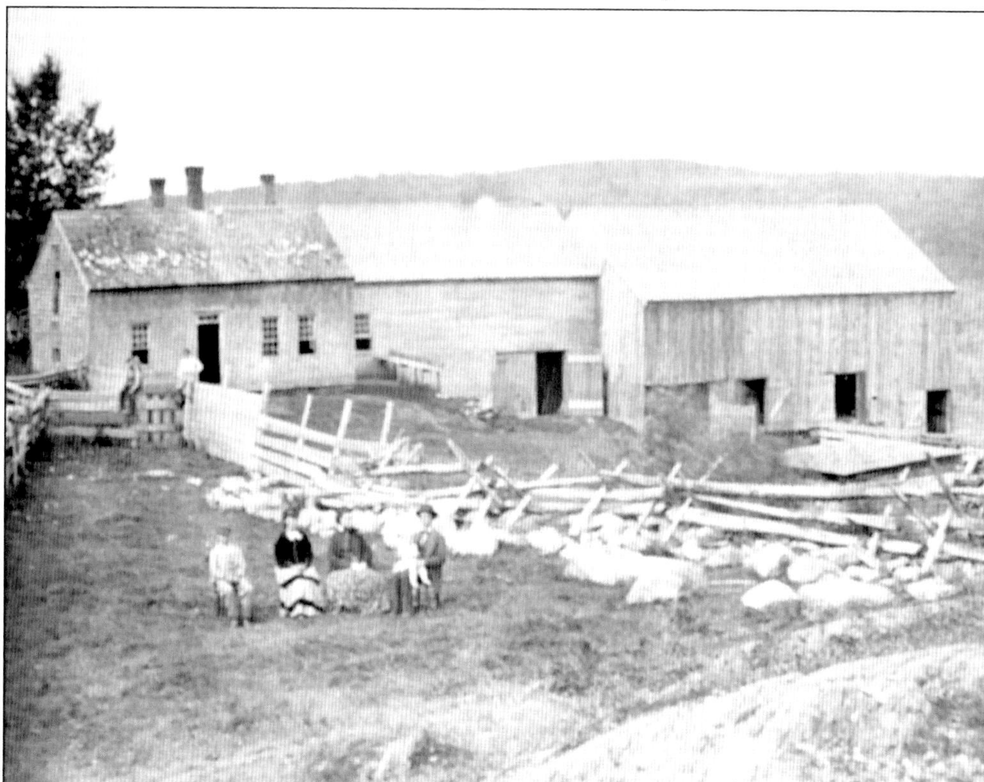

Boardinghouse at the Madison Slate Quarry. The five people who are seated appear to be posed. This was in the 1890s.

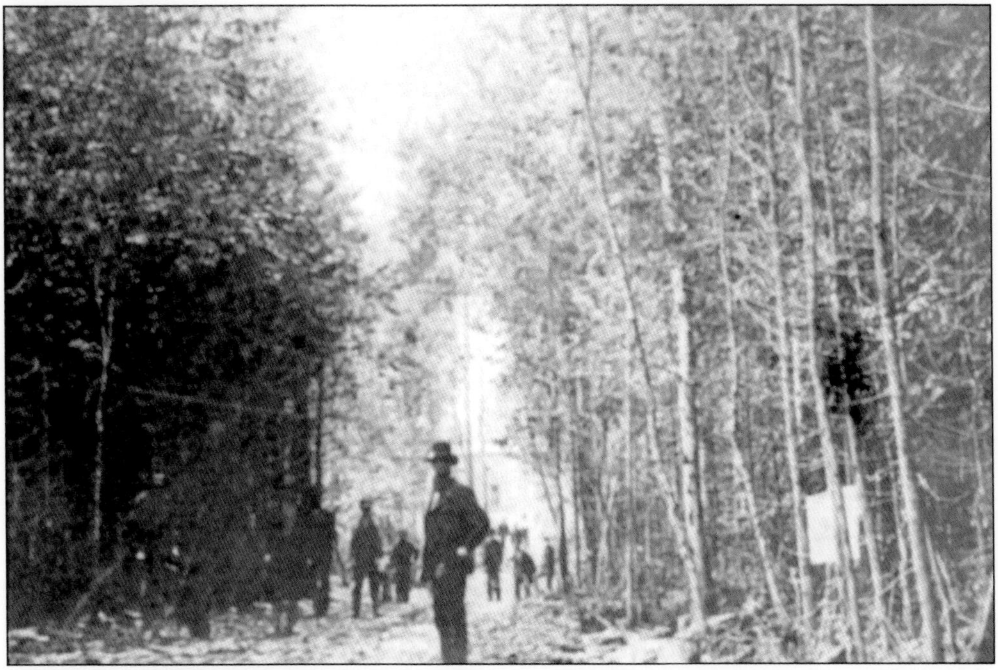

ROAD TO THE MADISON SLATE POND QUARRY IN THE 1870S OR 1880S. Note the tall man with the top hat in front.

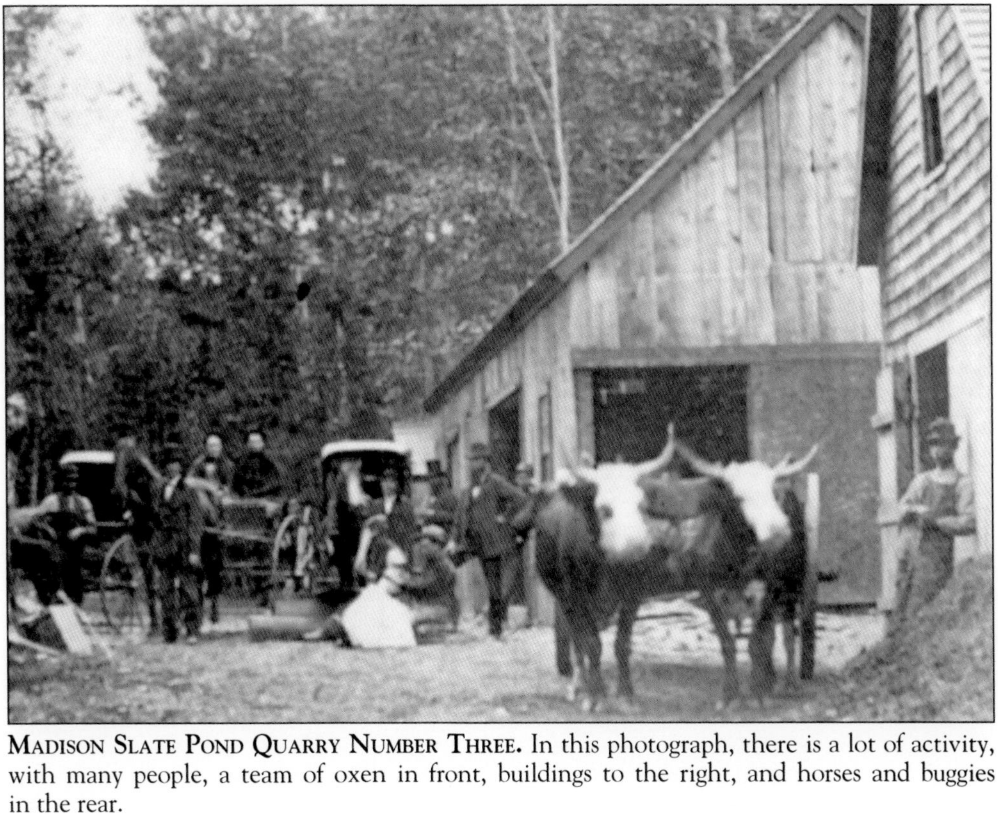

MADISON SLATE POND QUARRY NUMBER THREE. In this photograph, there is a lot of activity, with many people, a team of oxen in front, buildings to the right, and horses and buggies in the rear.

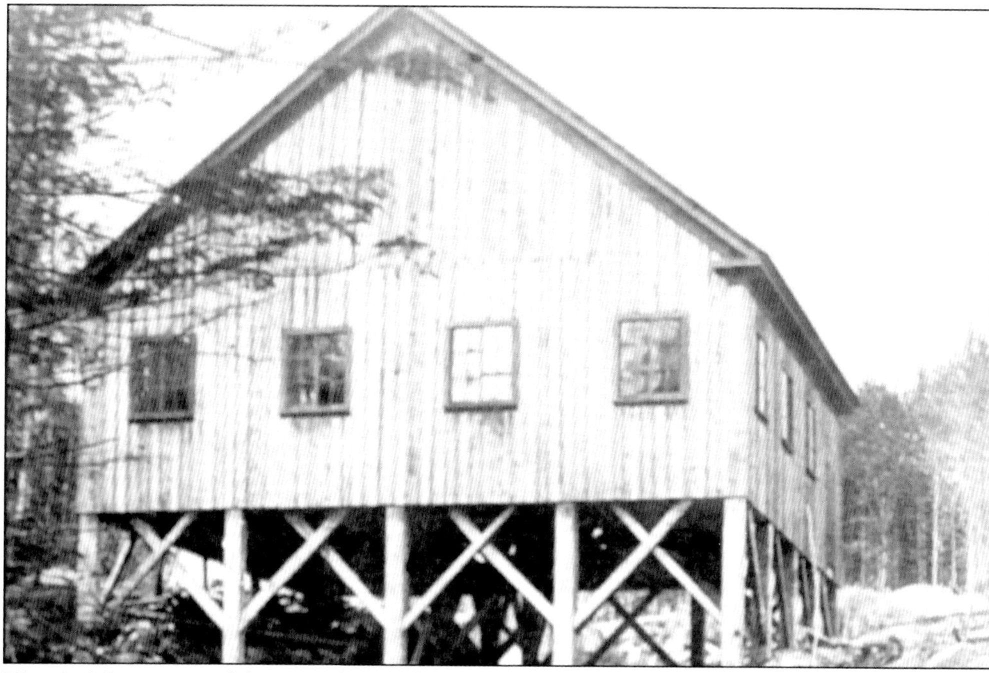

HALL'S MILL AT THE MADISON SLATE QUARRY IN THE 1880S. There is water coming down a sluice and a building standing on stilts.

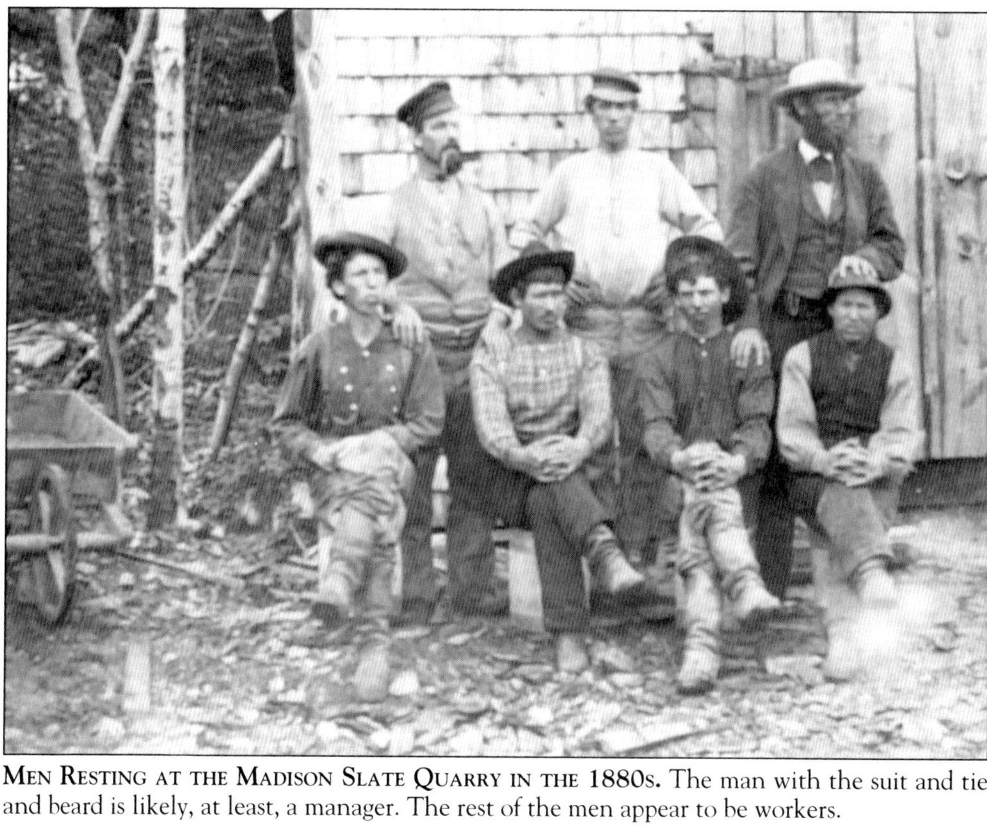

MEN RESTING AT THE MADISON SLATE QUARRY IN THE 1880S. The man with the suit and tie and beard is likely, at least, a manager. The rest of the men appear to be workers.

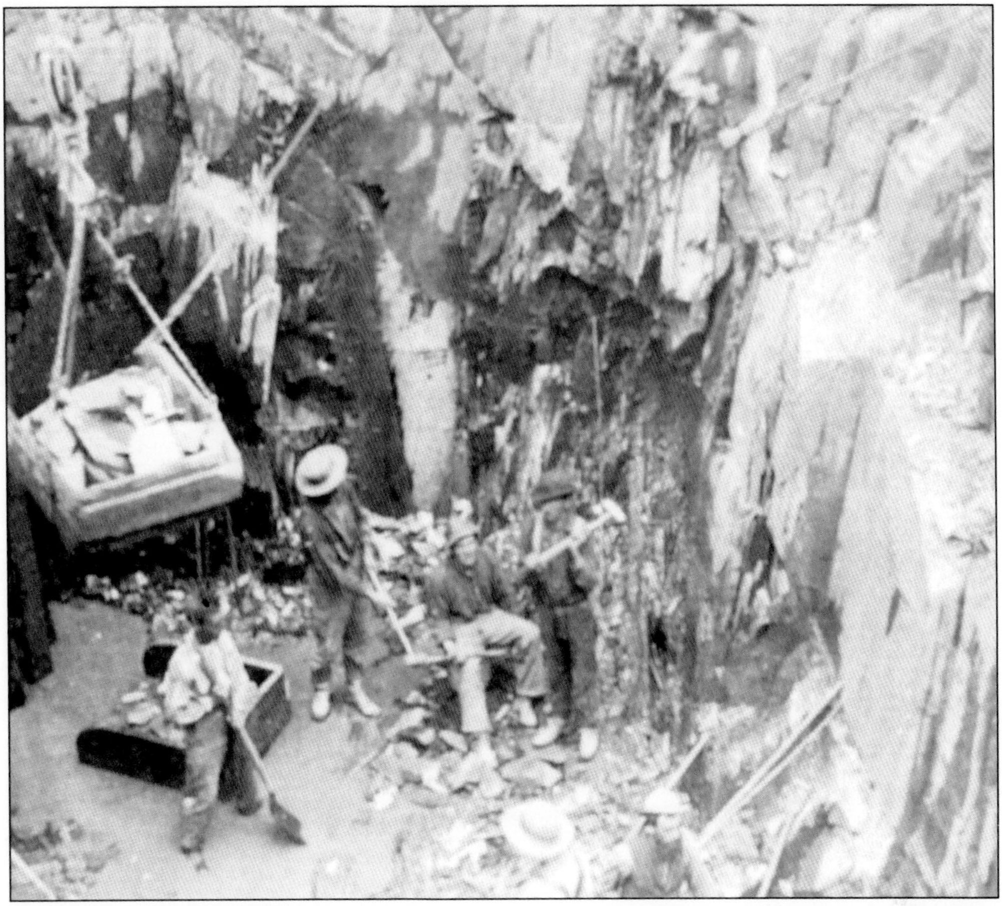

East Madison Slate Quarry in the 1890s. In this interesting picture, men pose here holding picks, shovels, and sledge hammers.

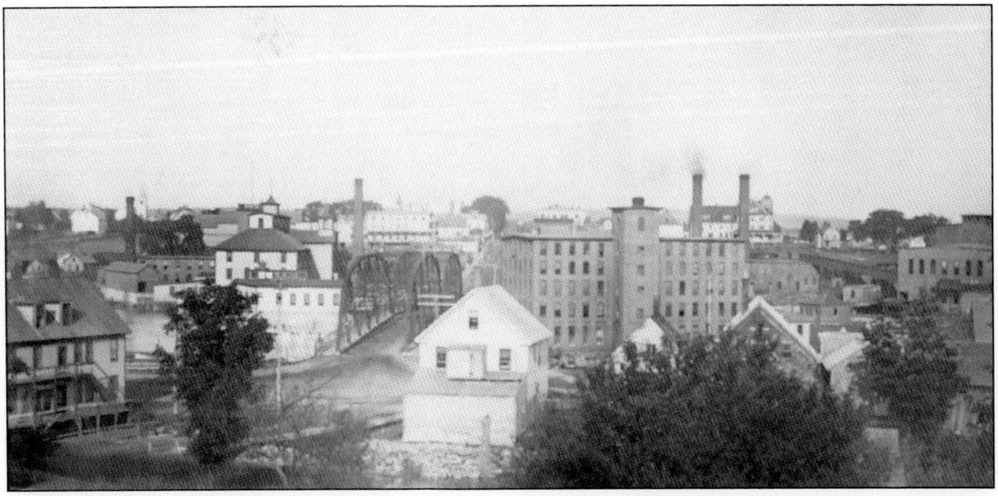

Madison Woolen Mill in the Late 1880s or Early 1890s. This photograph was taken not too long after the mill started operations. It was the first large manufacturing industry in the town.

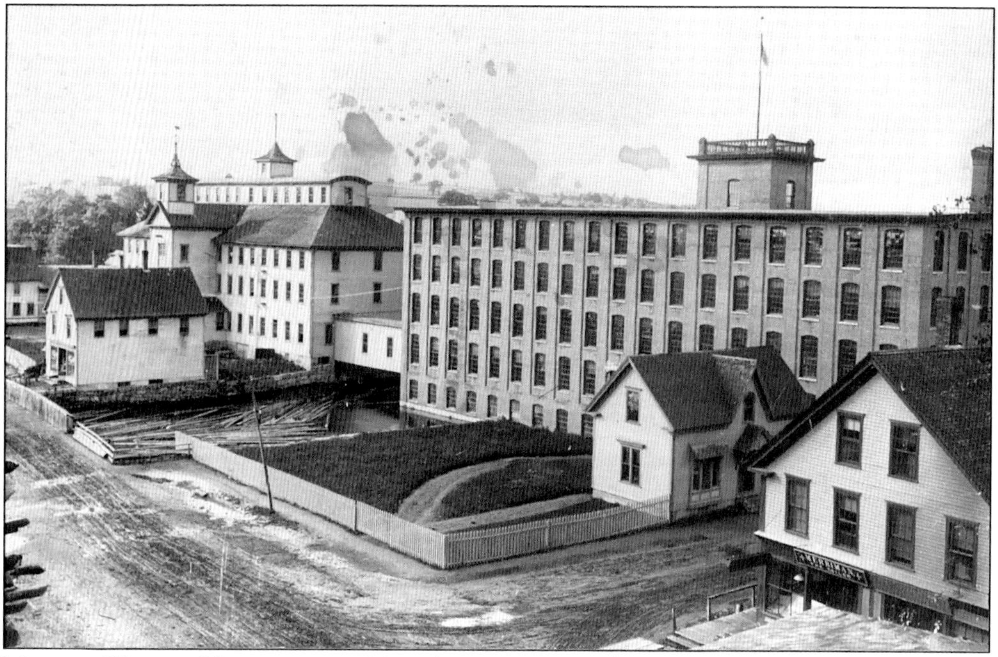

MADISON WOOLEN MILL, C. 1900S. Note the "Merriman," the tailor sign in the right foreground. Apparently, one didn't have to go far to get the woolen cloth made into a suit.

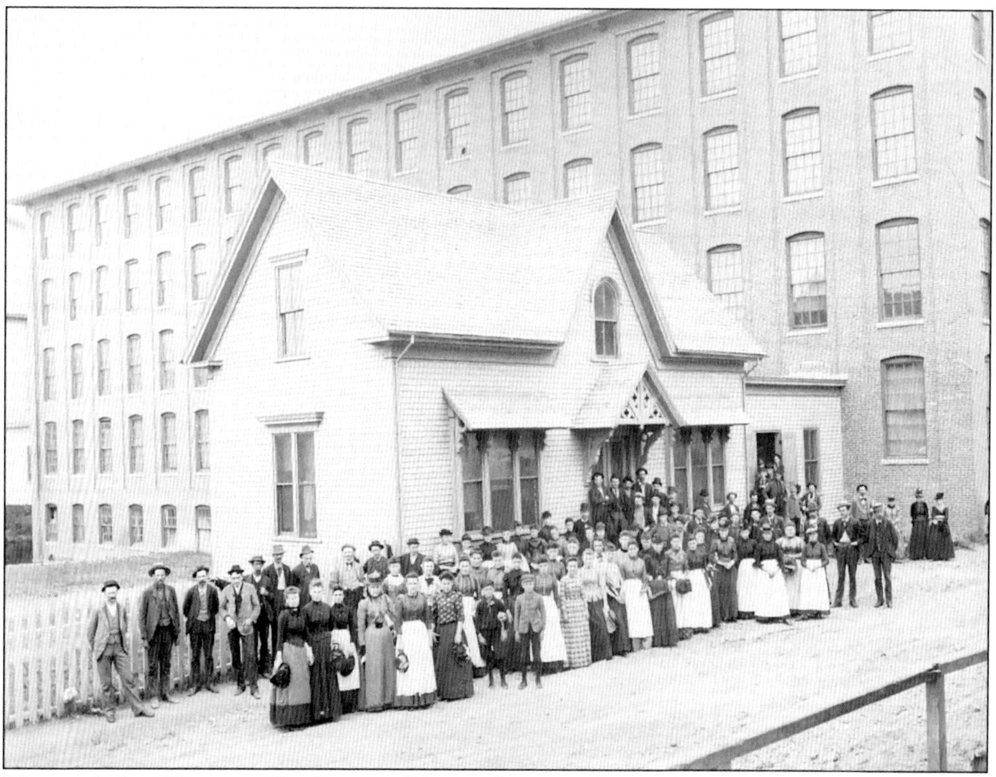

WOOLEN MILL WORKERS. Employees of the Madison woolen mill pose outside in the 1900s.

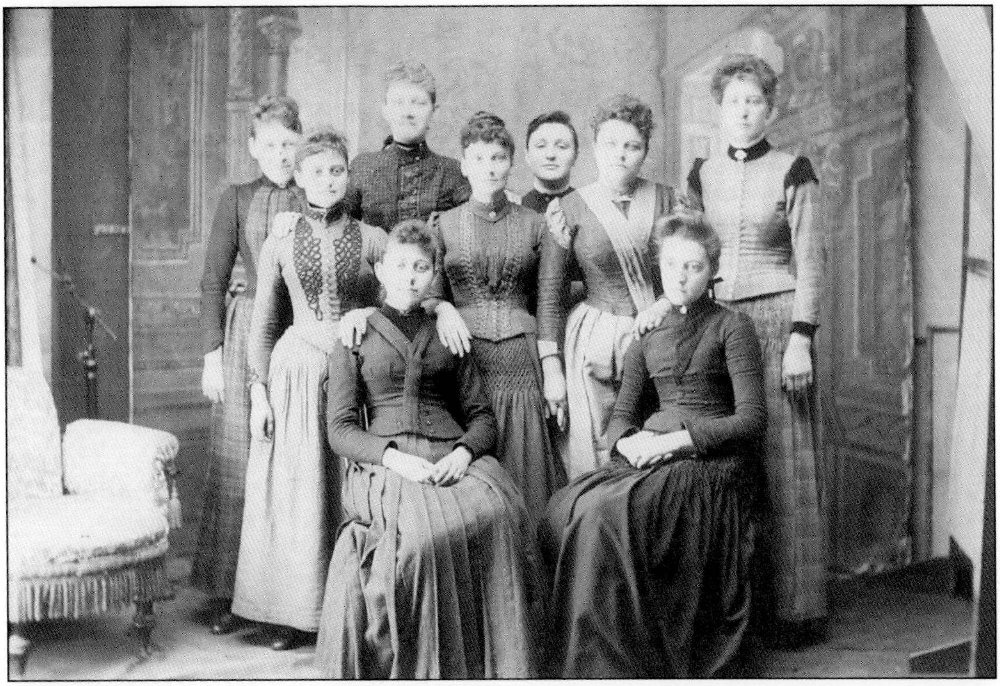

Female Workers at the Madison Woolen Mill in the 1890s. Eight of the nine pictured were Nellie Wade, Nettie Wade, Edith Nye, Lizzie Booker, Emma Wood, Mrs. Hinckley, Della Greenleaf, and Bertha Randall.

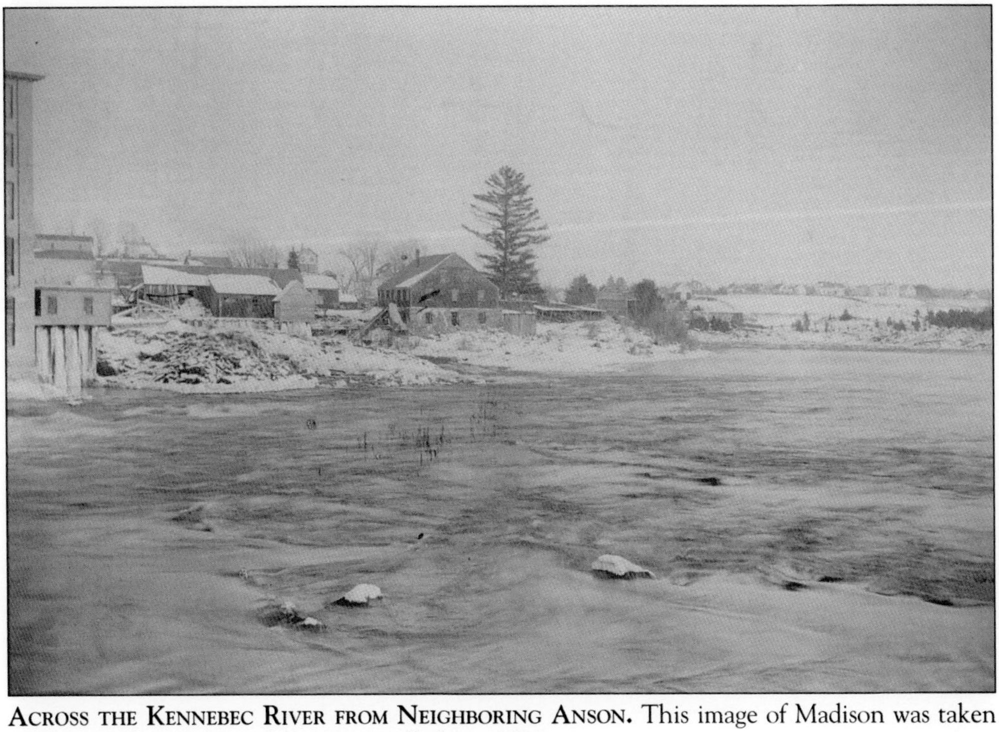

Across the Kennebec River from Neighboring Anson. This image of Madison was taken just before the coming of the paper mill about 1889.

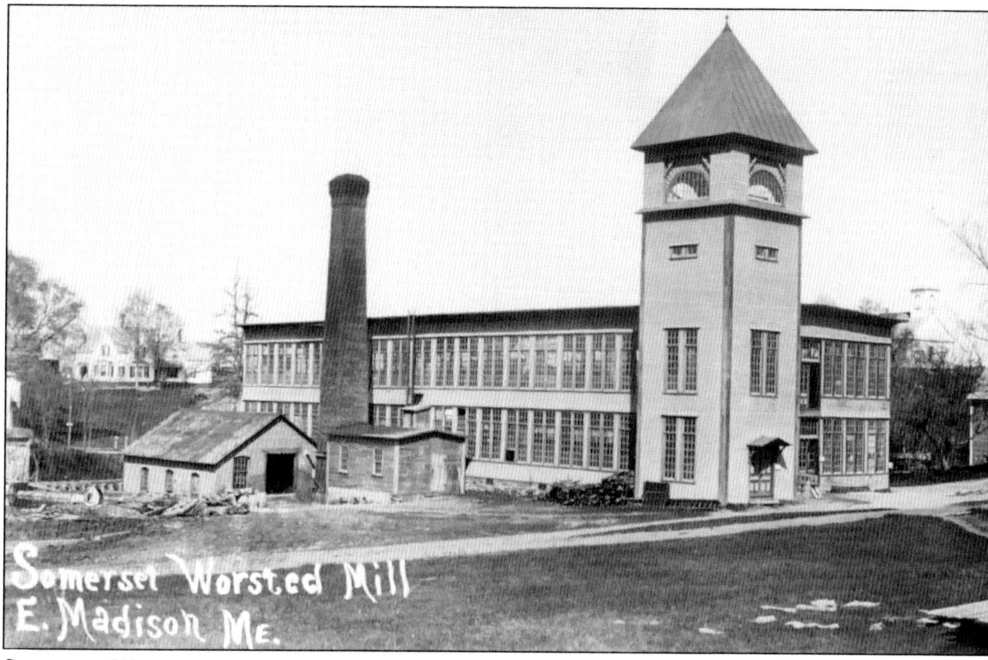

SOMERSET WOOLEN MILL IN EAST MADISON IN THE EARLY 1900S.

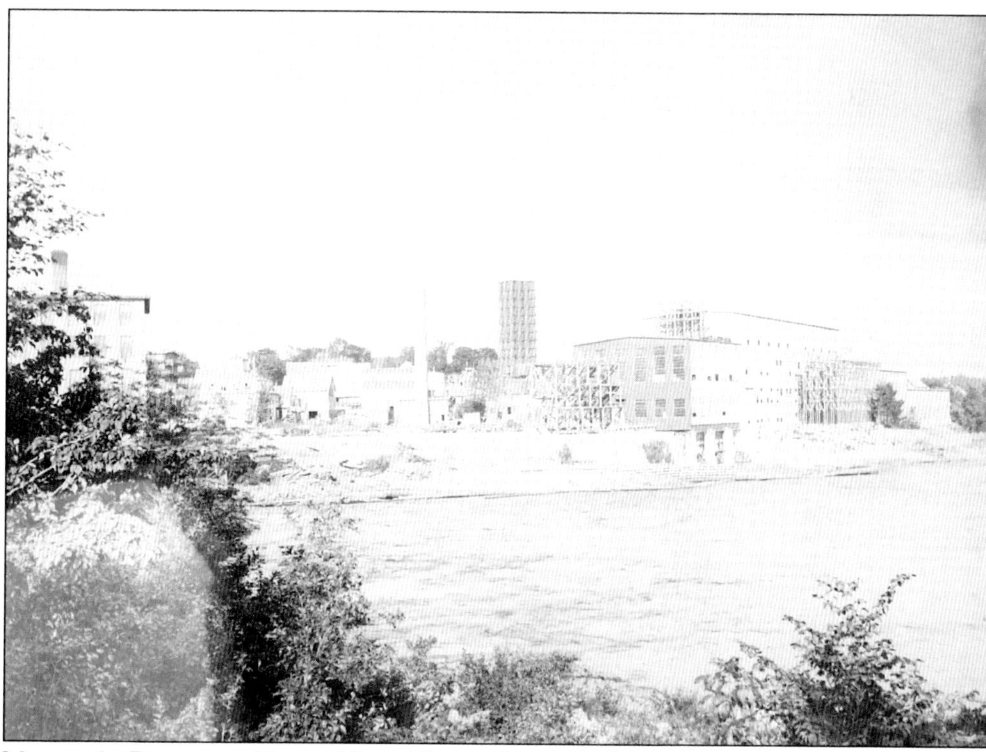

MADISON'S PULP AND PAPER MILL. The mill was under construction by Manufacturing Investment Company in the early 1890s. The acid tower is going up by the Kennebec River.

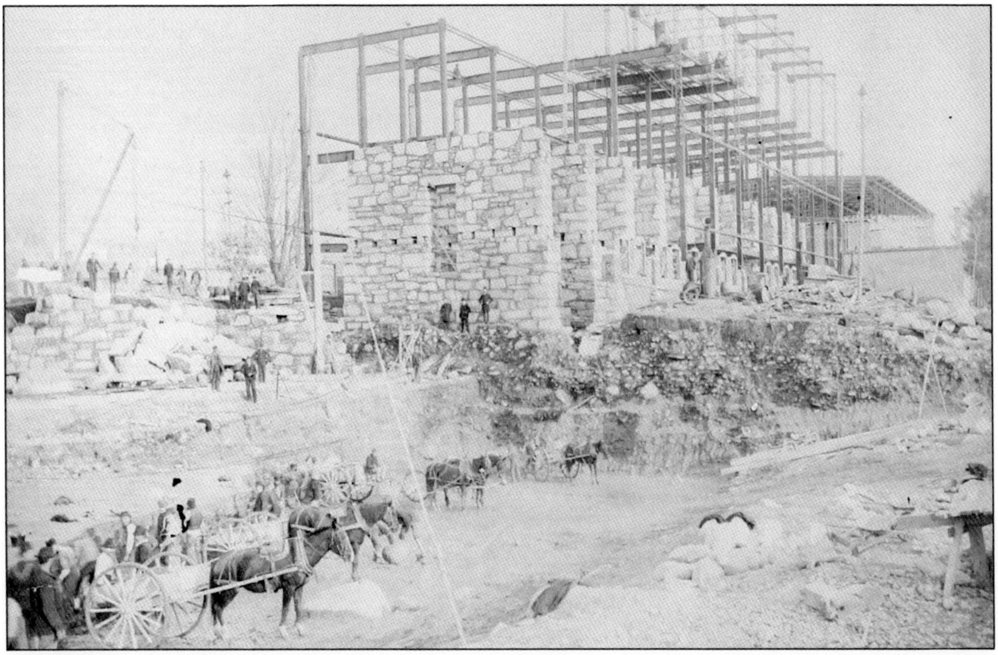

Madison Paper Mill, Early 1890s. This view shows construction of digester pits at the new paper mill in Madison. Note the construction workers and their horses.

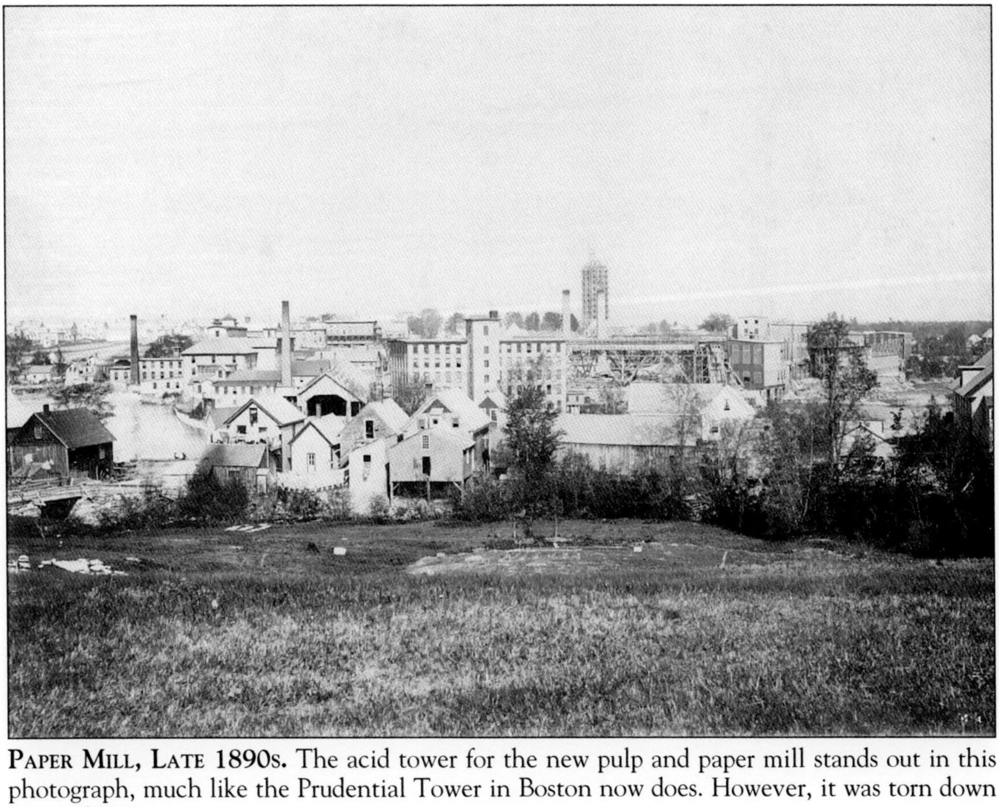

Paper Mill, Late 1890s. The acid tower for the new pulp and paper mill stands out in this photograph, much like the Prudential Tower in Boston now does. However, it was torn down after a few years.

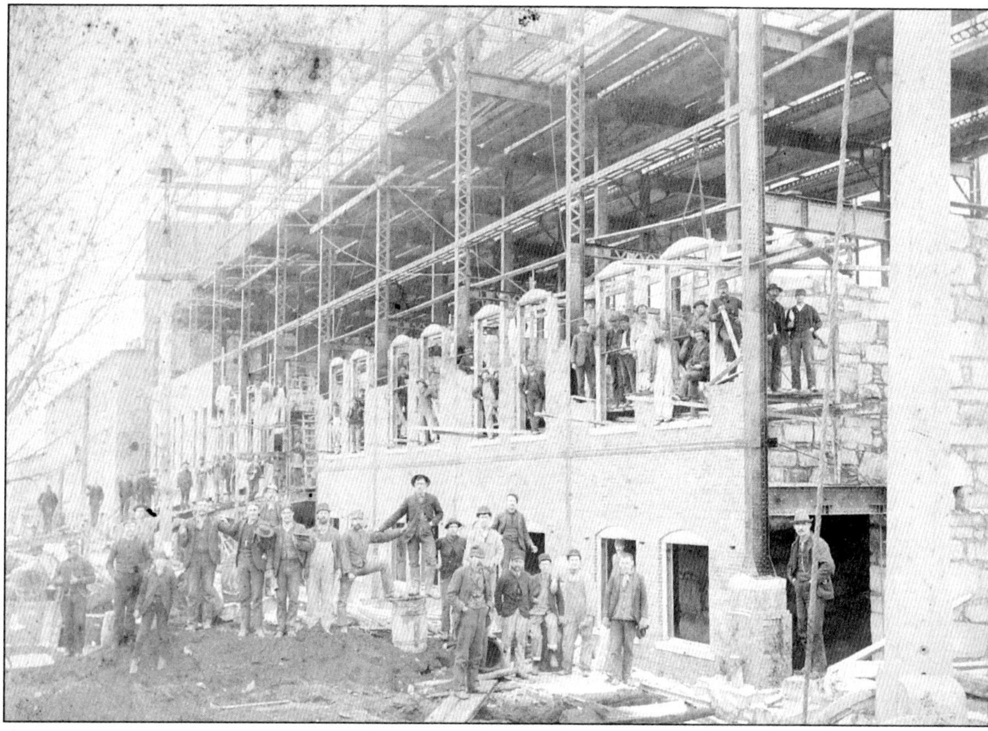

ANOTHER PICTURE OF CONSTRUCTION ON THE MADISON PAPER MILL. Owned first by Manufacturing Investment Company, the mill went through some hard times and was eventually taken over by Great Northern Paper Co.

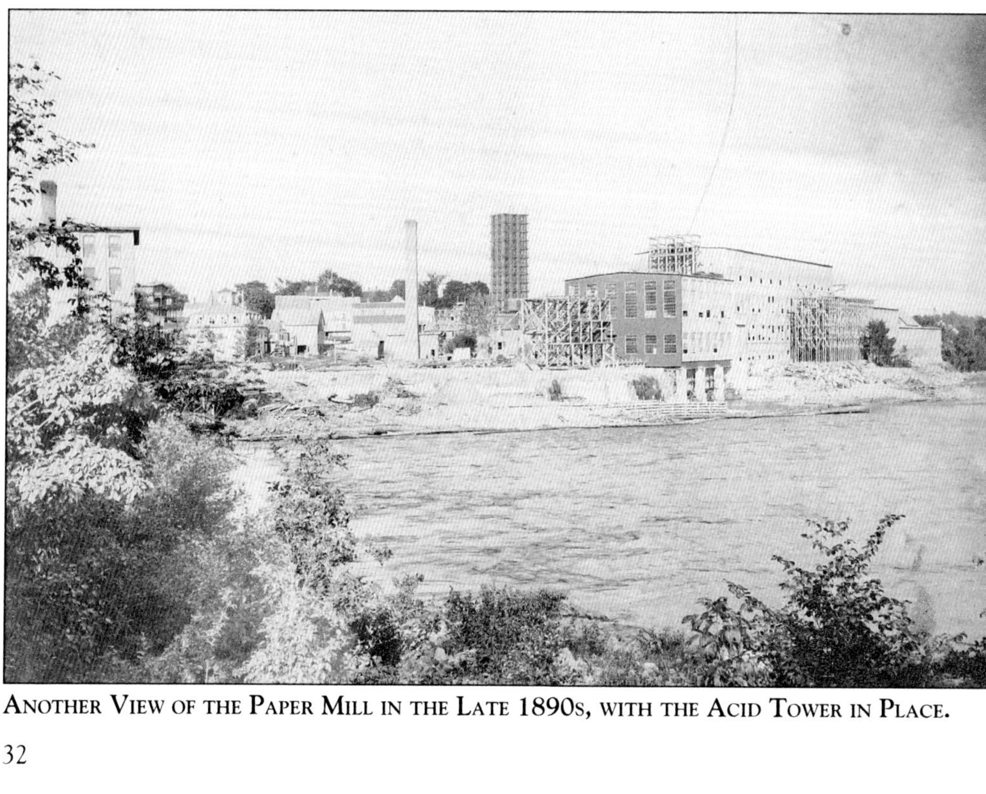

ANOTHER VIEW OF THE PAPER MILL IN THE LATE 1890S, WITH THE ACID TOWER IN PLACE.

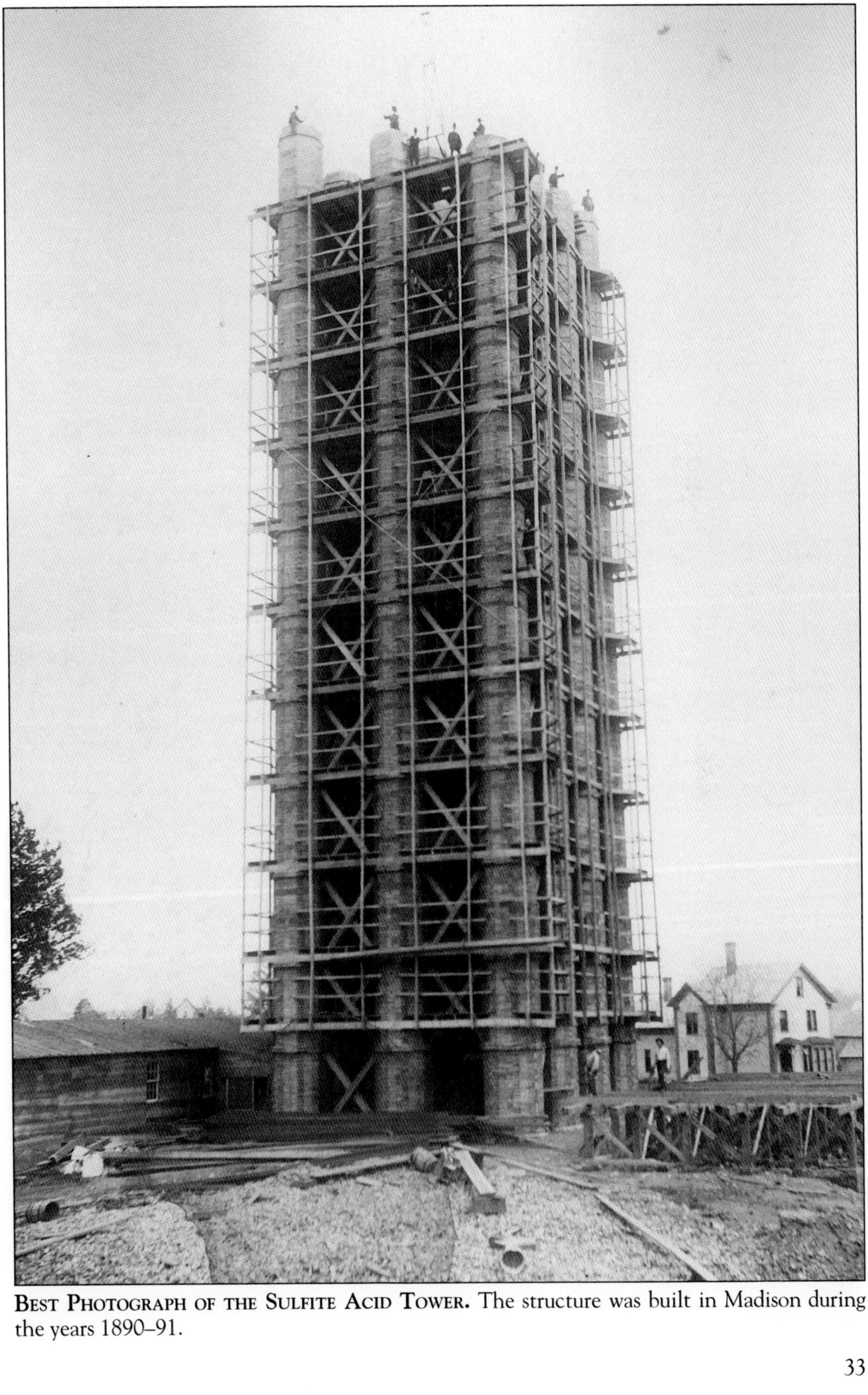

Best Photograph of the Sulfite Acid Tower. The structure was built in Madison during the years 1890–91.

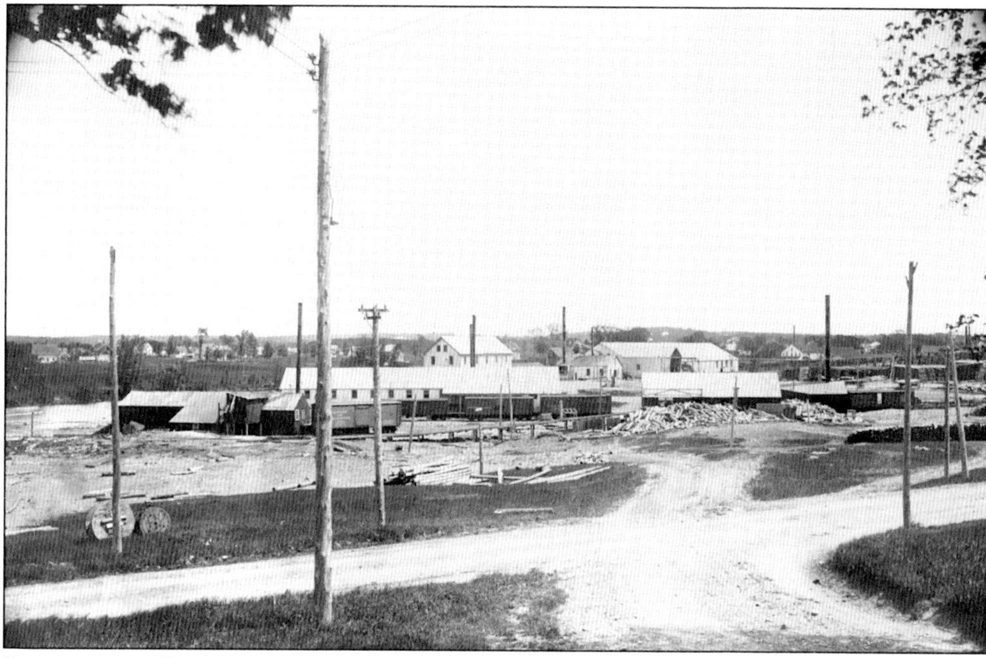

RAILROAD AND LUMBERYARD IN MADISON IN THE 1900S.

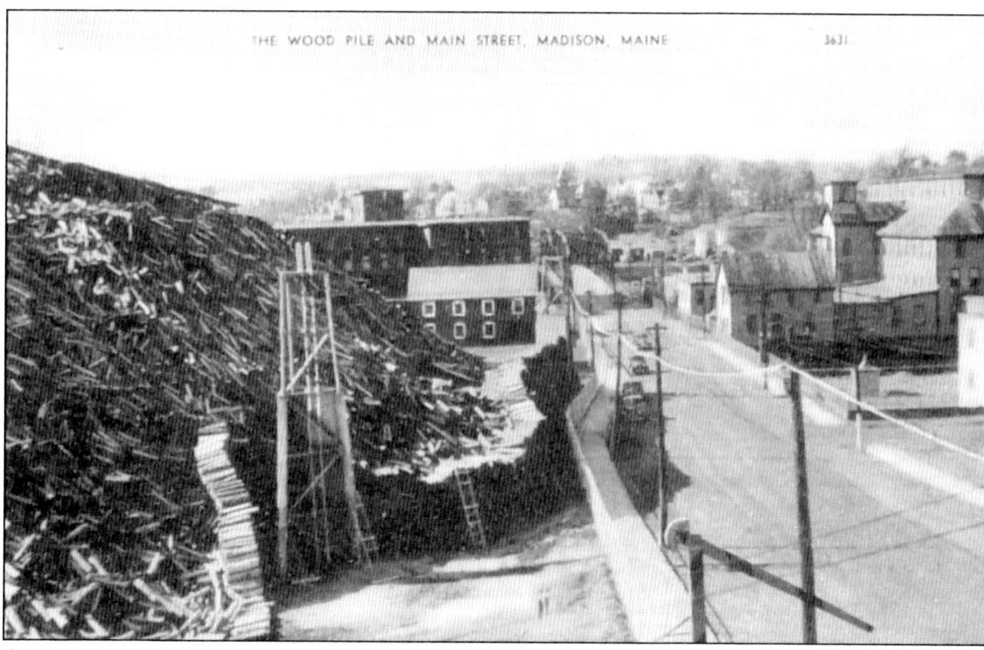

GREAT NORTHERN PAPER COMPANY'S WOOD PILE ON MAIN STREET, MADISON, IN THE 1920S.

Three

Norridgewock

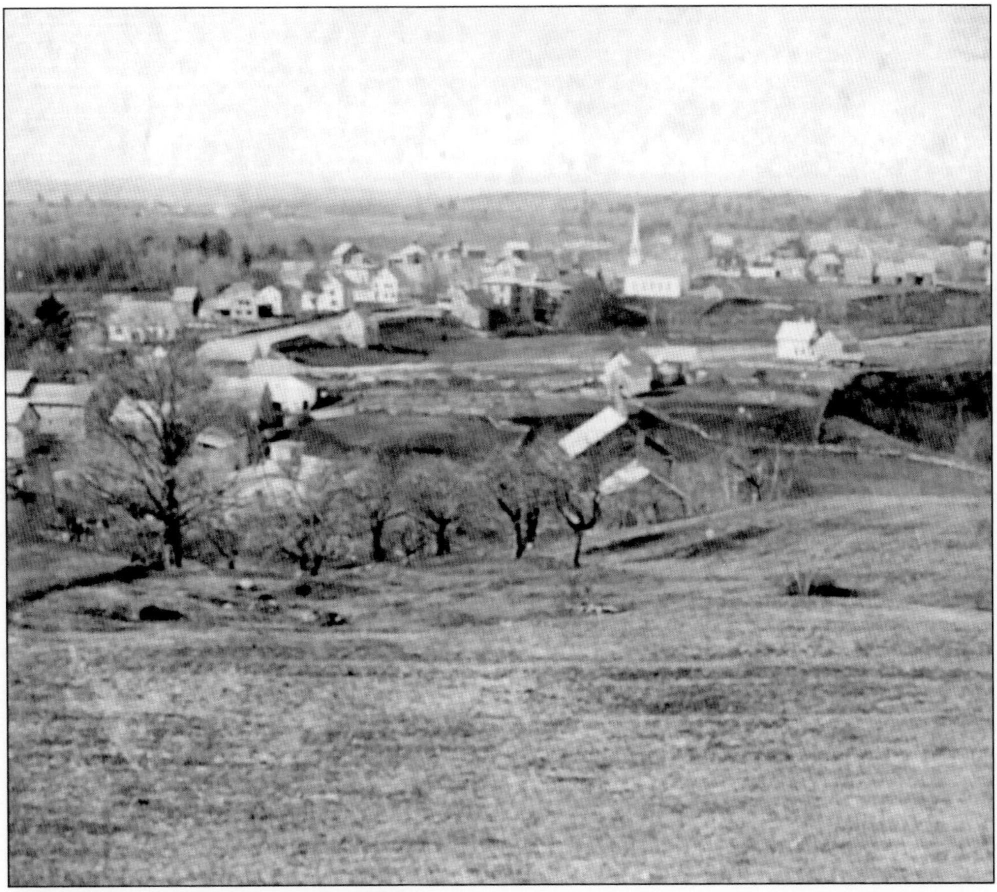

VIEW OF NORRIDGEWOCK IN THE 1880S.

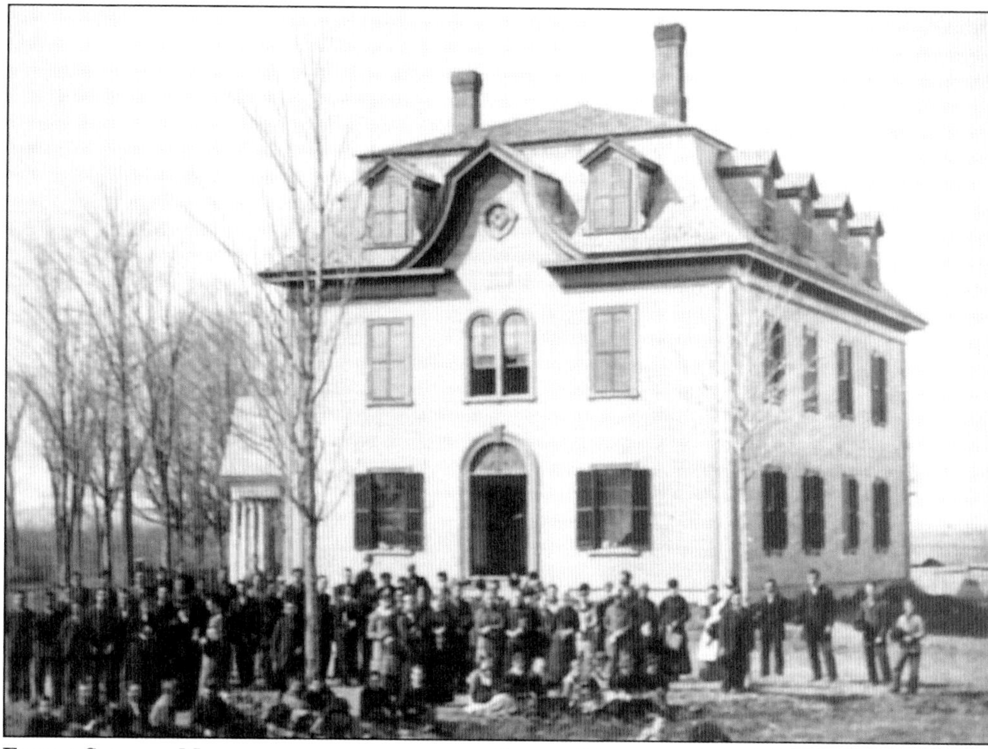

EATON SCHOOL, NORRIDGEWOCK, DURING THE SPRING TERM IN 1880. All the students are in front of the school. The front row is seated and the rest are standing. Founded by Hamlin Eaton in 1865, the school was at this location from 1866 to 1883, when it closed and the building was used as the public high school. This school building, in turn, was taken over by the local Grange in a 1916 swap for the then Grange building.

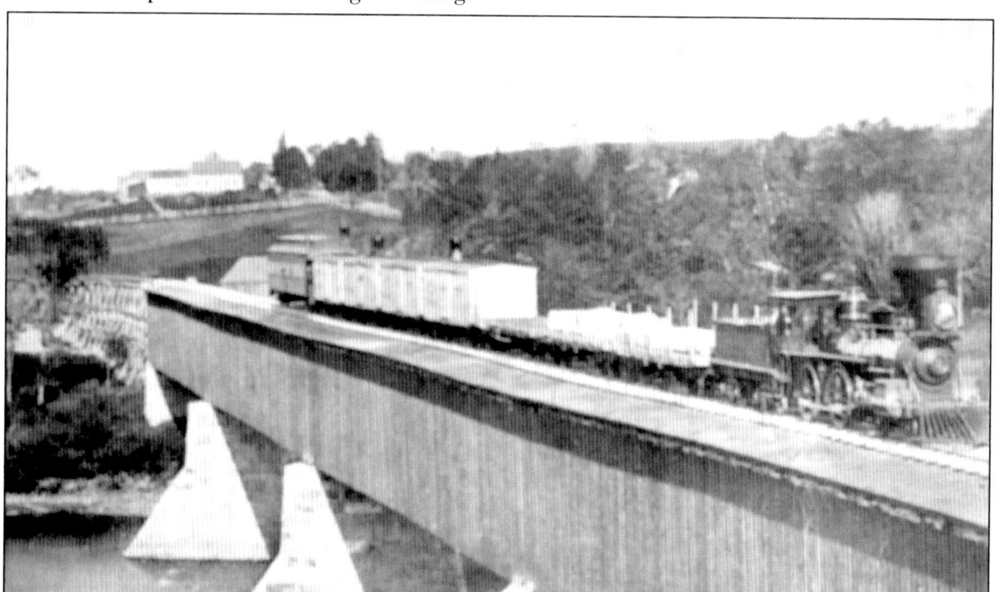

A FREIGHT TRAIN. With one passenger car at its end, this train goes over the railroad bridge at Norridgewock in the 1900s.

FATHER RASLE MONUMENT AT OLD POINT IN NORRIDGEWOCK IN THE 1900S. The Native American village that was once located here was wiped out by the British. Father Rasle, long a missionary to the Native Americans, was killed here August 27, 1724.

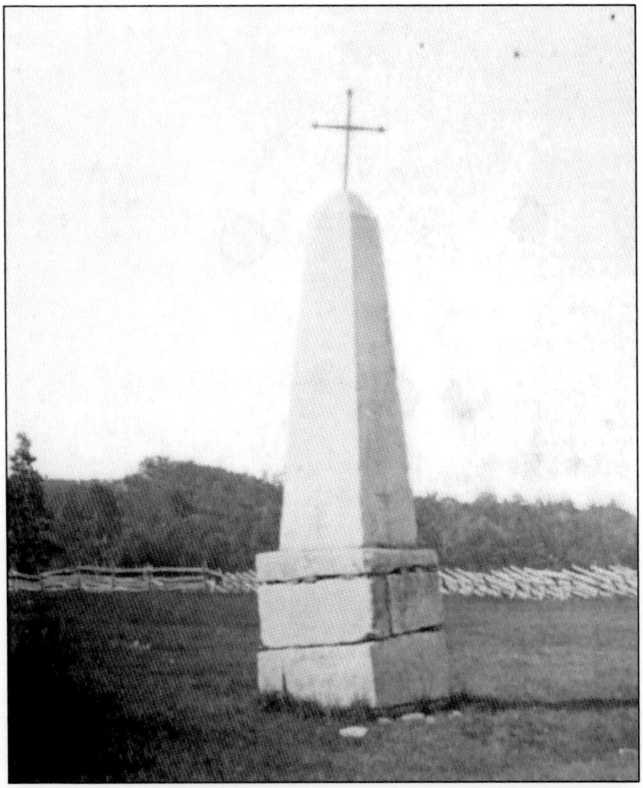

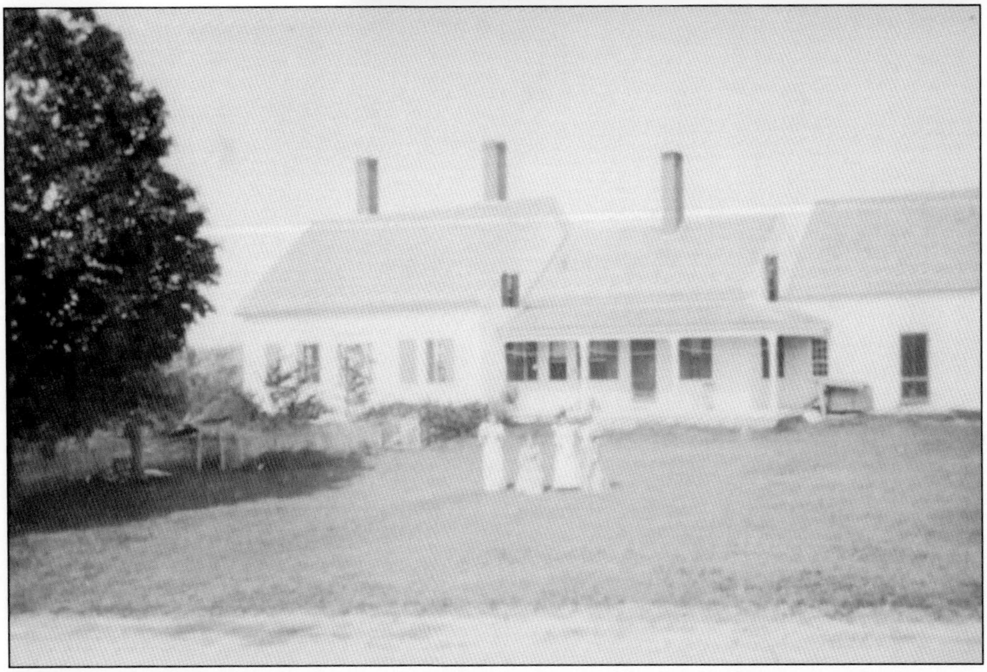

RESIDENCE IN NORRIDGEWOCK OF ISAAC MORSE ON AUGUST 29, 1897. Four women pose in front of this home—one seated and three standing. Note the three chimneys on this beautiful house.

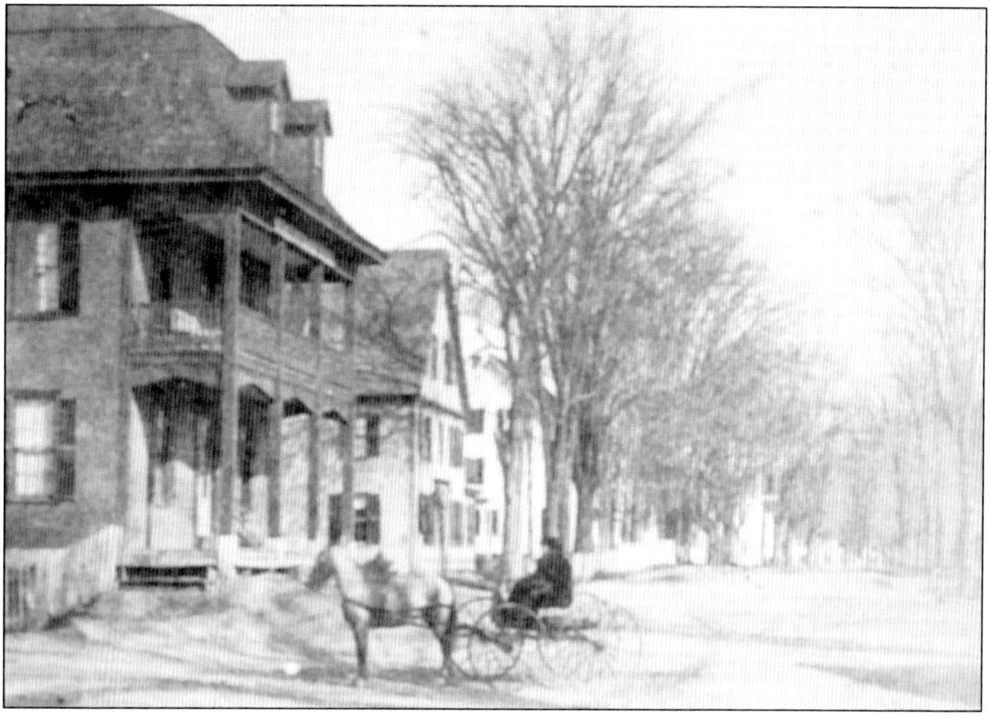

Main Street, Norridgewock in the 1890s. This view doesn't look too busy with only one horse and buggy on the road.

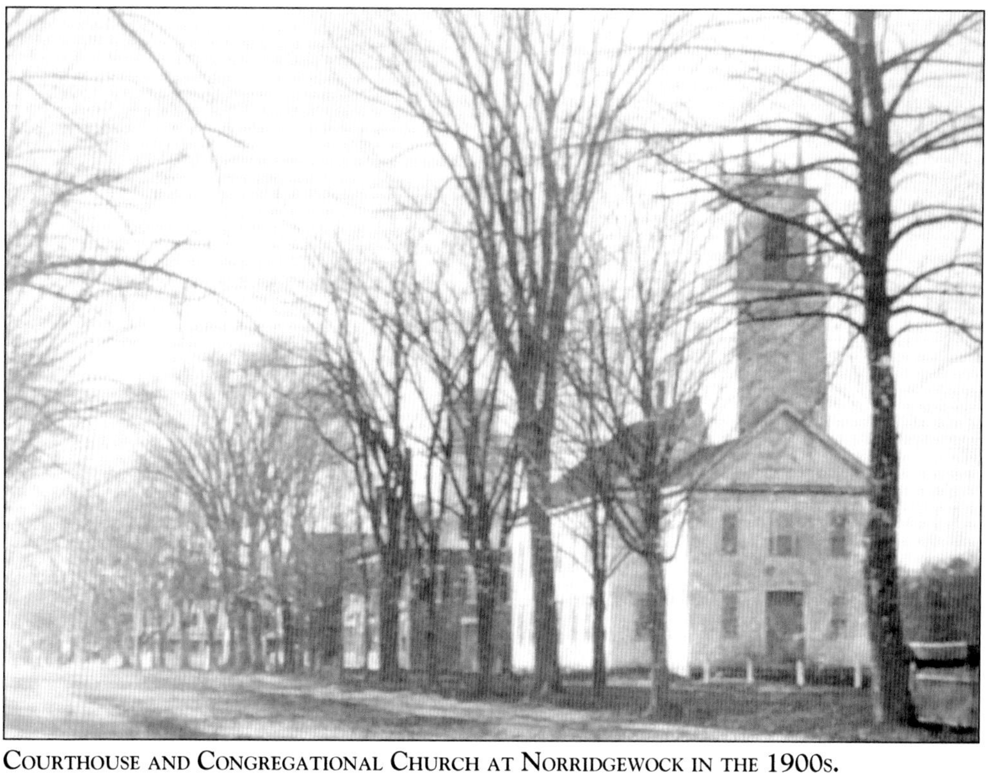

Courthouse and Congregational Church at Norridgewock in the 1900s.

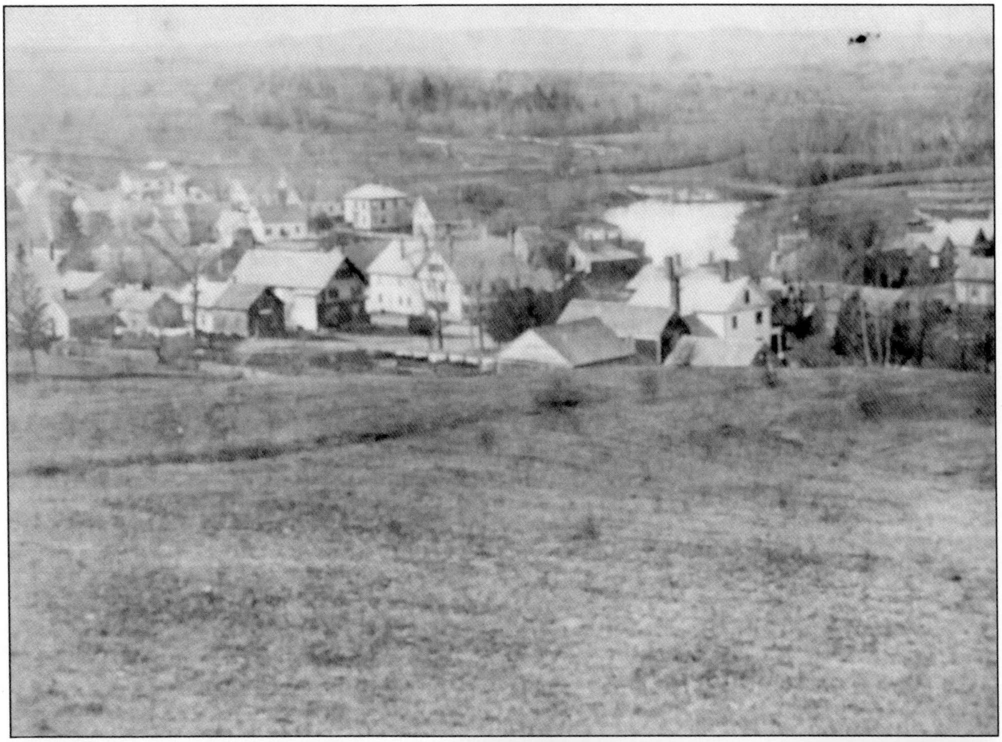

NORRIDGEWOCK FROM GILMAN HILL IN THE 1890S.

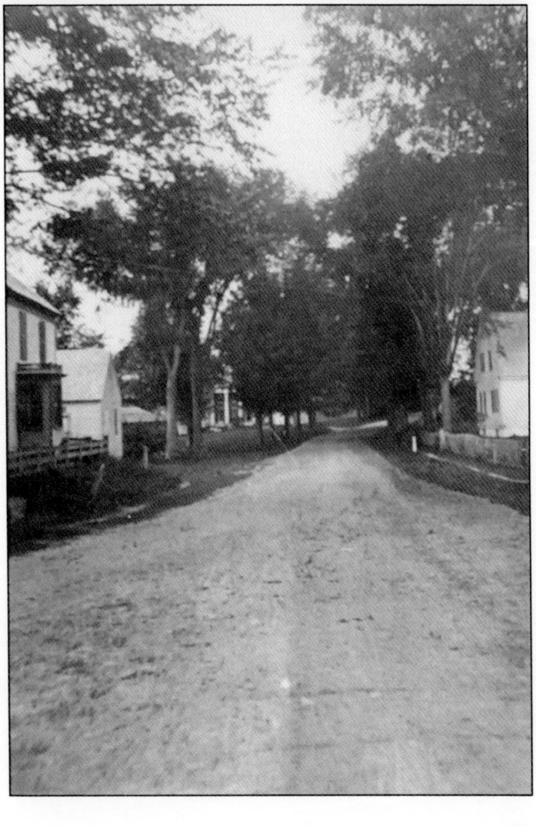

NORRIDGEWOCK, AGAIN IN THE 1890S. Note the dirt road.

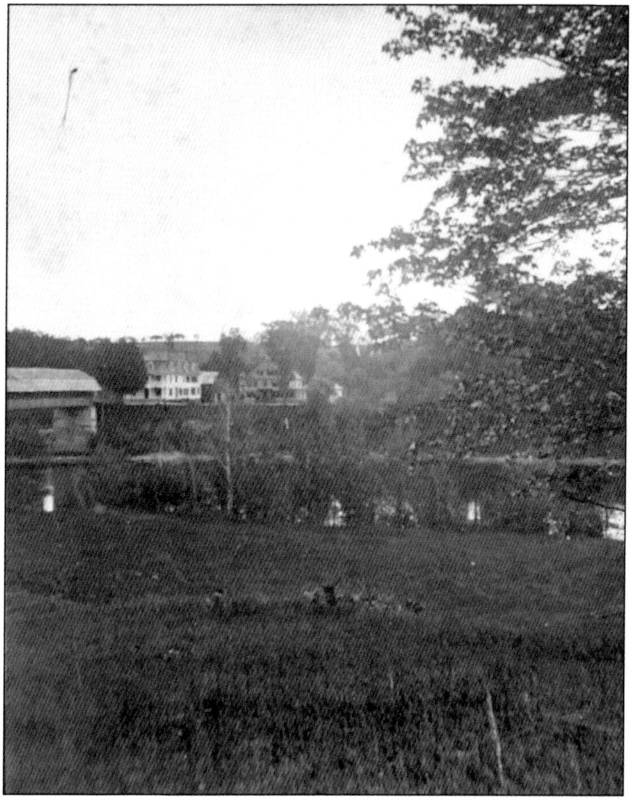

Norridgewock with the Kennebec River in the Foreground in the 1890s. The Norridgewock House may be in the distance.

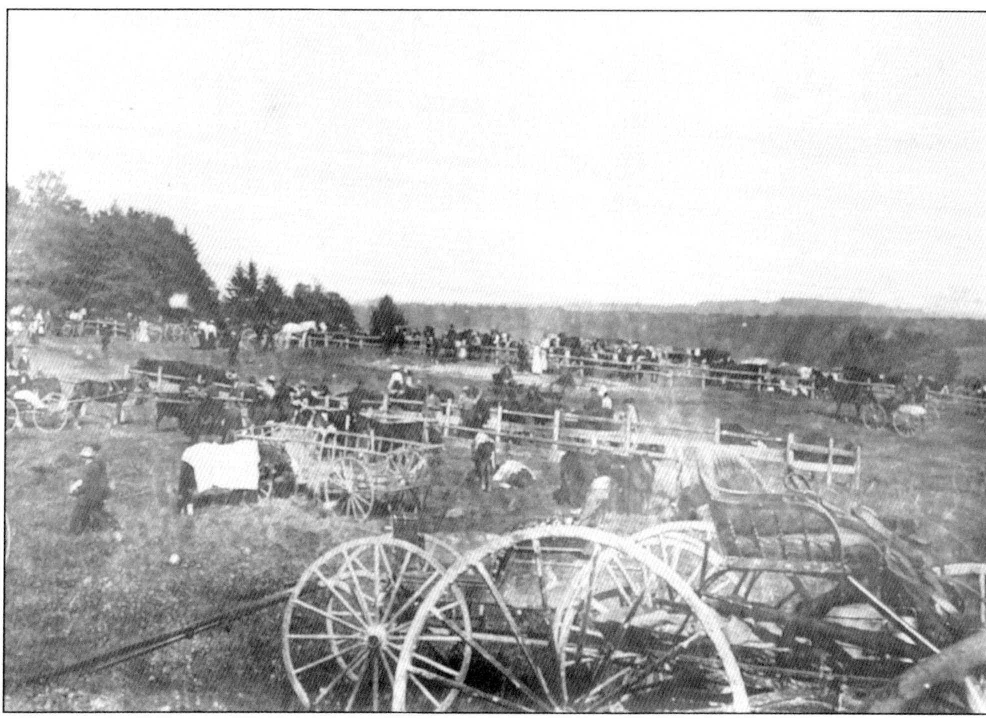

A Norridgewock Gathering in the 1900s. Dodlin Mountain is visible on the far right.

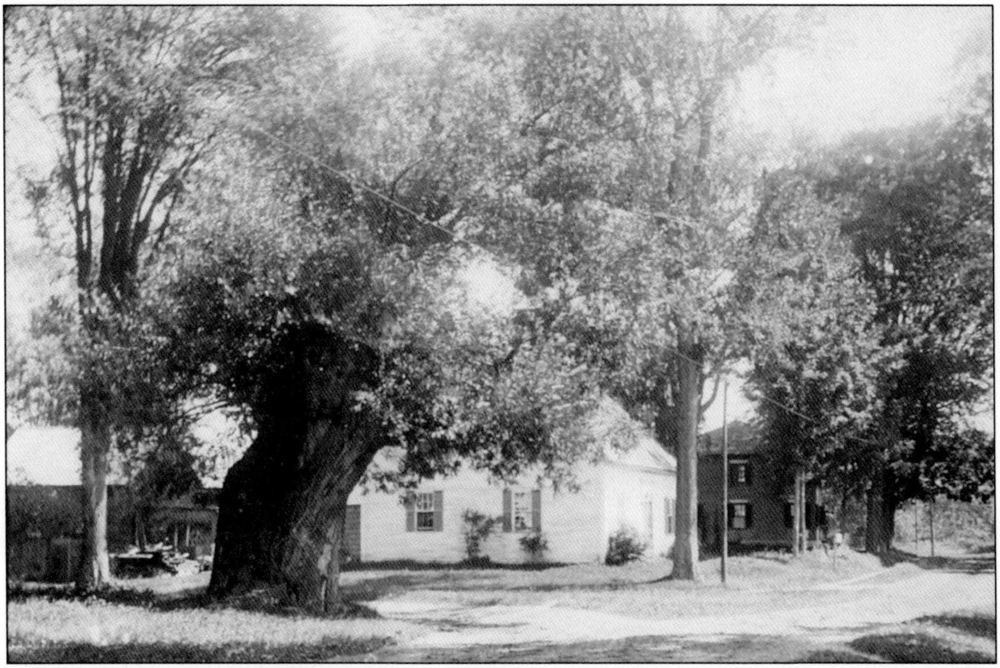

Norridgewock, in the Early 1900s. This huge willow tree was on the north side of the Kennebec River in Norridgewock. The first house on the left was once owned by Everett Rowe. Farther along on the left center, to the rear is the brick house once owned by the Dole family, ancestors of the Dole pineapple family in Hawaii.

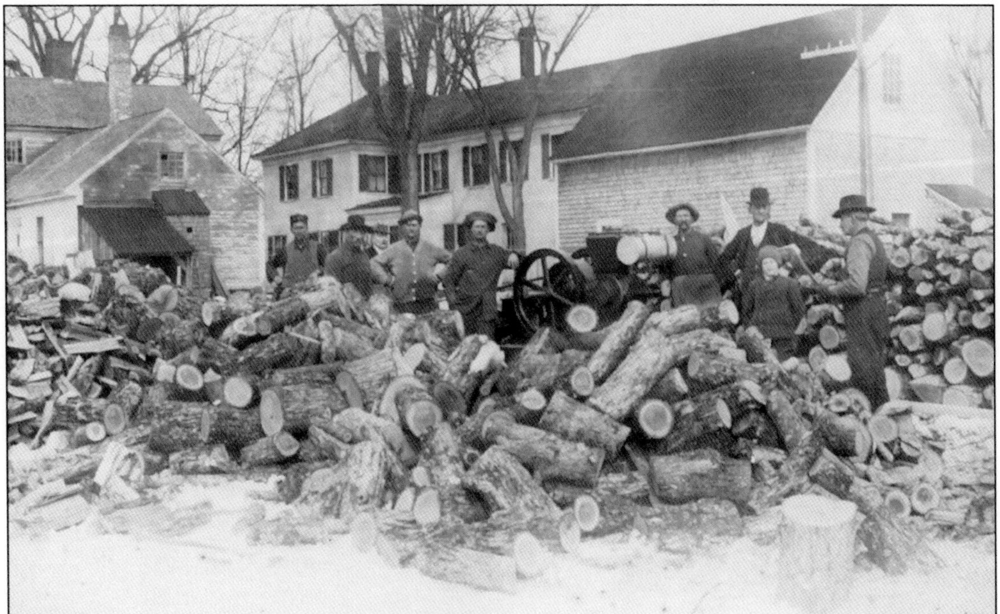

Edward Burgess's Home on Main Street, Norridgewock in 1912. Wood was hauled there and cut on this machine into a size to fit a wood stove.

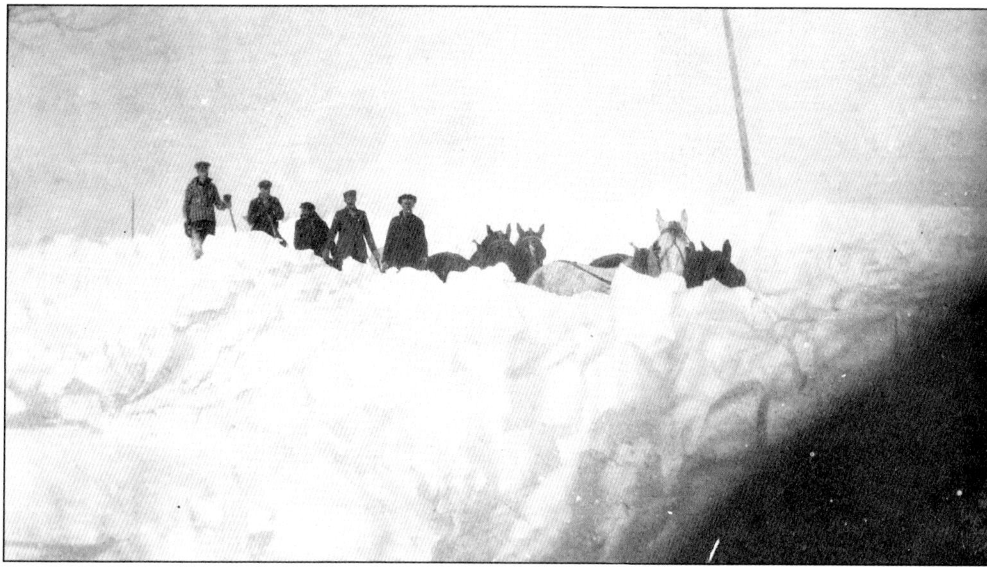

Norridgewock in the 1930s. Snow really piled up in front of the Clinton Watson home on Winding Hill Road. Note how high the snow is on the horses.

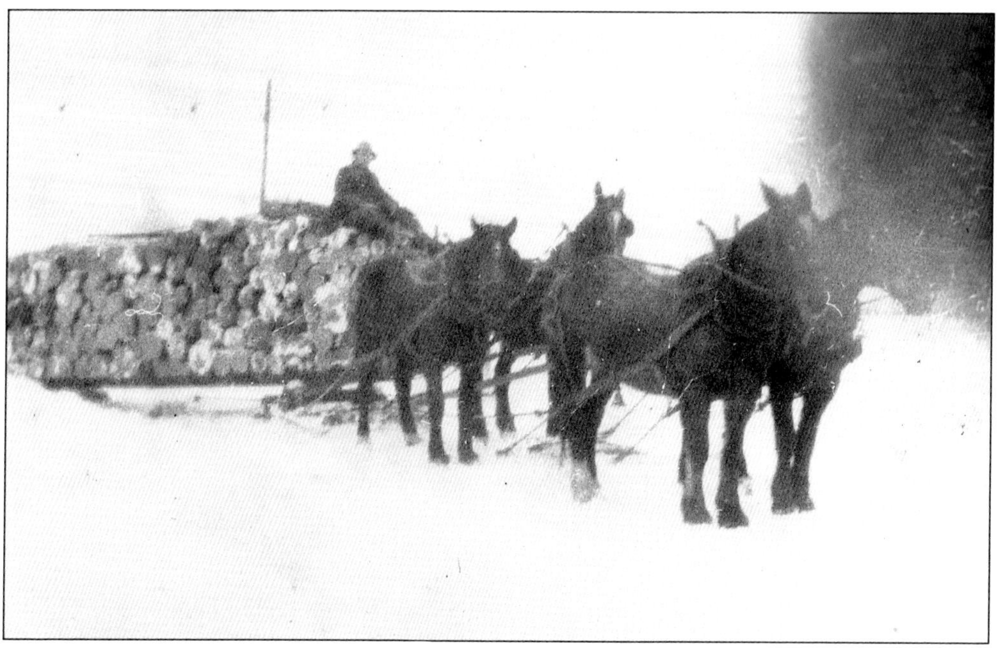

Clinton Watson, Hauling Pulp in 1930. The four horses are hauling 3 3/4 cords.

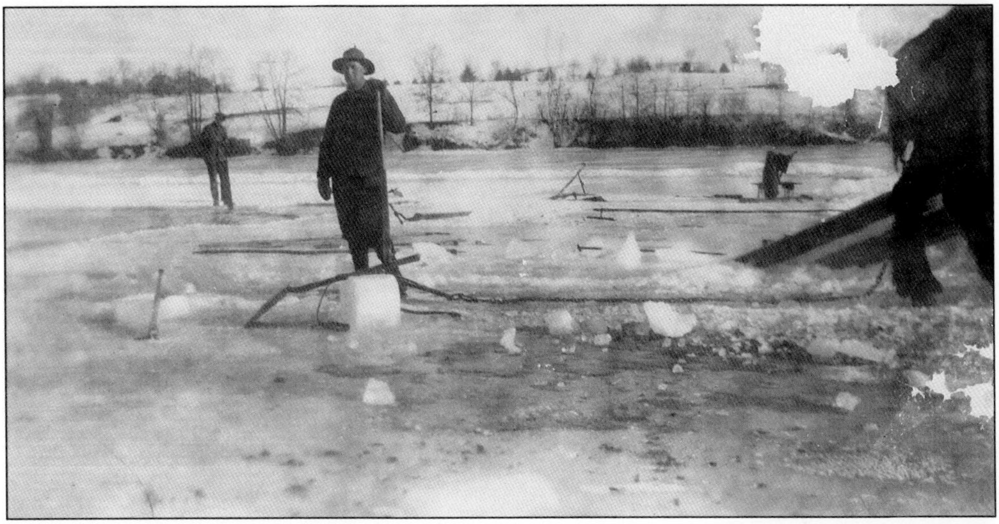

Clayton Albee and Frank Esty in 1928. The two men cut ice, as the icehouse was still popular then. Stored in such a house with sawdust to help keep it from melting, the ice was used in the family icebox during the warmer months of the year.

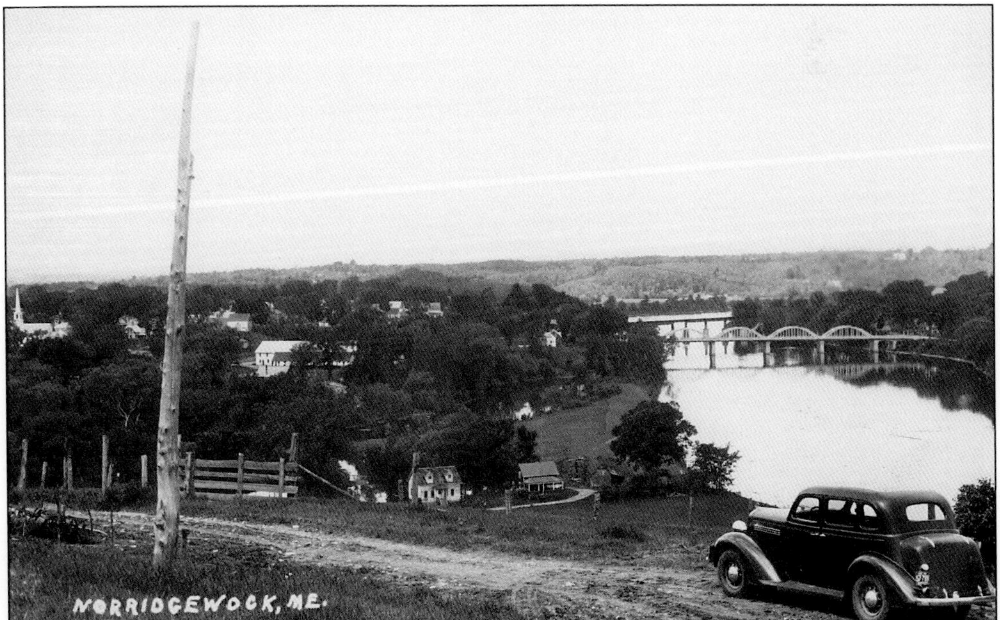

Looking down from the Top of Sunset Hill. Sophie May Lane, of Norridgewock, is shown here at the Kennebec River in the 1930s.

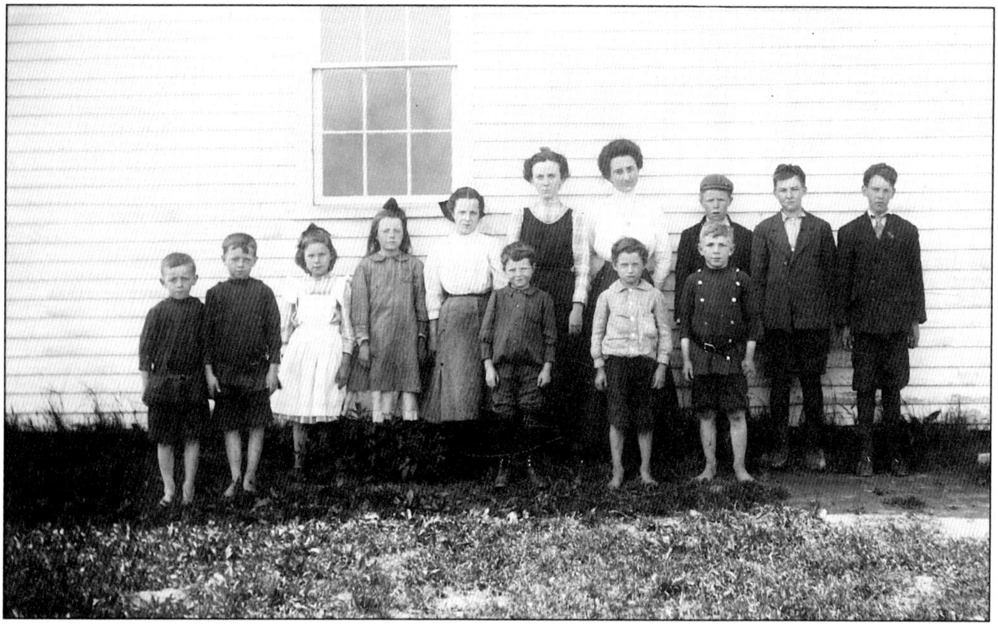

PUPILS AND TEACHERS AT THE ATKINSON SCHOOL, WILDER HILL ROAD, IN THE 1900S.

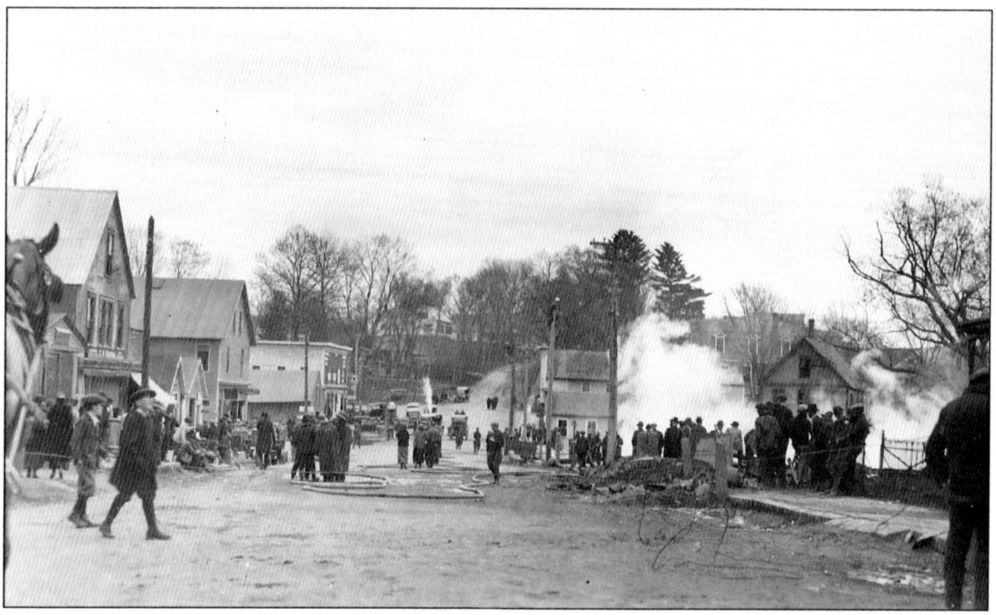

GREAT FIRE OF MARCH 1924 IN NORRIDGEWOCK. It destroyed most of Main Street.

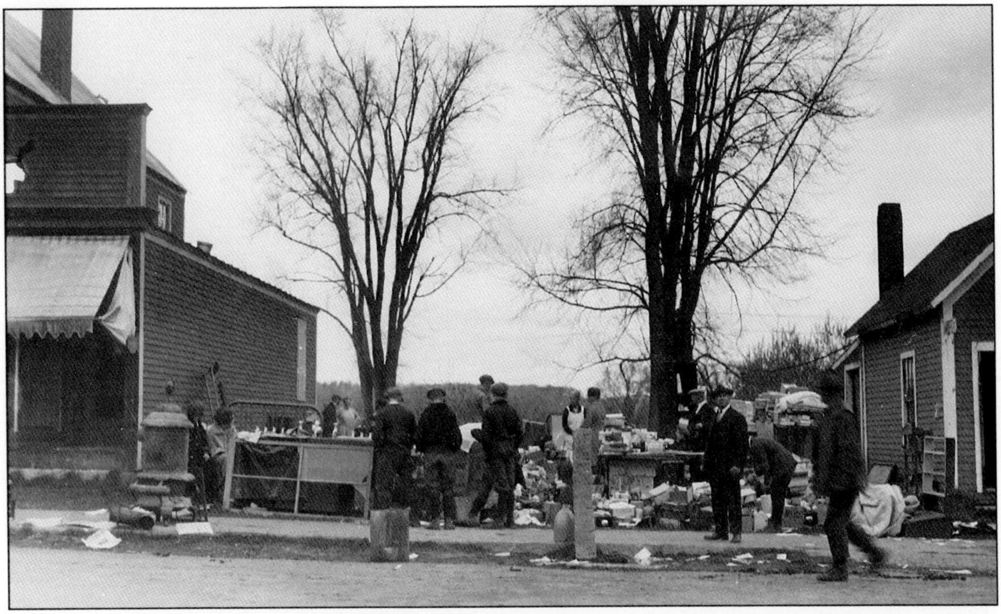

AN UNUSUAL FIRE PHOTOGRAPH. This is the side of Main Street that didn't burn with materials moved from inside some of the buildings that did burn.

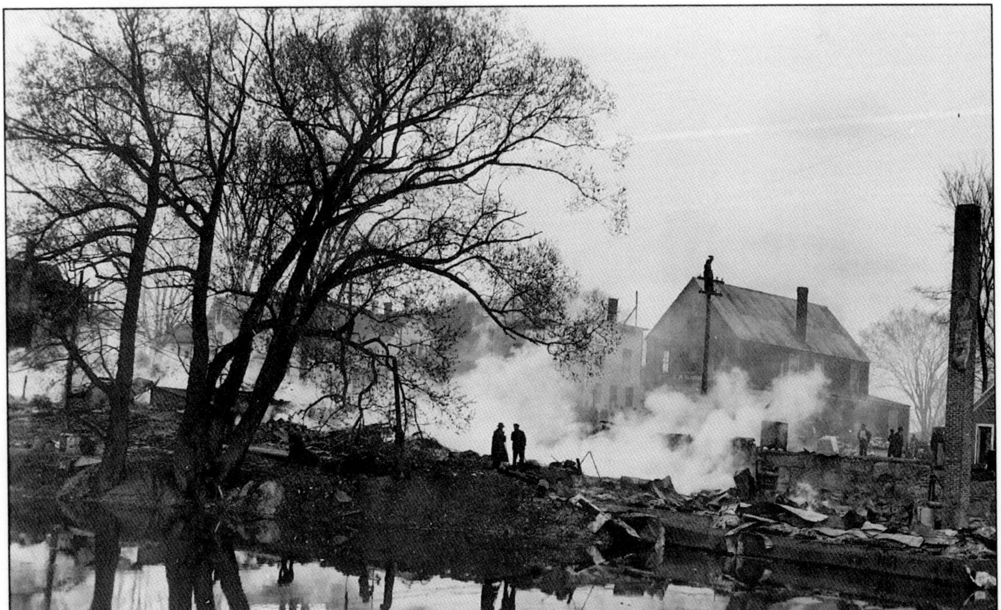

NORRIDGEWOCK FIRE, 1924. Two men are silhouetted against the smoke during the big fire.

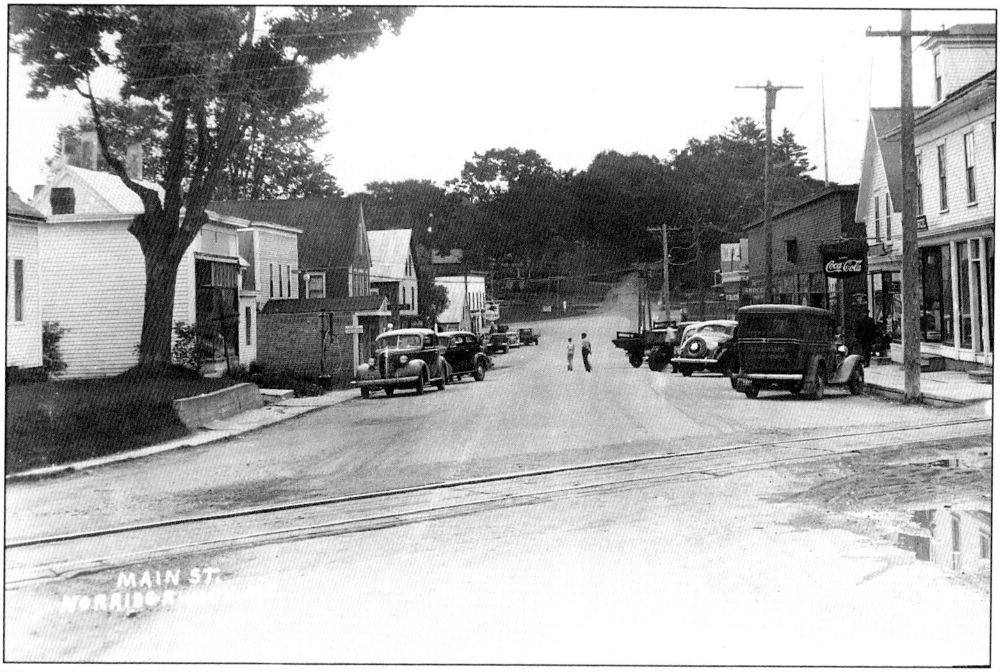

MAIN STREET, NORRIDGEWOCK, IN THE 1930S. The automobile had obviously taken over.

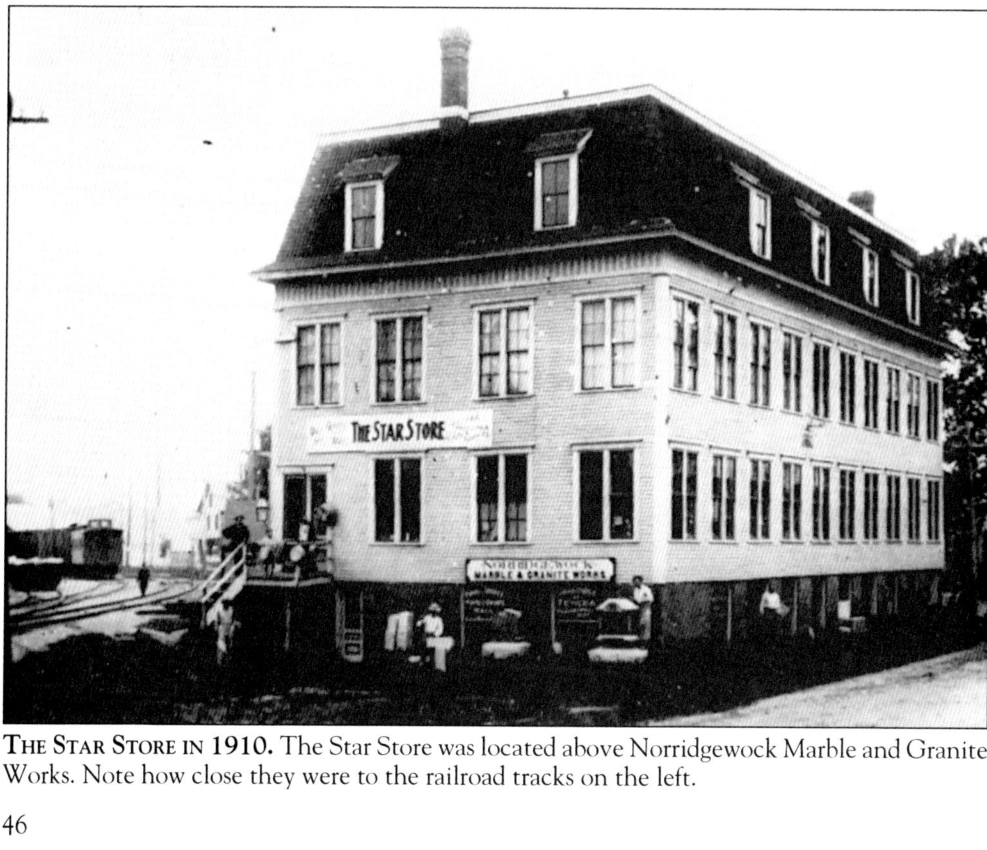

THE STAR STORE IN 1910. The Star Store was located above Norridgewock Marble and Granite Works. Note how close they were to the railroad tracks on the left.

Four

Smithfield

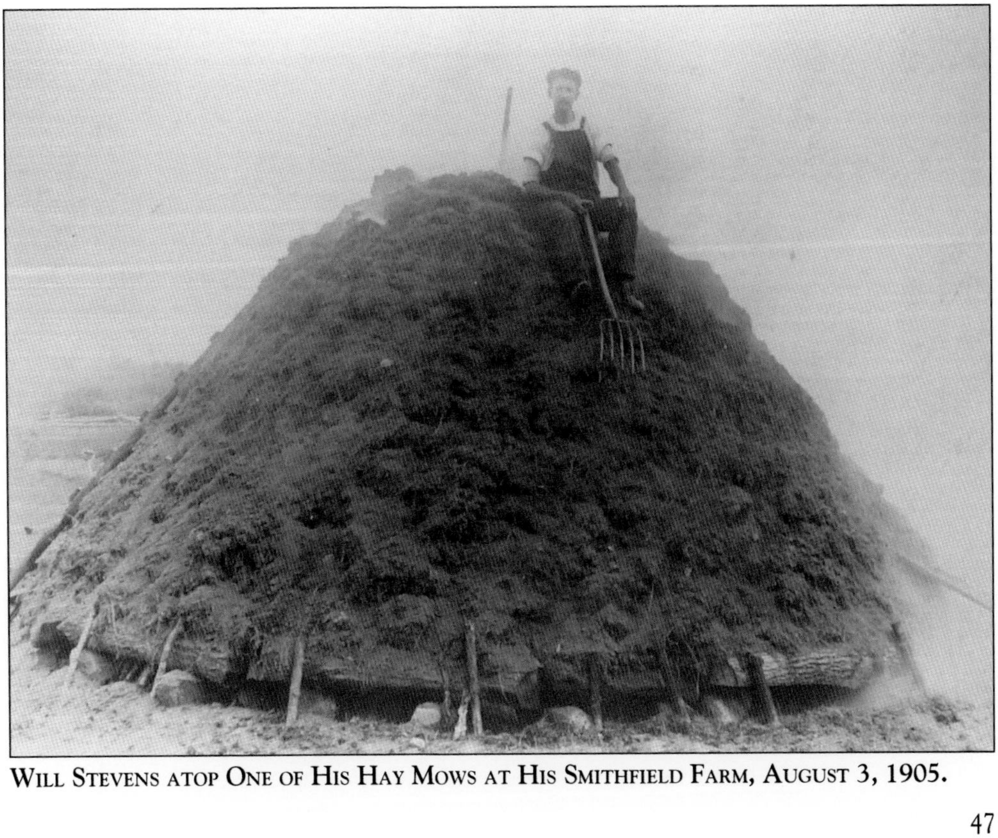

WILL STEVENS ATOP ONE OF HIS HAY MOWS AT HIS SMITHFIELD FARM, AUGUST 3, 1905.

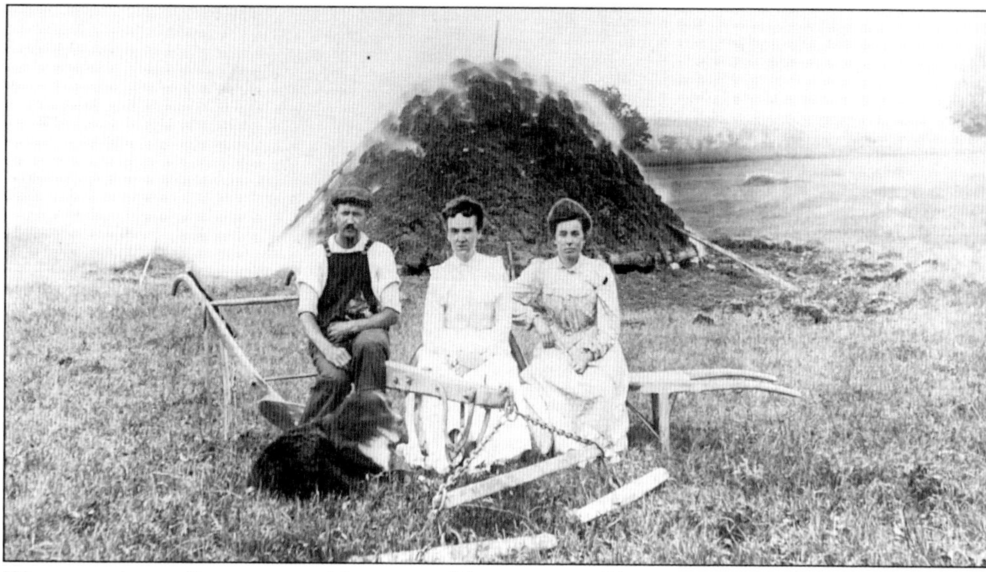

Will and Addie Stevens and Margaret Ham with an Unnamed Dog. The trio sits in front of a hay mow at the Stevens farm in the summer of 1906.

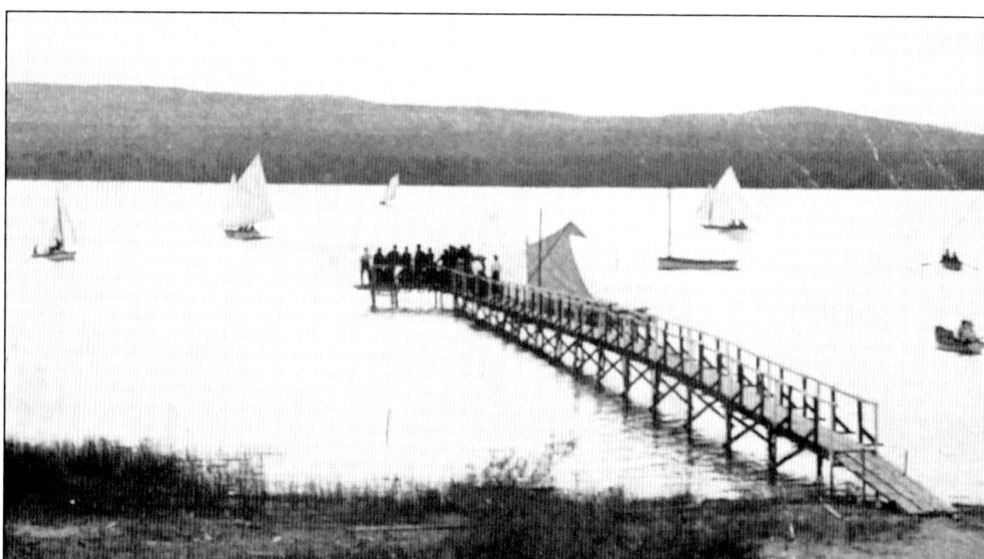

North Pond in Smithfield with Long Wharf and Sailboats in the 1920s.

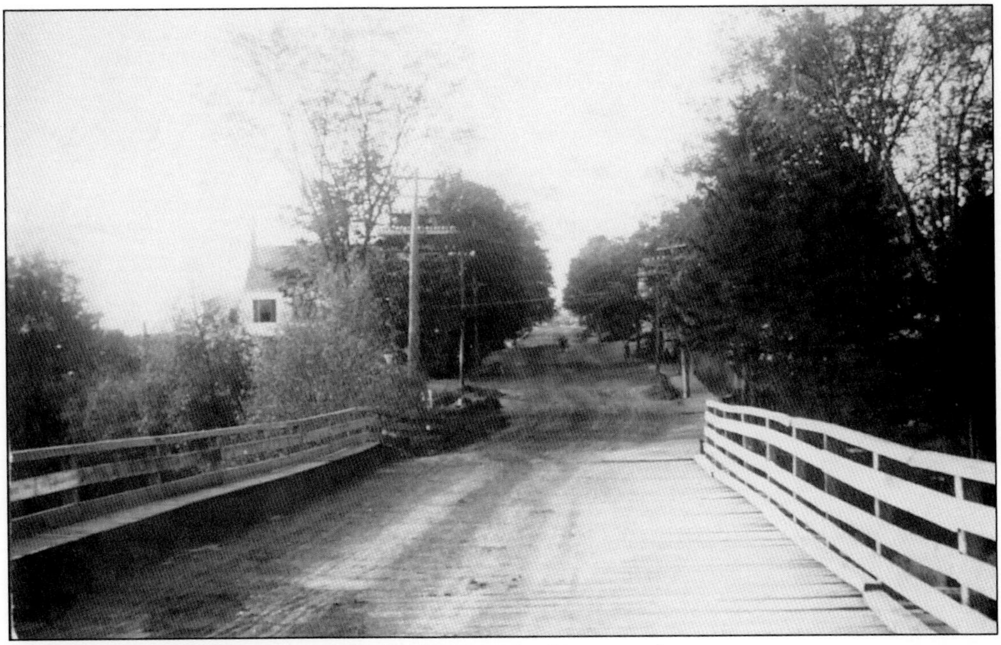

SMITHFIELD IN 1914 OR 1915. The bridge is in the foreground.

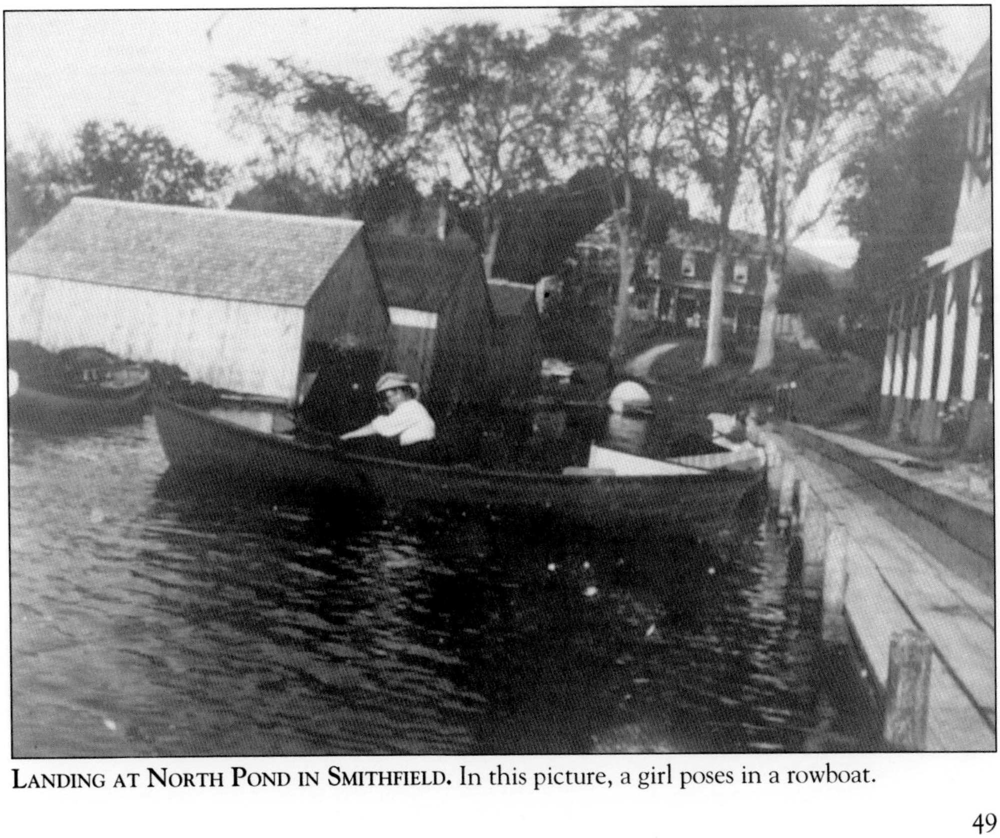

LANDING AT NORTH POND IN SMITHFIELD. In this picture, a girl poses in a rowboat.

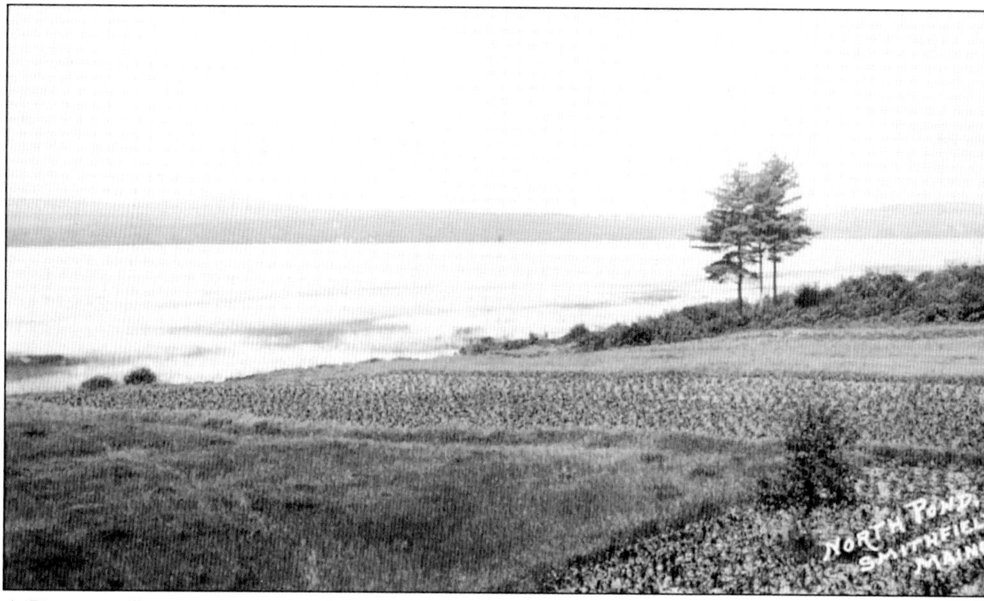

A FIELD OF CORN IN FRONT OF BEAUTIFUL NORTH POND.

SCENIC NORTH POND IN THE 1940S. This photograph was taken from the Corson home on Route 8 in Smithfield.

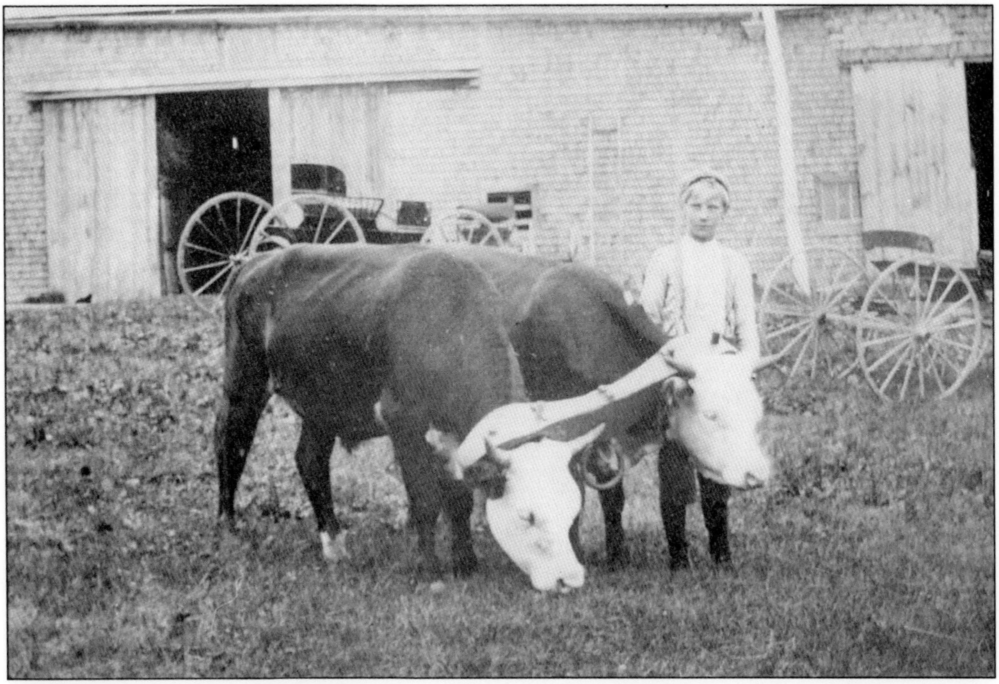

Ernest Stevens, About Age 13. He stands with two yoked oxen in front of the barn at the Fred Stevens Farm on Route 8 in 1908.

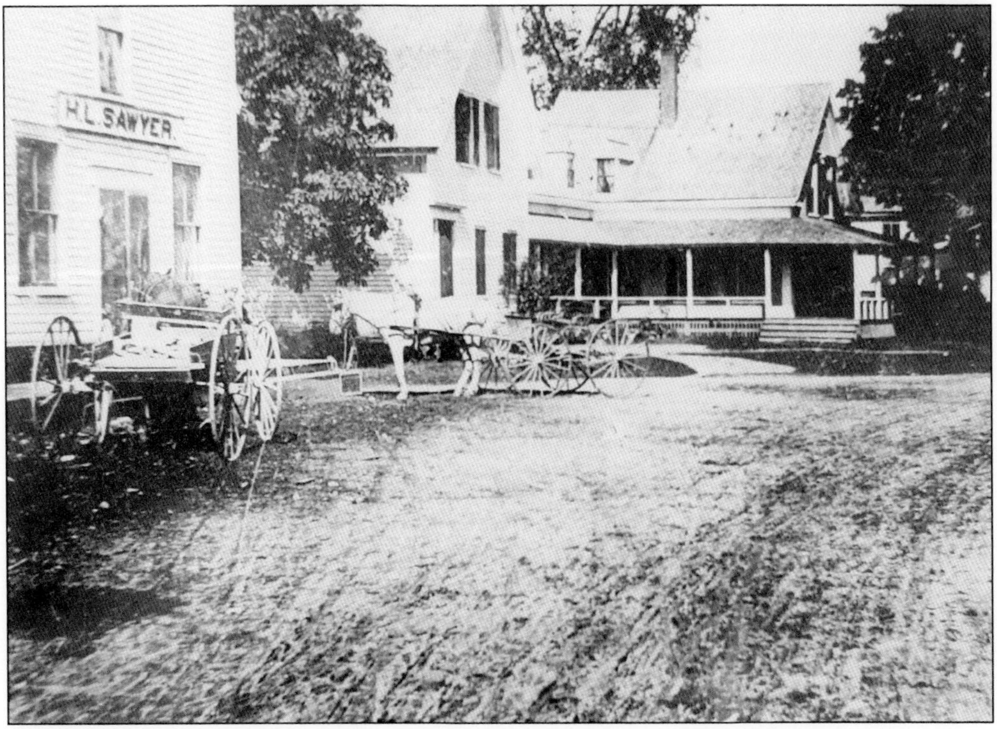

Smithfield Village, About 1910. The H.L. Sawyer store is on the left with the old hotel on the right. There are two horses and two buggies in front of Sawyer's.

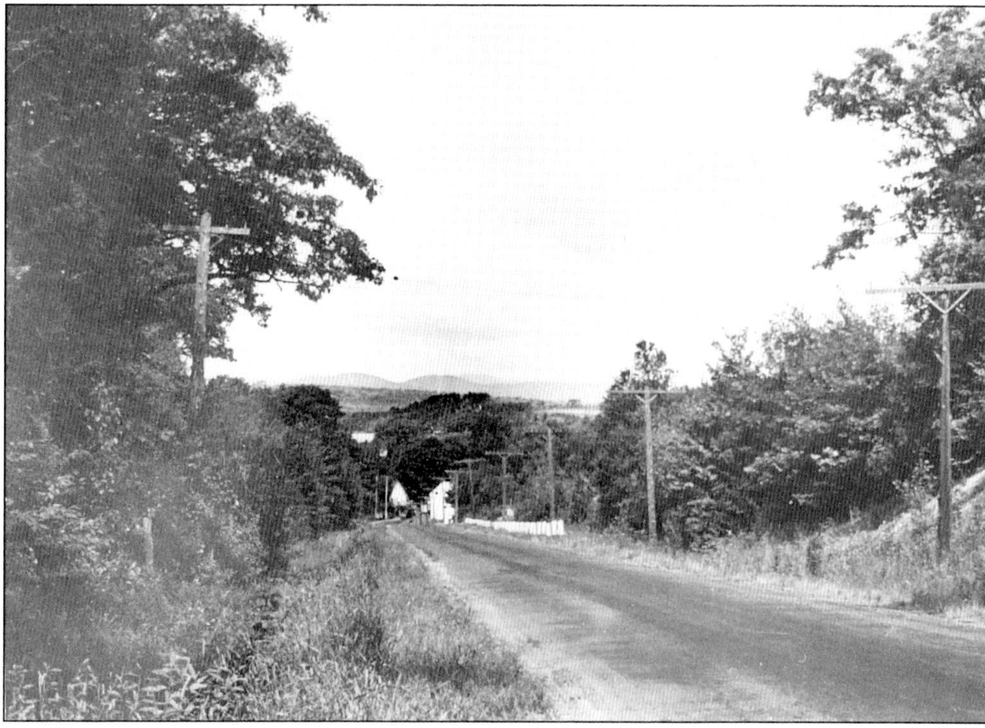

FROM ROUTE 8 LOOKING TOWARD SMITHFIELD VILLAGE IN THE 1940S.

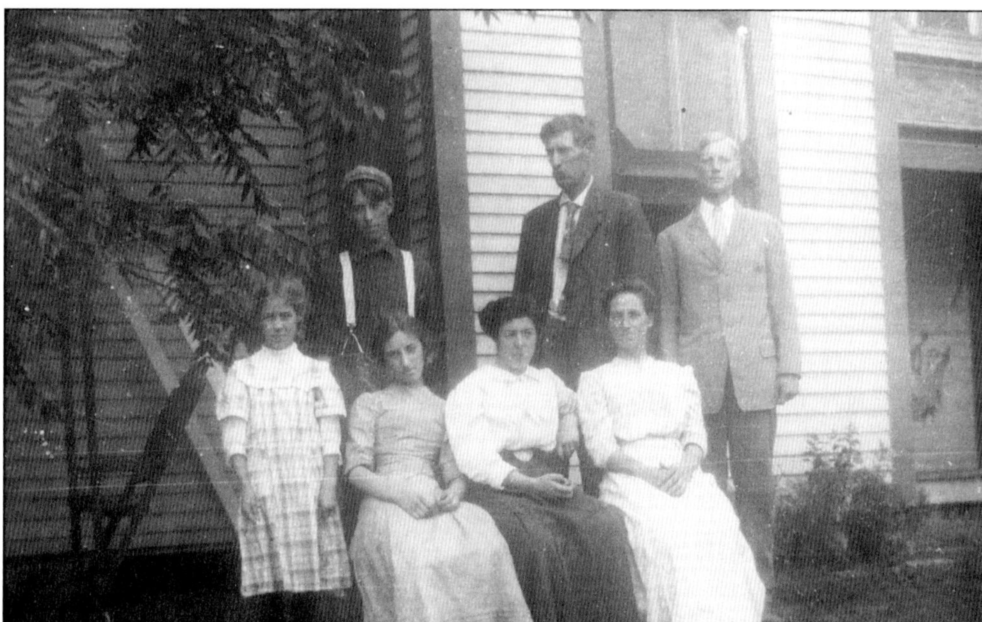

STEVENS FAMILY PORTRAIT. This 1910 image was taken near the Stevens home, on top of the hill just south of Smithfield Village on Route 8. The house, built in the late 1700s, is now a garage, with the present house constructed about 1850. In the photograph are Lindsey Stevens, Fred D. Stevens, Ernest M. Stevens, Eula Stevens Witham, Bessie L. Stevens Corson, Mabel Winegartner (daughter), and Lizzie G. Stevens (Lindsey's wife).

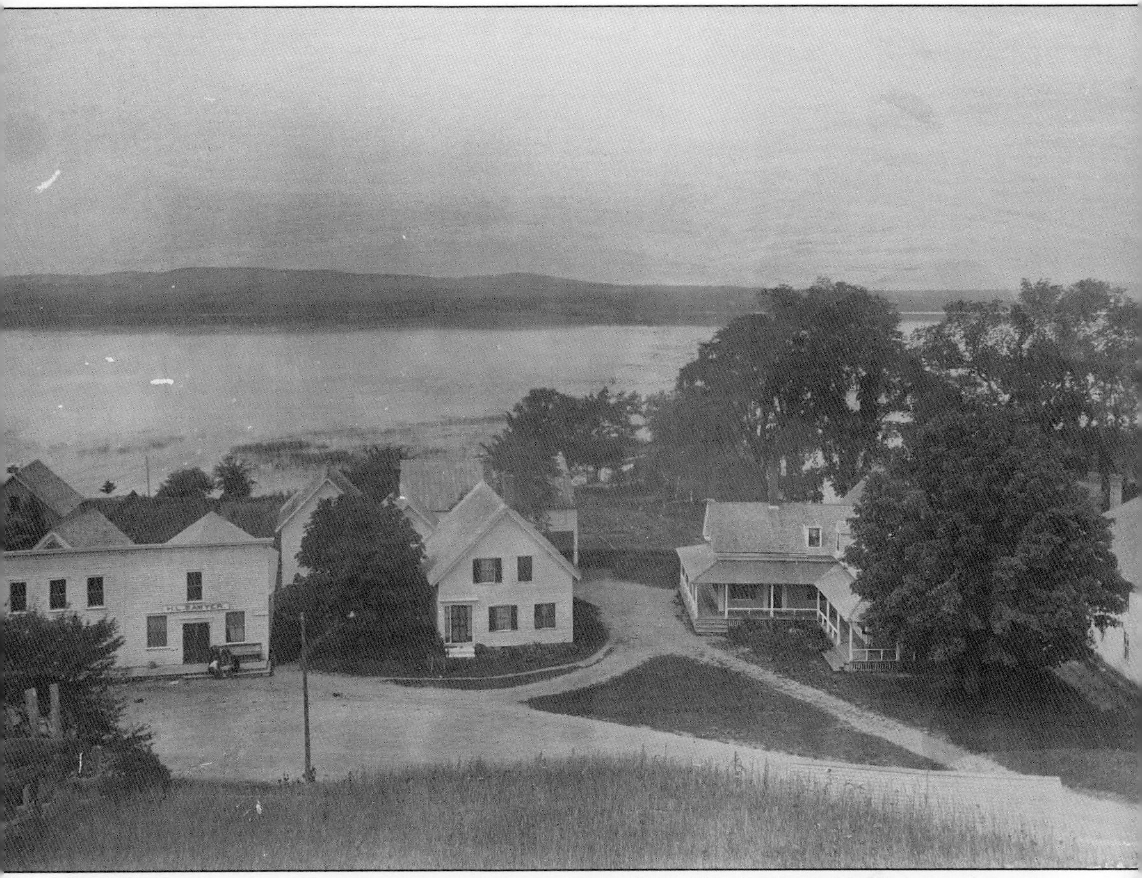

North Pond in the Background, About 1910. The North Pond Hotel, owned by the Hartford family, is pictured on the right. Sawyer's Store is on the left, with a home in between the store and the hotel. Fred Stevens, a lifelong farmer with many children and many descendants, seems to have been an excellent photographer also, for he took this photograph.

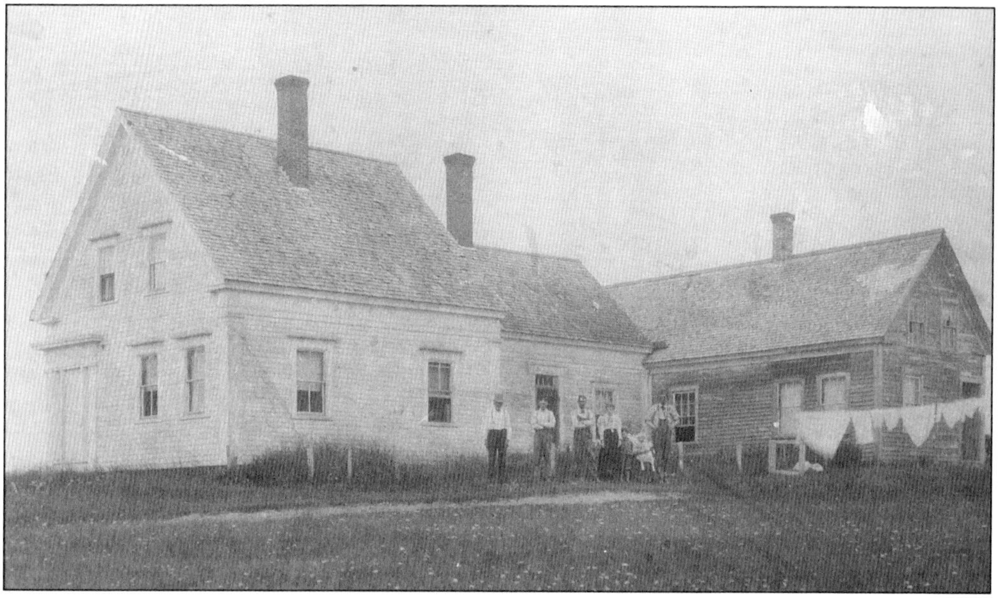

Fairview Farm, atop the Hill Just South of Smithfield Village. The farm is now the Doris Haines home. Fairview Farm is now called Windy Ridge but was once known as Stevens Hill when the Stevens family lived there.

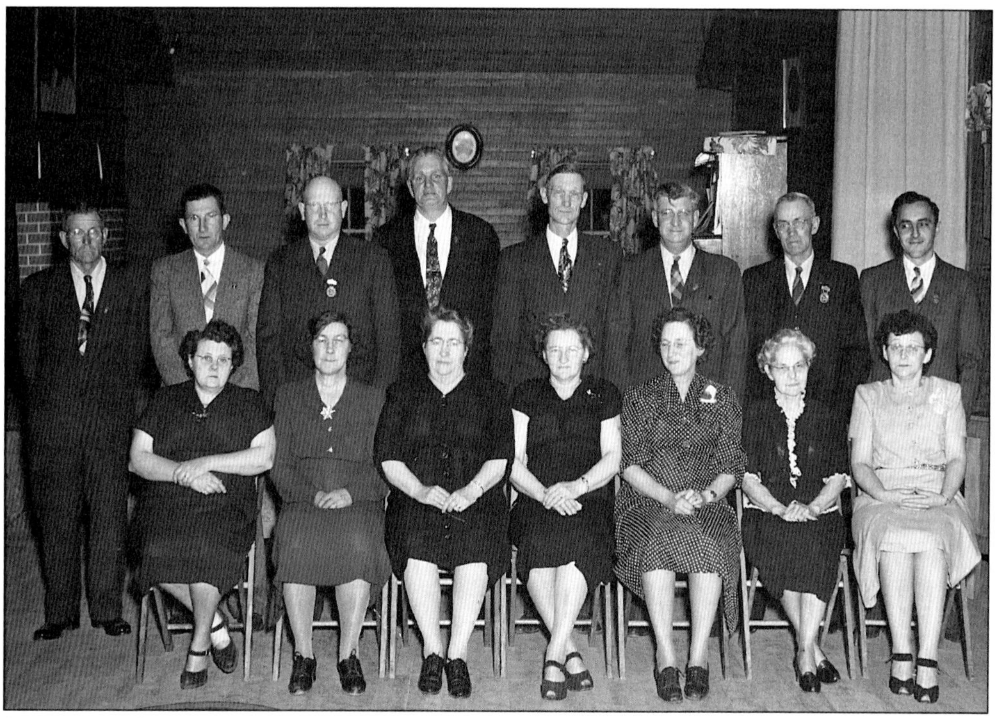

Smithfield Grange in the Mid-1940s at the Grange Hall. Pictured from left to right are as follows: (front row) Lillian Charles, Eula Witham, Bessie Abbott, Stella Stevens, Bessie Corson, Mabel Hartford, and Julia Taylor; (back row) George Hartford, Eugene Charles, Leon Witham, Theopolis Abbott, Ernest Stevens, Robert Corson, Luther Hartford, and Emery Taylor.

Five

The Parker Family

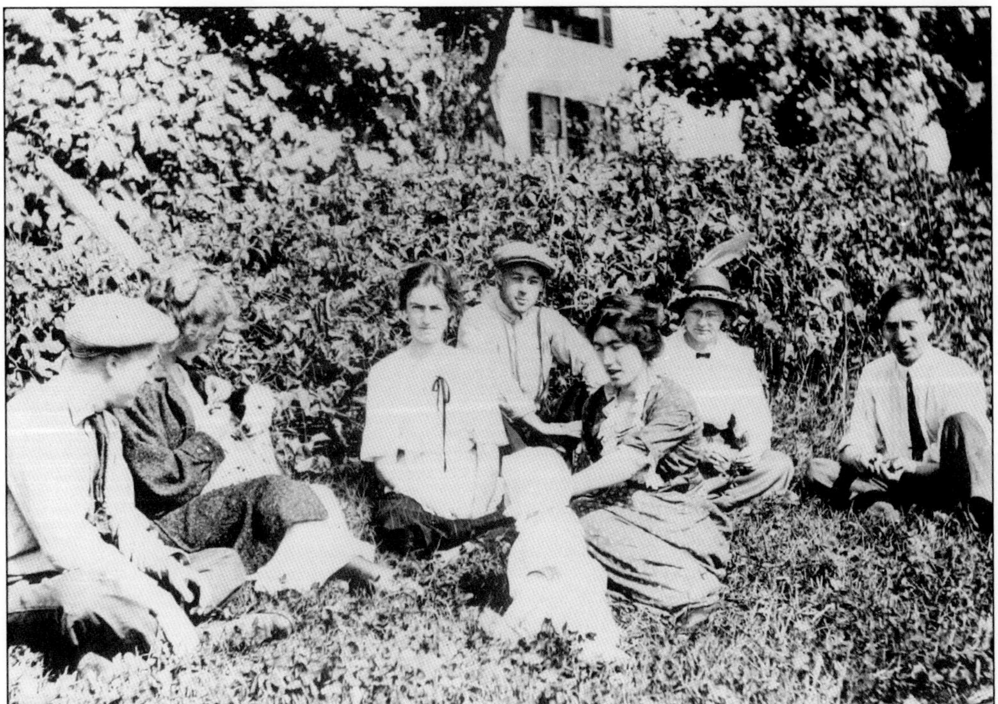

Parker Homestead on Tarbell Hill, Norridgewock, About 1914. A group of Parker family relatives sits in front of the house. The couple on the left are unknown. Florence Parker Barstow is the woman in front with her baby, Richard Barstow. Those in the rear, left to right, were Elizabeth Cook, George Moore, Ethel Moore, and Philip Barstow (Florence's husband). Philip was a pharmacist in nearby Skowhegan. The barns at the farm burned in 1951. The farm remained in the Parker family from about 1770 (except when the Parkers went to Massachusetts during the Revolutionary War) until 1958.

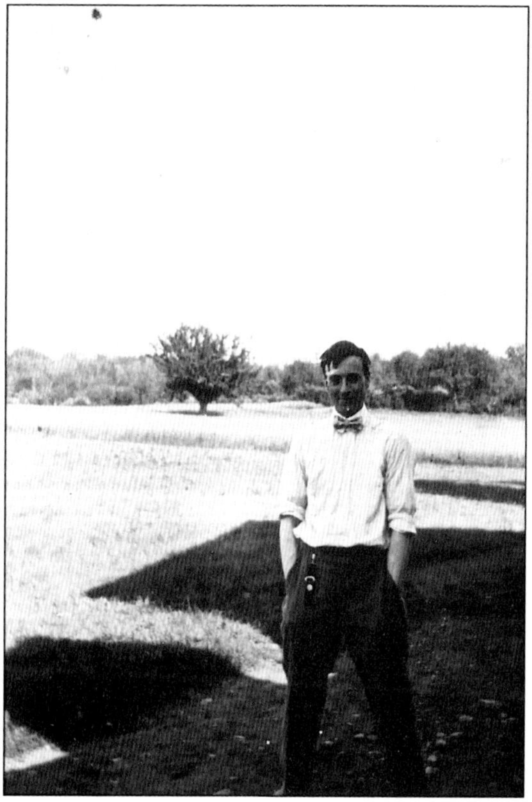

PHILIP BARSTOW EAST OF THE PARKER FARM IN 1915.

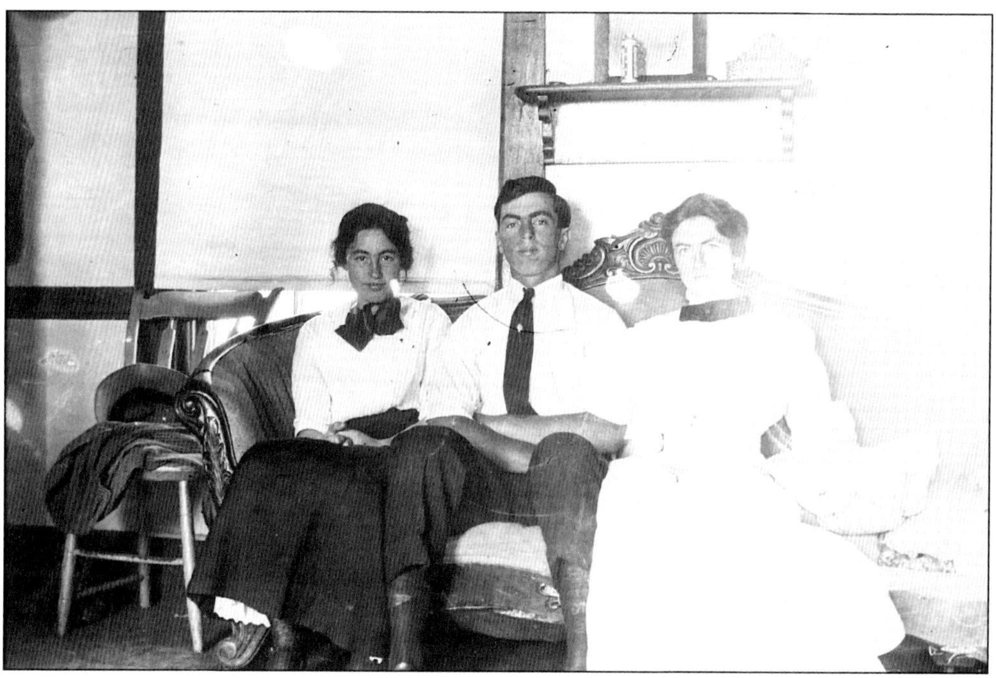

IN THE KITCHEN AT THE PARKER FARM, ABOUT 1912. From left to right are Florence, George, and Mary Elizabeth Parker.

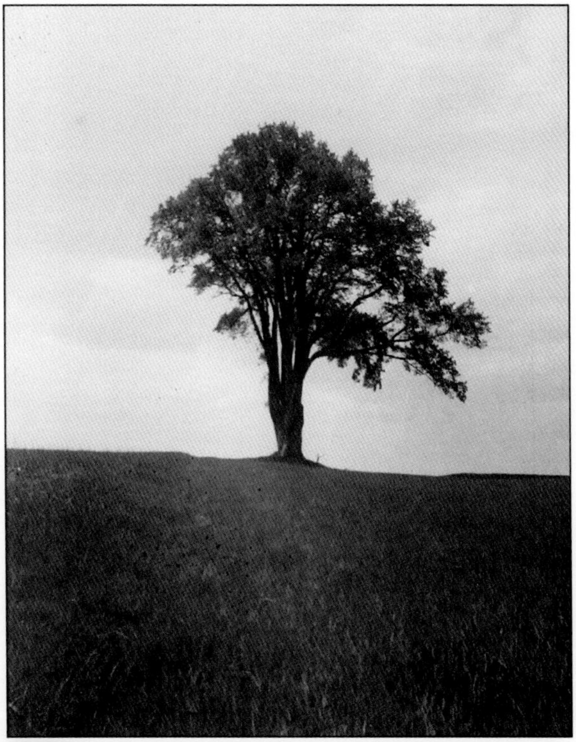

Giant Elm Tree at Elmcrest Farm, the Name of the Parker Farm. The tree could have been planted when the land was cleared in the 1700s. The photograph was taken about 1935, and the tree was still standing in 1958 when the farm passed out of the Parker name. The tree no longer exists.

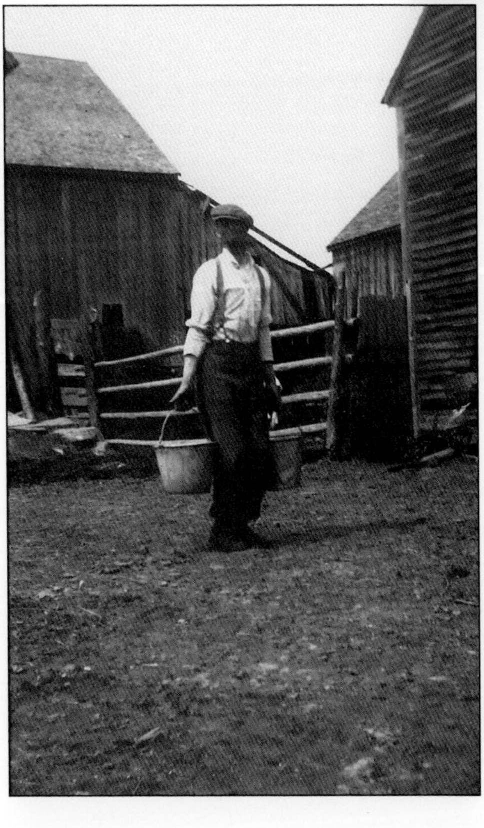

Parker Farm, About 1925. George Parker carries water on this primarily dairy farm.

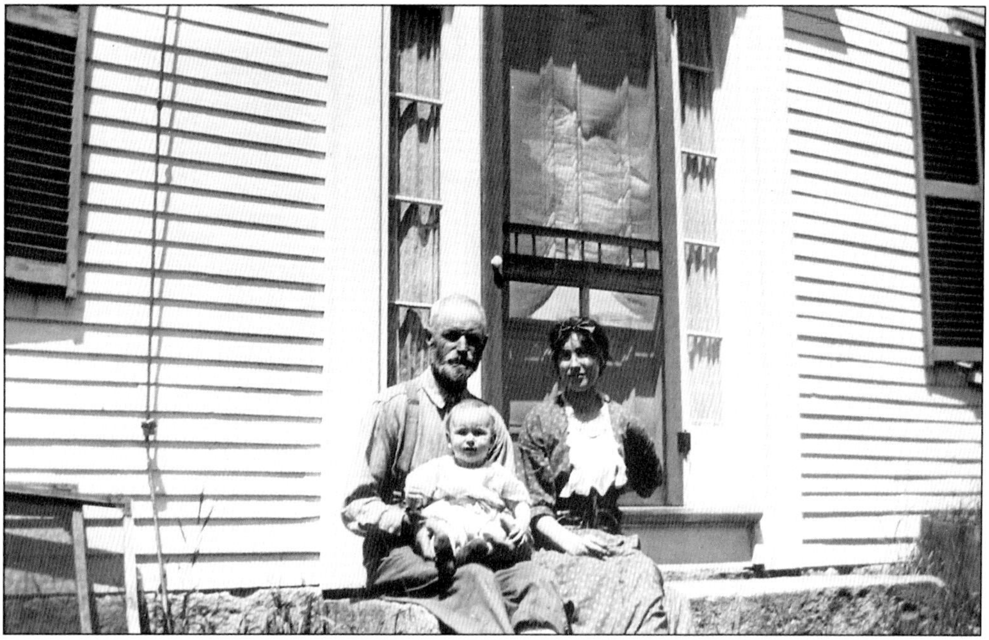

Three Generations of the Parker Family, About 1914. On the front steps of the Parker homestead are, from left to right, as follows: Frank Parker (grandfather), Richard Barstow (grandchild), and Florence Parker Barstow (daughter and mother).

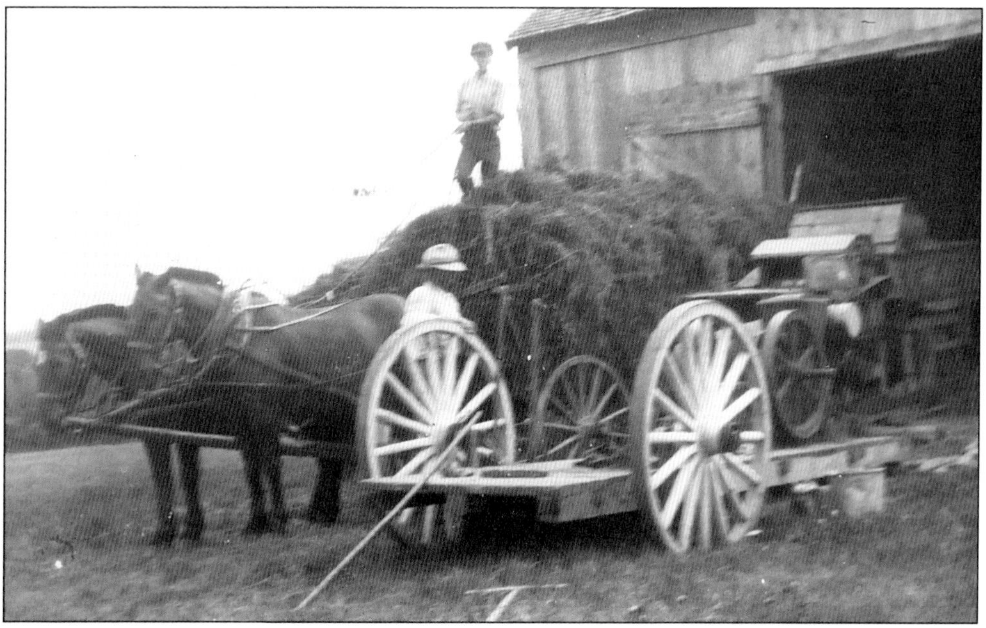

A Parker Storage Barn in the 1920s. George Parker is on the ground and an unknown hired hand unloads hay. A second barn, down by the fields, was used to store hay and straw.

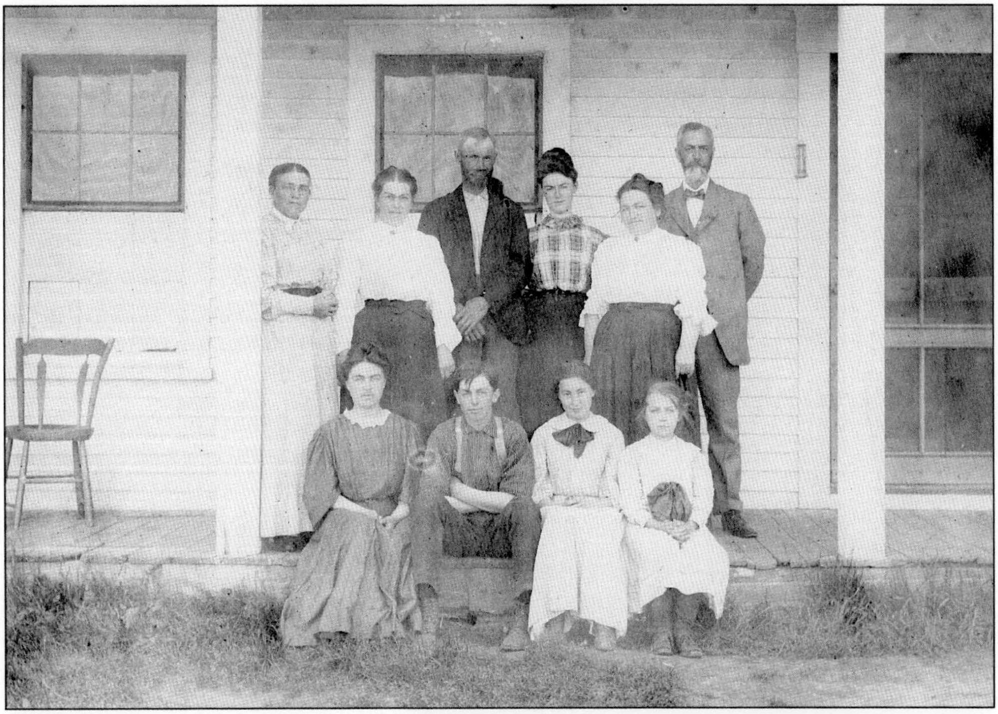

AT THE PARKER FARM IN THE 1900s. Pictured from left to right are as follows: (front row) Hazel Leavitt, George Parker, Florence Parker, and Marion Adams; (back row) Clara Leavitt, Thankful Parker (Clara's daughter), Frank Parker, Beth Parker, Hannah Flint, and Walter Flint.

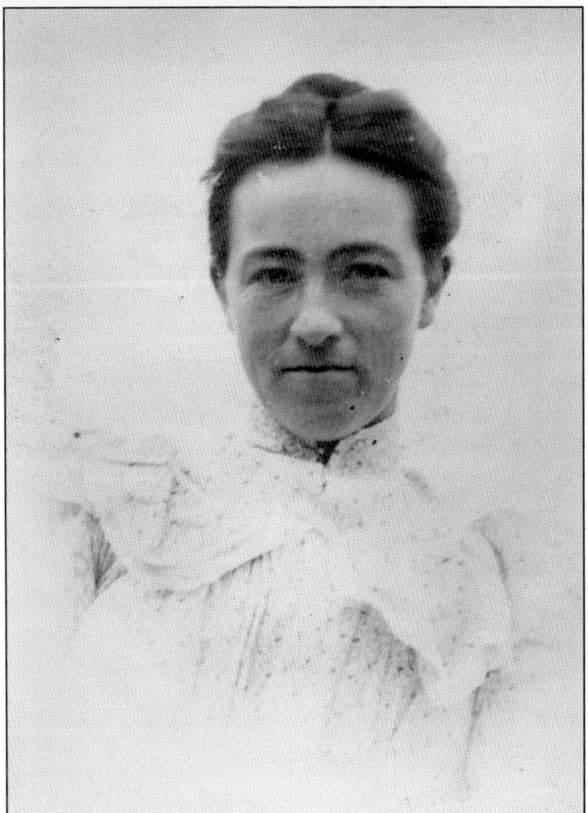

CORA LEAVITT PARKER, FRANK PARKER'S FIRST WIFE, C. 1900.

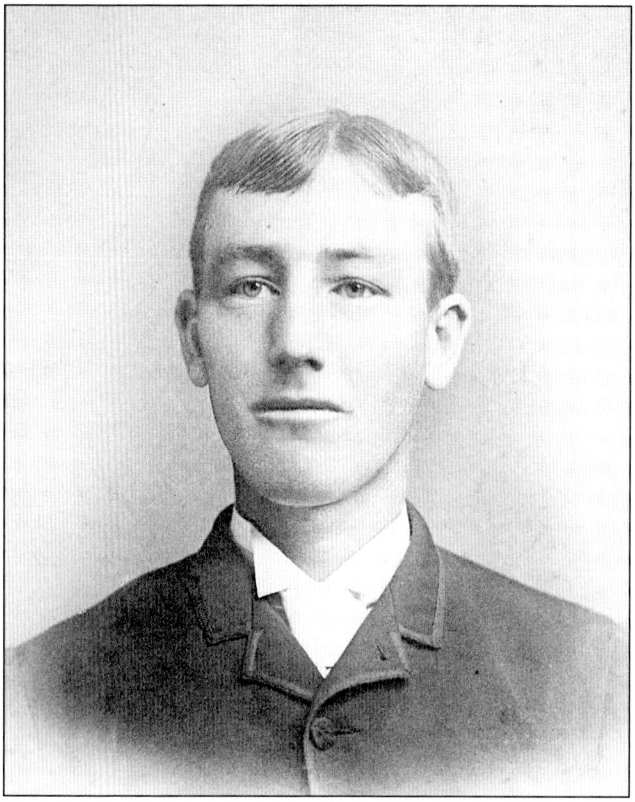

GEORGE PARKER, BROTHER OF FRANK PARKER. He ended up living in Minnesota. This was taken in the 1860s at Norridgewock.

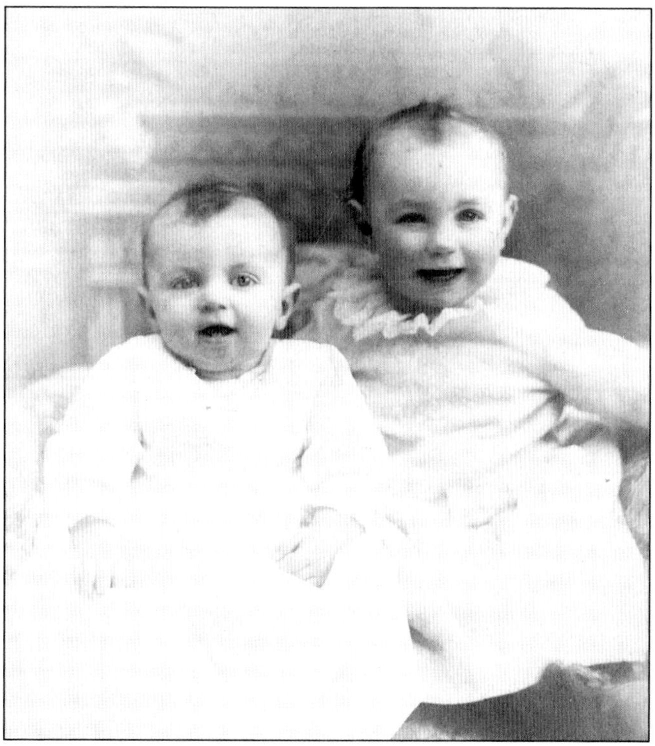

GEORGE LEAVITT PARKER AND MARY ELIZABETH PARKER IN 1888.

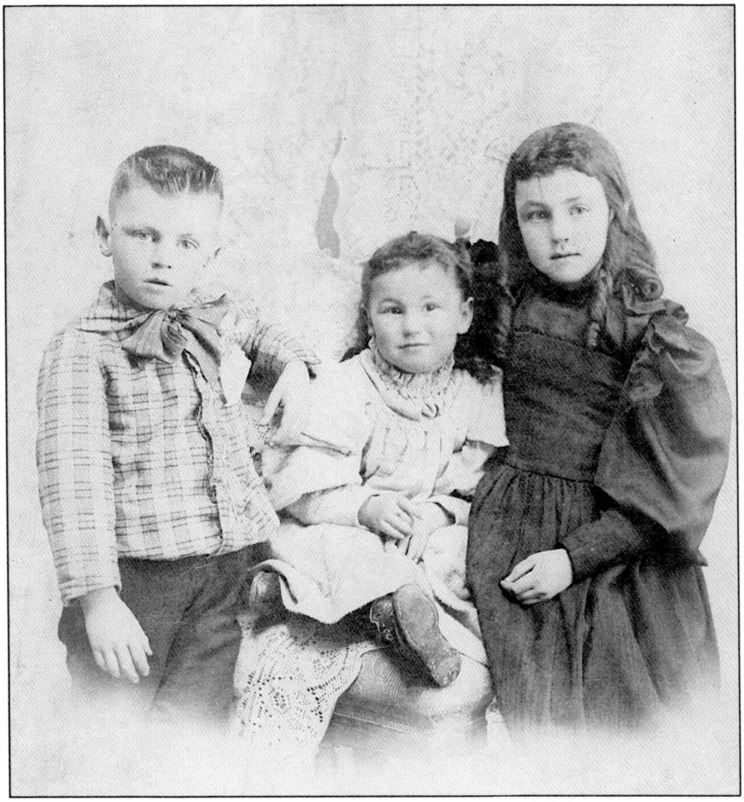

The Children of Frank and Cora Parker. In 1893, they are as follows: George Parker, five and a half years old; Florence Parker, three and a half years old; and Beth Parker, six and a half years old.

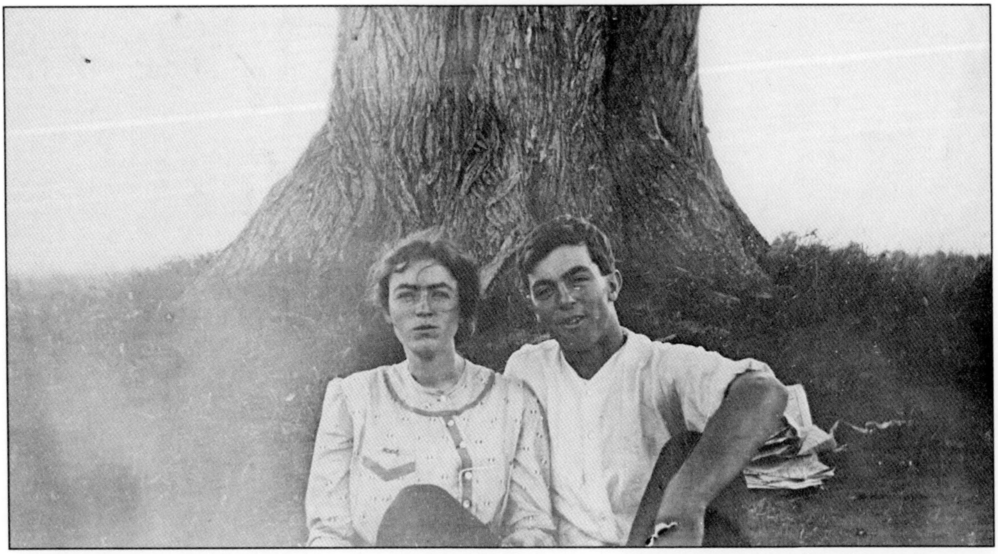

On the Parker Farm. This big elm tree was 27 feet around its stump. Seated in front of it were Beth and George Parker about 1912.

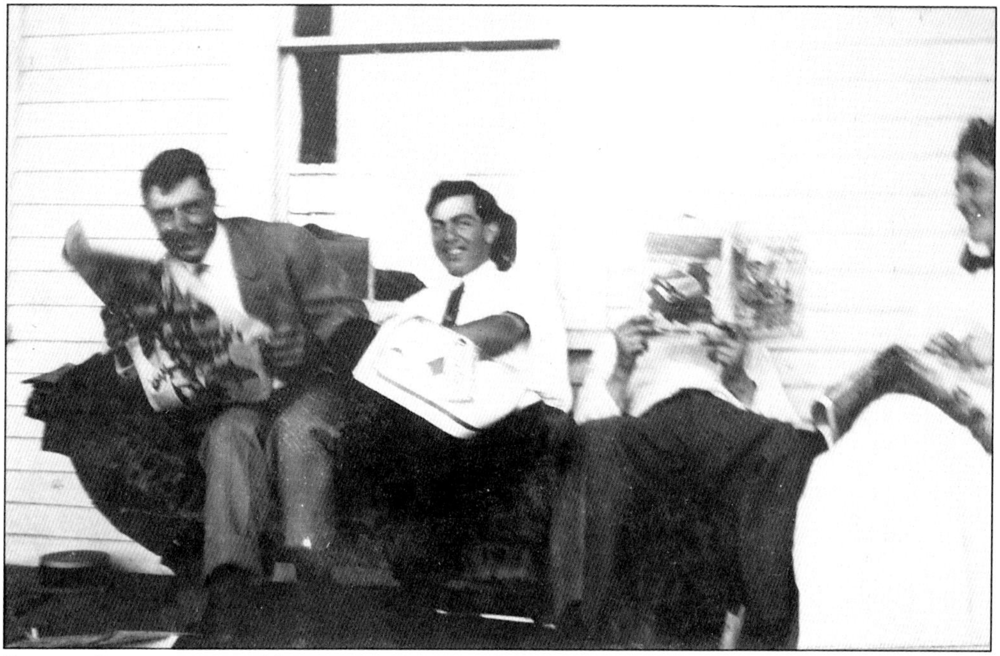

DENNIS BOUCHARD, A NEIGHBOR; GEORGE PARKER; AN UNKNOWN PERSON BEHIND THE NEWSPAPER; AND BETH PARKER IN THE 1910S AT THE PARKER FARM.

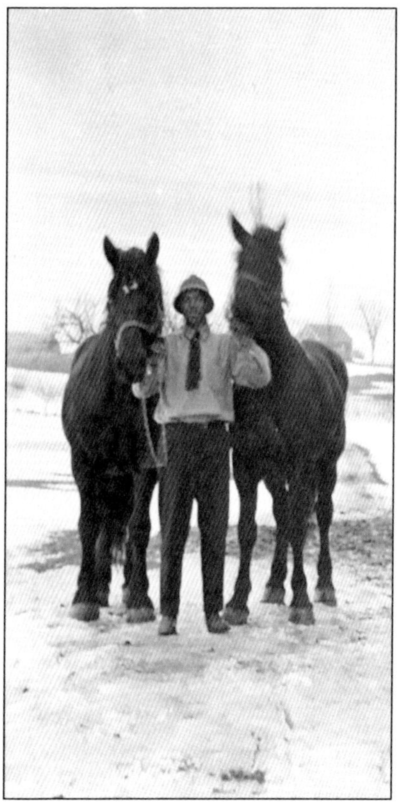

GEORGE PARKER AND HORSES. George diversified in 1916, going into the woods at Flagstaff, where he took lumber off Flagstaff Mountain to Flagstaff Lake. He is shown with his first pair of horses, Pete and Dick.

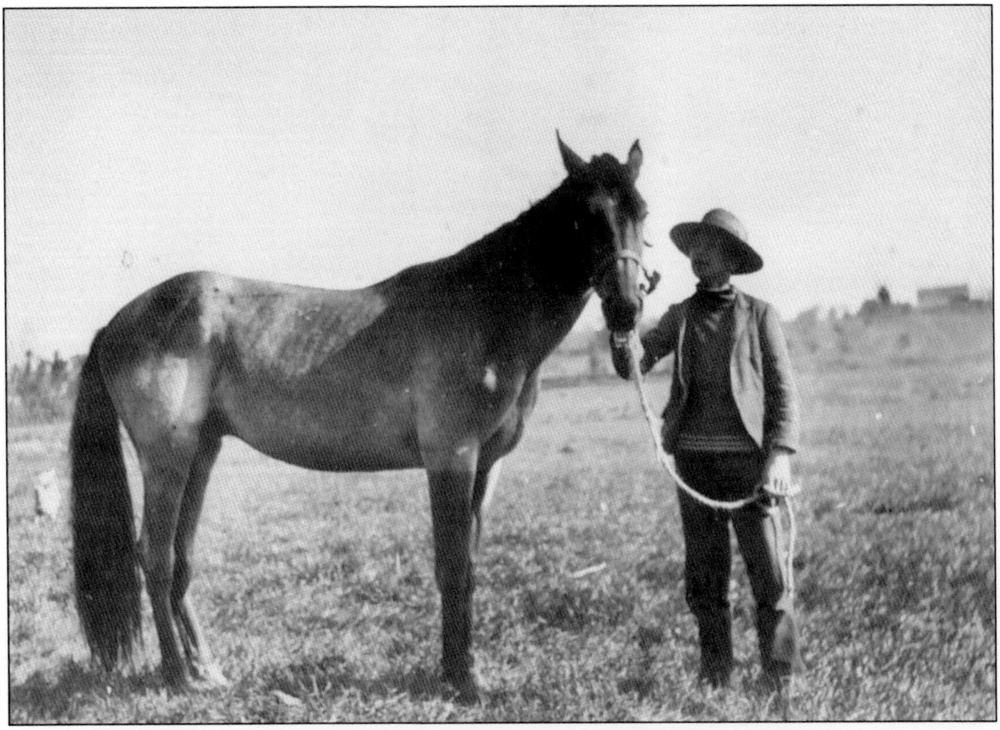

GEORGE PARKER WITH ONE OF HIS MORGAN HORSES, C. 1900. These were only used as driving horses, to pull sleighs and wagons.

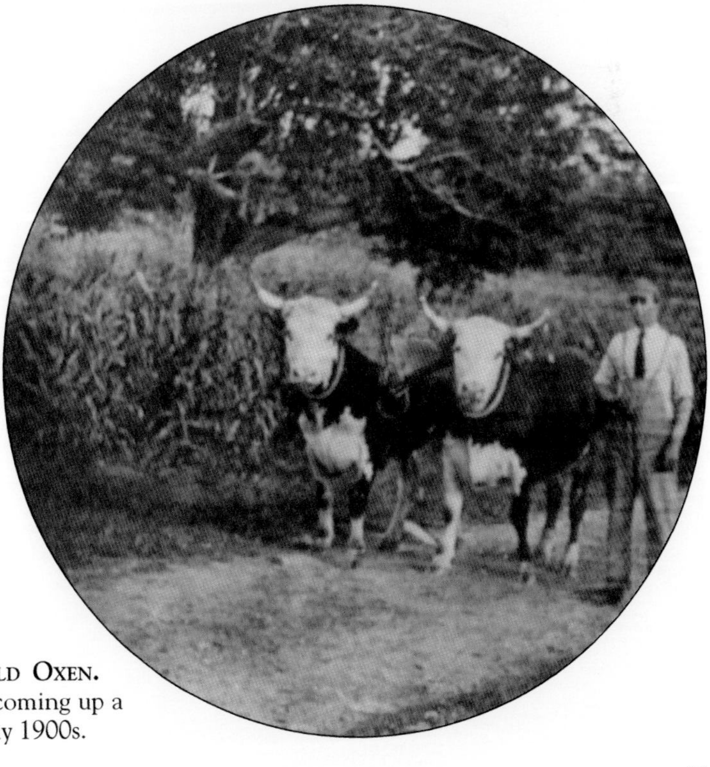

GEORGE PARKER WITH OLD OXEN. In this image the team is coming up a lane at the farm in the early 1900s.

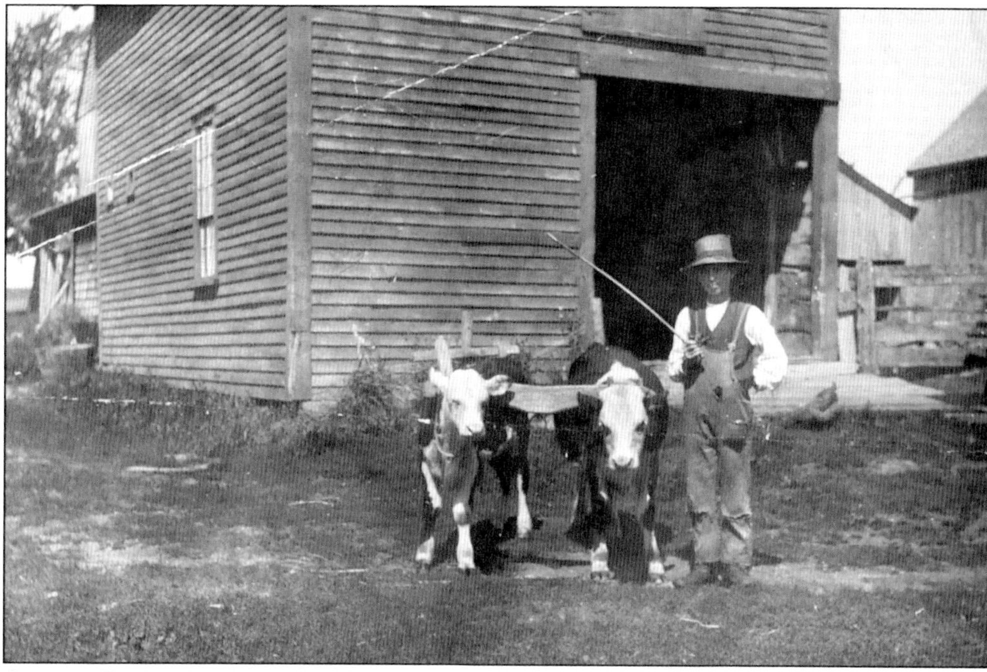

George Parker with a Yoked Team of Young Oxen at the Parker Farm in the Early 1900s.

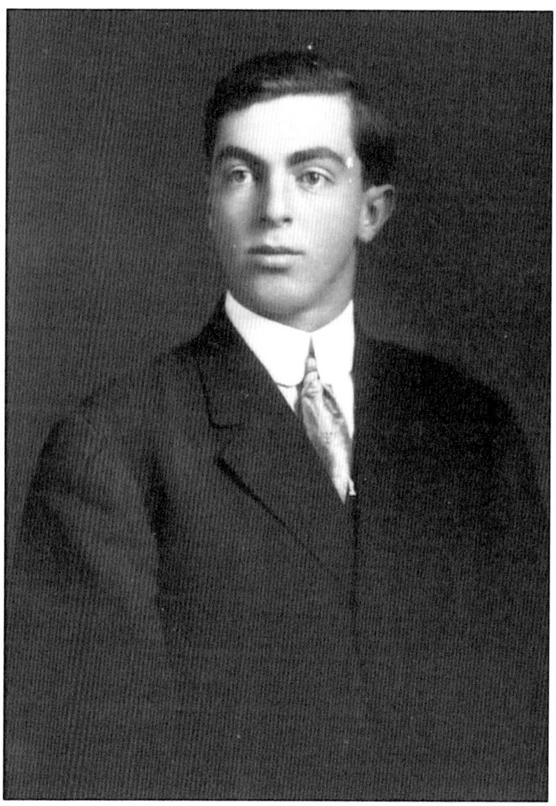

George Parker, Class of 1912.

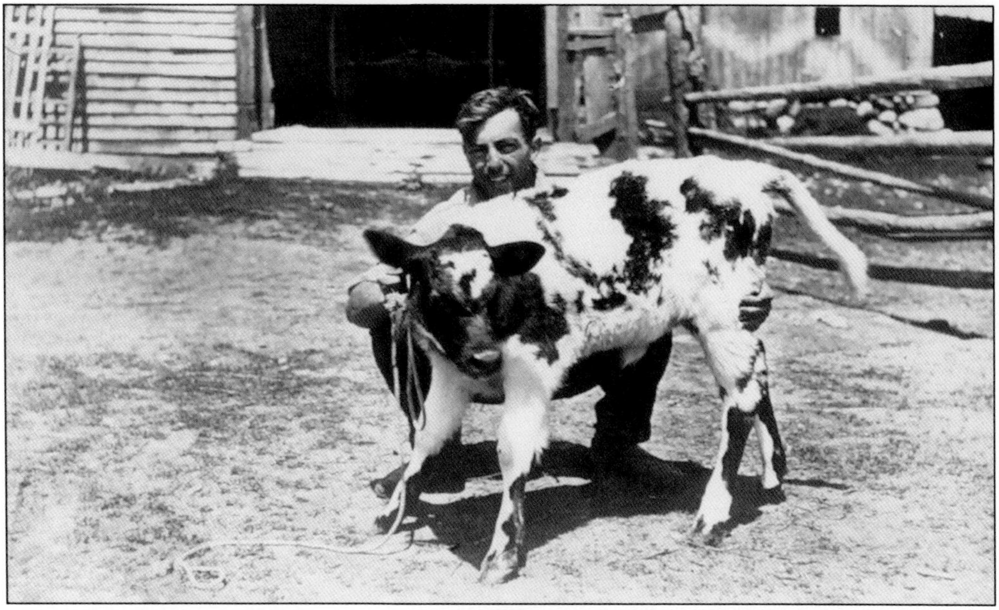

George Parker with a Holstein Calf on the Parker Farm in the 1930s. He was a member of the Maine Milk Commission for a period of time.

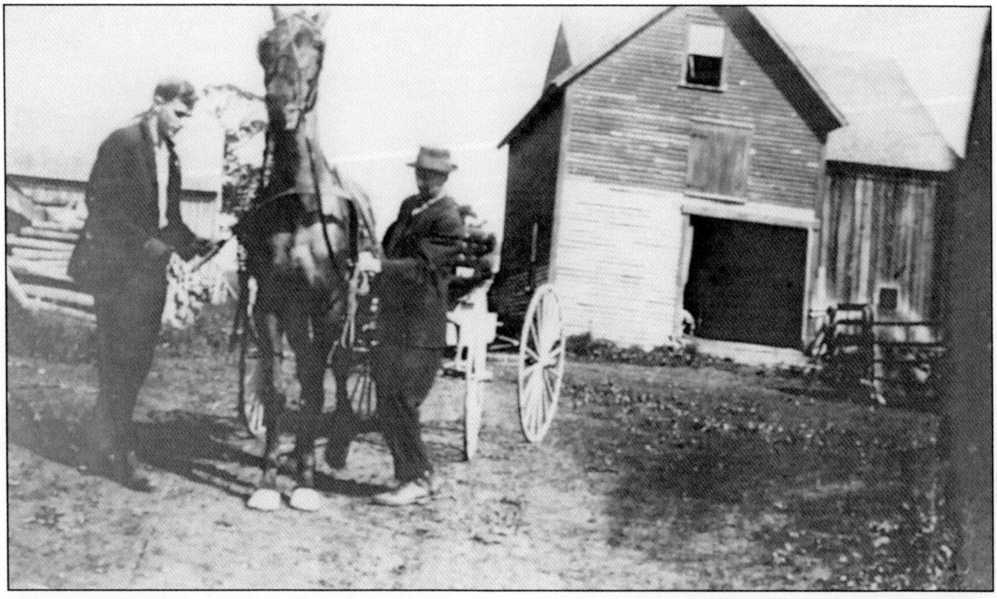

George and Hired Man. George is hitching up Colonel, a Morgan horse, to his wagon. They were on their way to town about 1930.

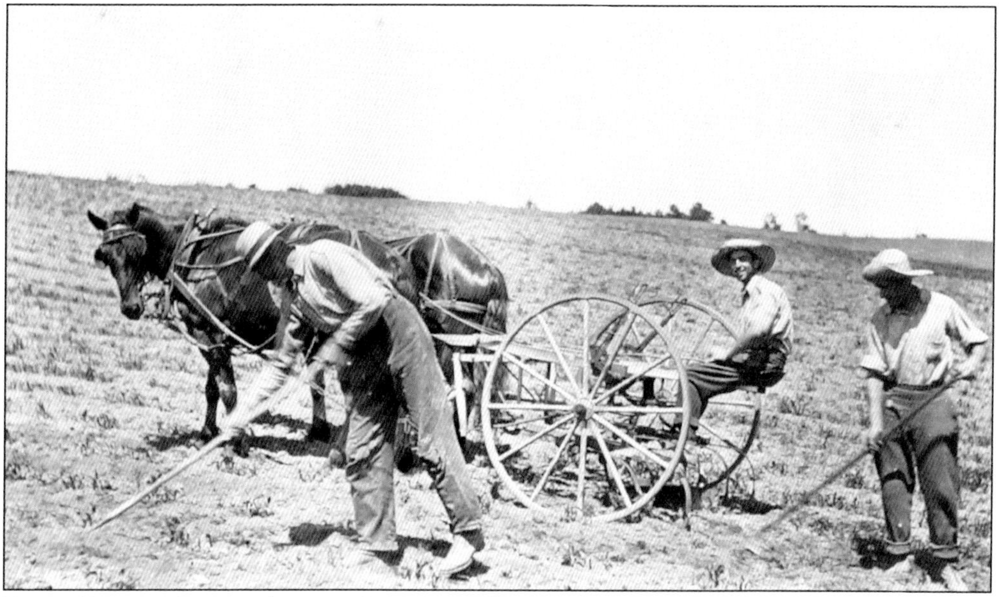

Frank Parker, George (on the Cultivator), and Pat Austin (the Hired Man), at the Parker Farm, About 1920.

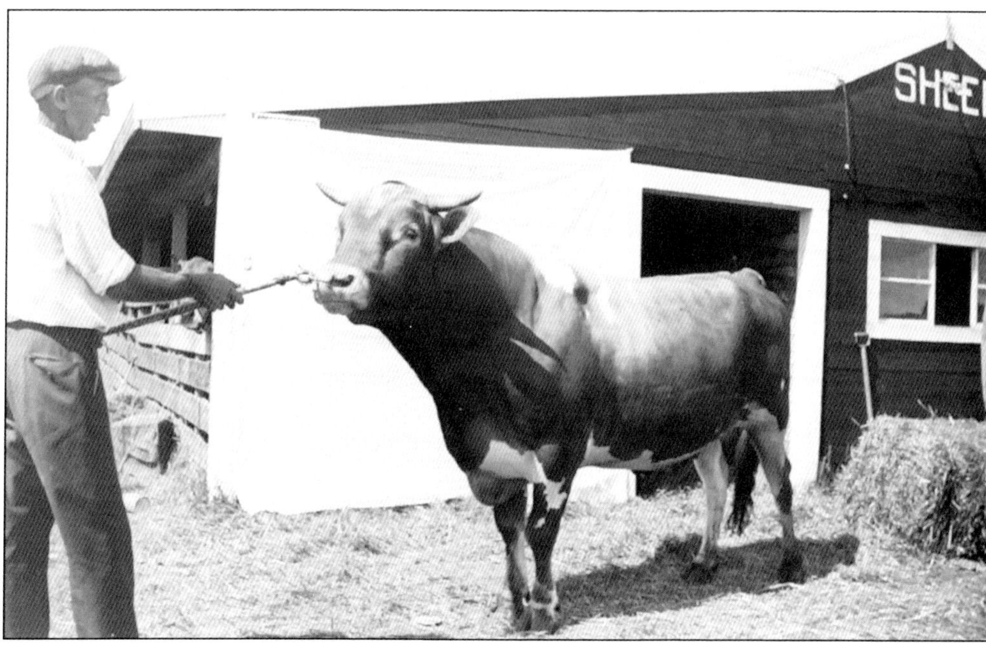

George Shows a Bull at the Skowhegan Fair in the Early 1940s.

Violet (Robinson) Parker, George's Wife, in 1915.

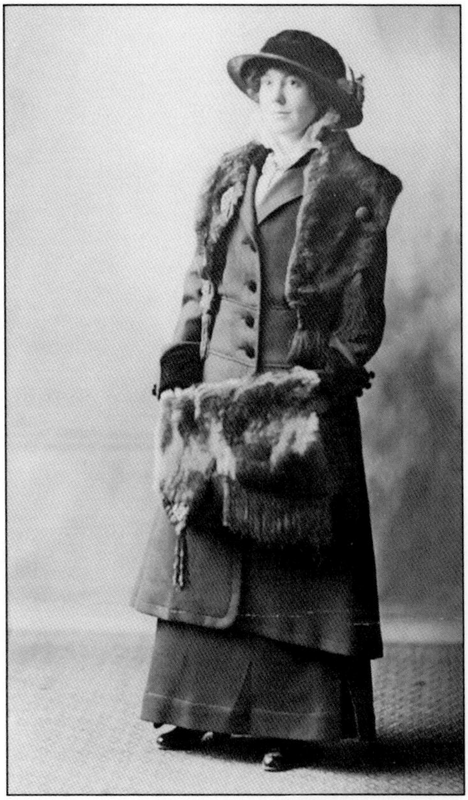

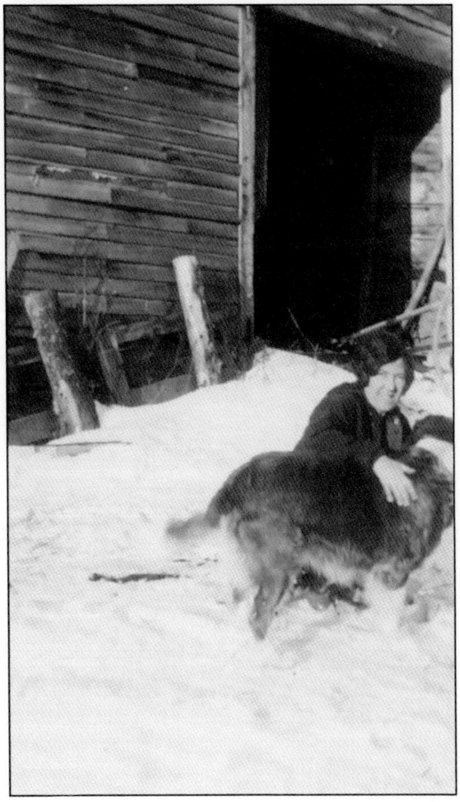

Violet in the 1940s on the Parker Farm with Donny, a Dog of Collie-shepherd Mixed Breed.

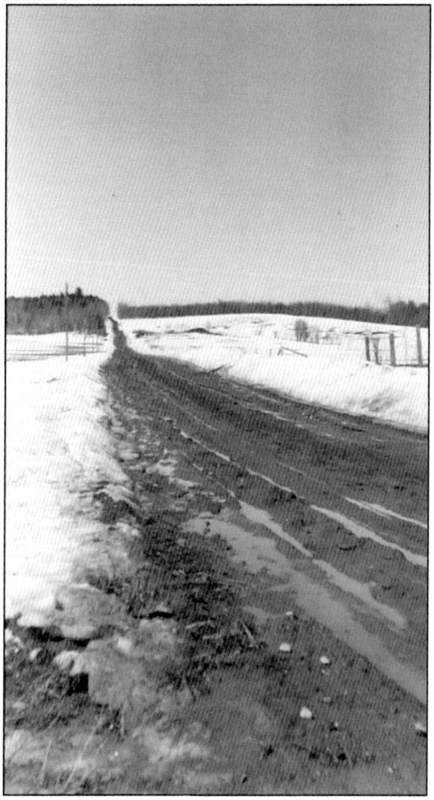

Road from Laney's Corner (a Section of Norridgewock) up over Beech Hill near the Parker Farm. That road was still unpaved as late as 1958.

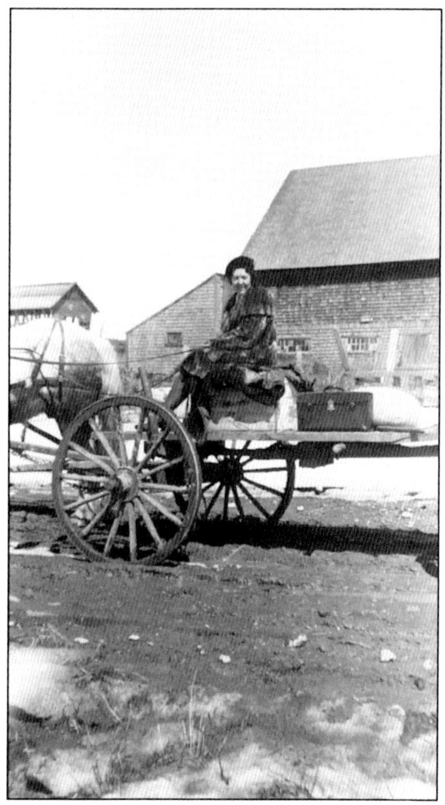

Violet Parker, in the Early 1940s. She is ready to go to Laney's Corner. Violet is pictured by one of the barns at the Parker Farm.

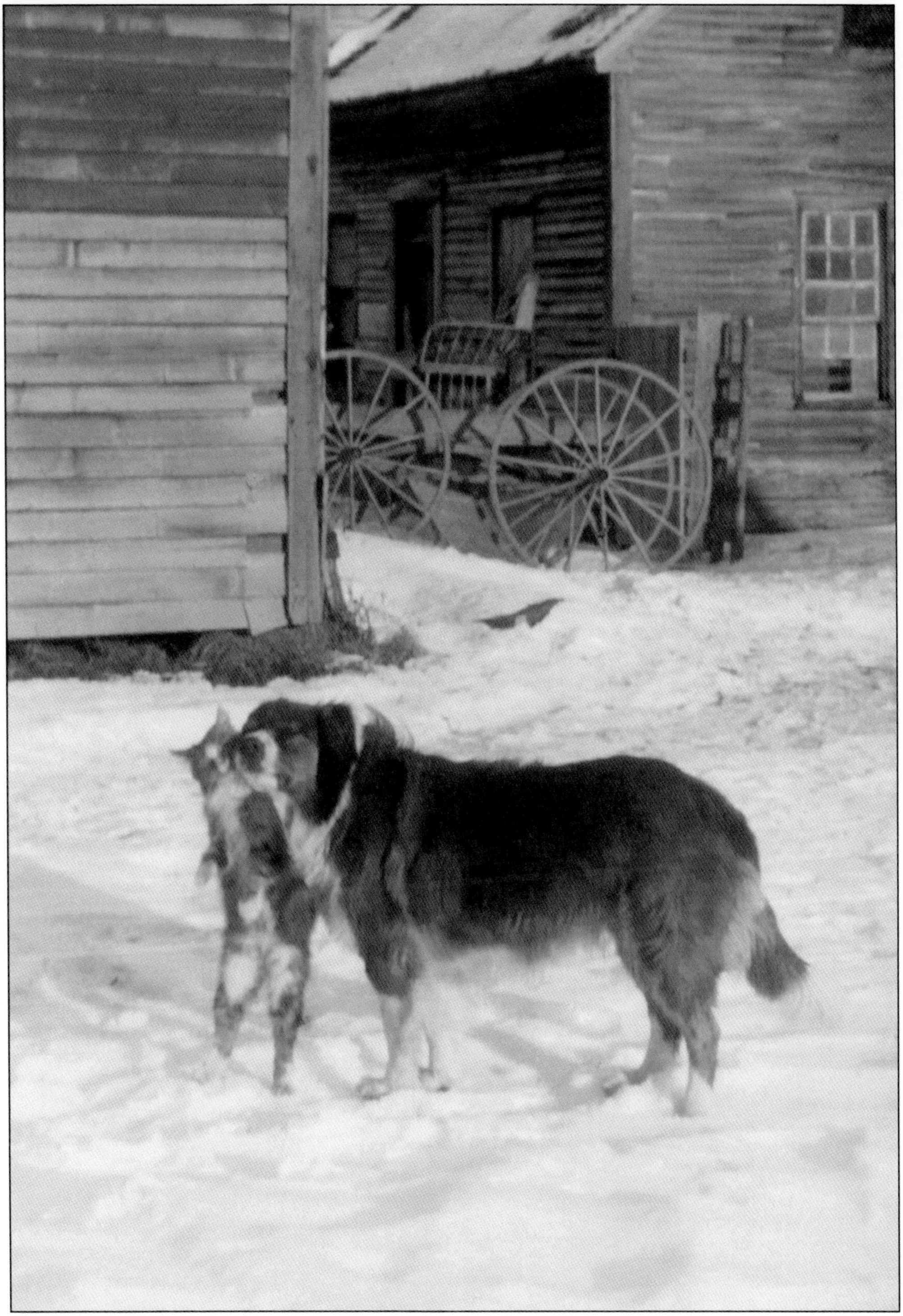

MOUSIE (THE PARKER CAT) AND DONNY (THE PARKER DOG), FRATERNIZING BY THE PARKER FARM BARN AND HOUSE IN 1935. Ever seen a cat on its hind legs holding itself up with one of its paws on a dog? Mousie and Donny obviously got along well.

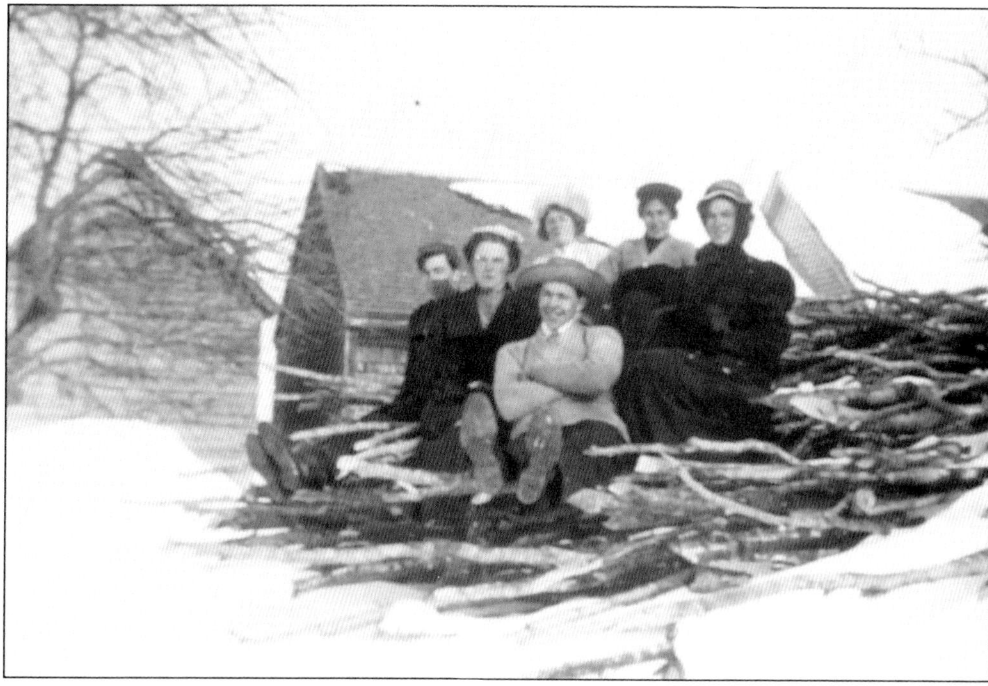

Part of the Parker Wood Pile in 1914. The wood was hauled down in tree lengths and then cut to fit stoves and fire places. In the photograph at the Parker Farm backyard were George and Beth Parker, Philip Barstow, and three others.

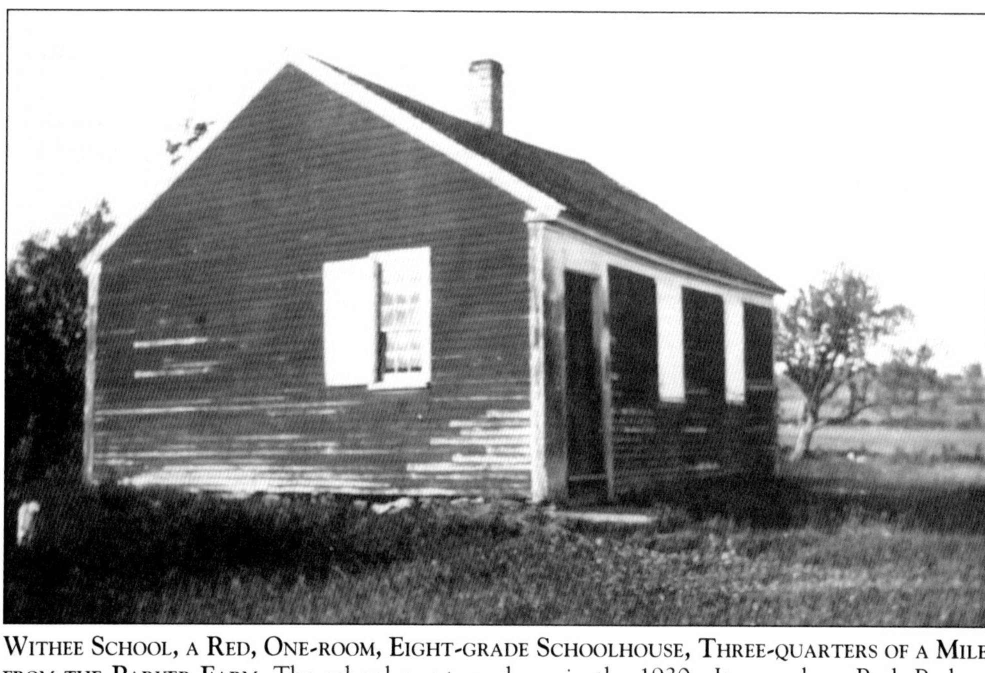

Withee School, a Red, One-room, Eight-grade Schoolhouse, Three-quarters of a Mile from the Parker Farm. The school was torn down in the 1930s. It was where Beth Parker, George Parker, Florence Parker, and Richard Barstow went to school. This photograph was taken in the early 1900s.

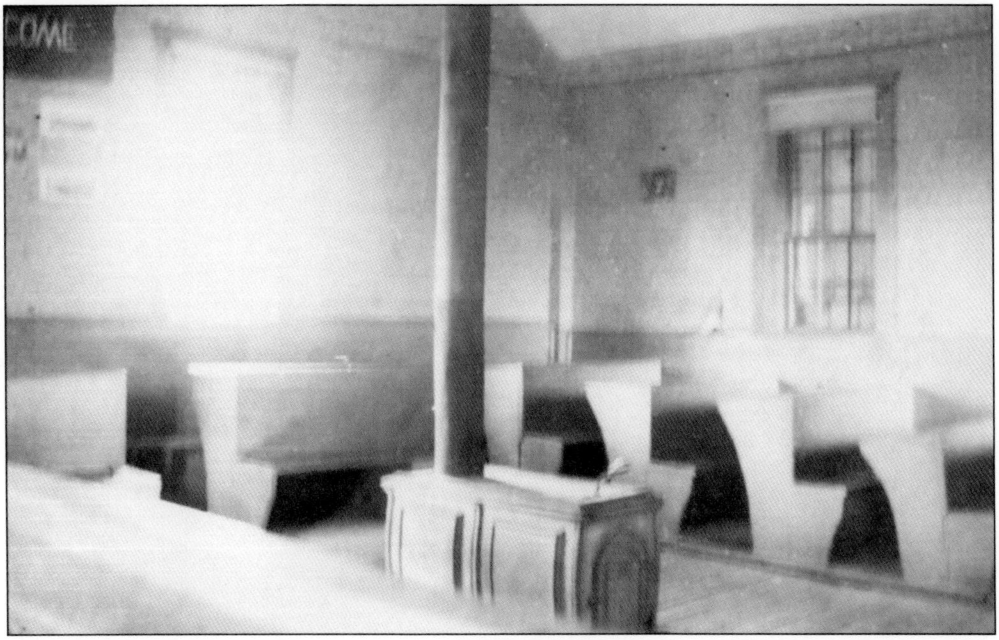

INTERIOR OF THE WITHEE SCHOOL IN THE EARLY 1900S.

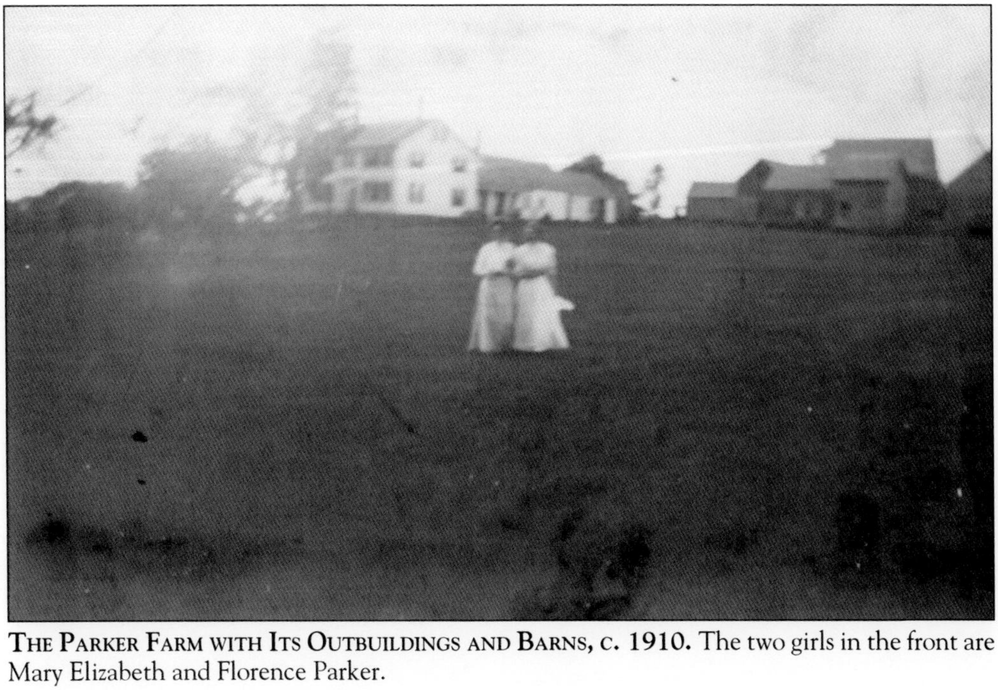

THE PARKER FARM WITH ITS OUTBUILDINGS AND BARNS, C. 1910. The two girls in the front are Mary Elizabeth and Florence Parker.

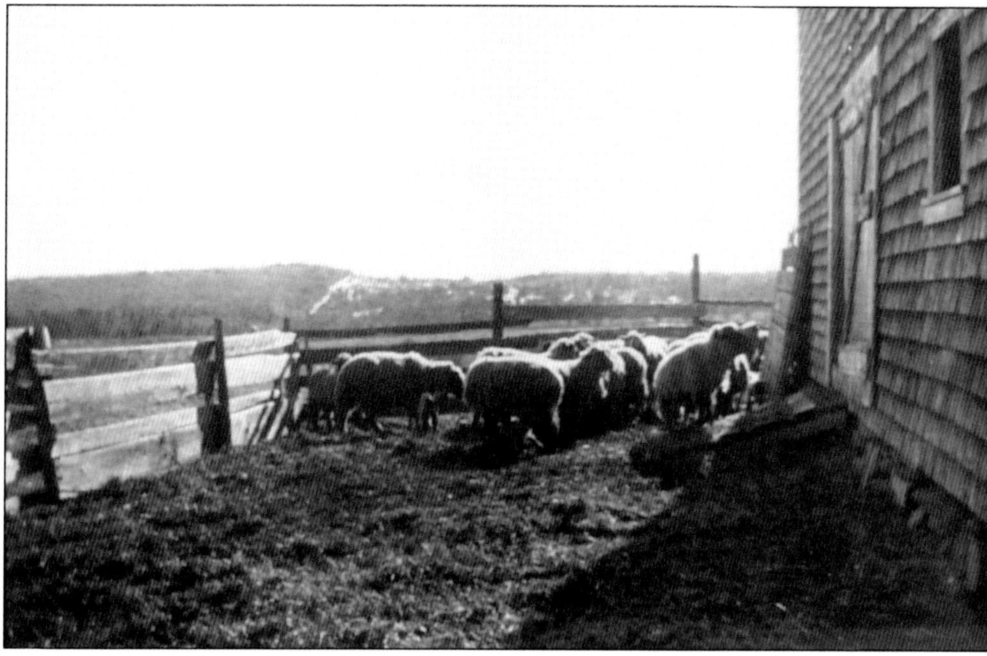

Sheep on the Parker Farm , c. 1900.

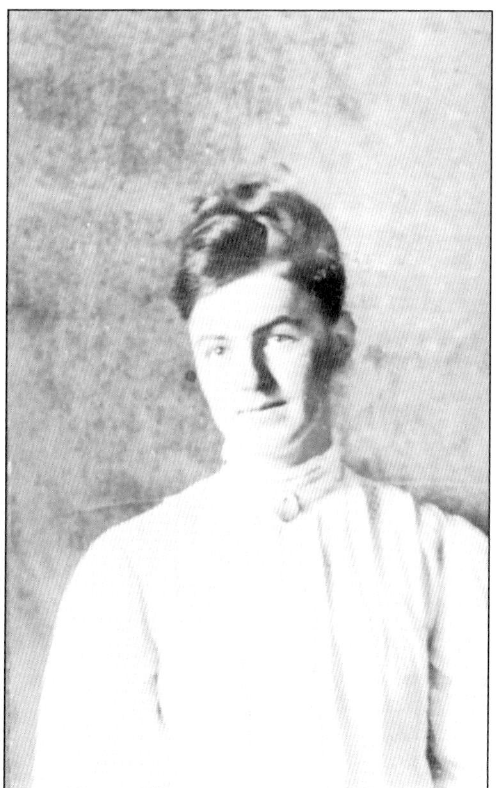

Mary Elizabeth Parker, c. 1912.

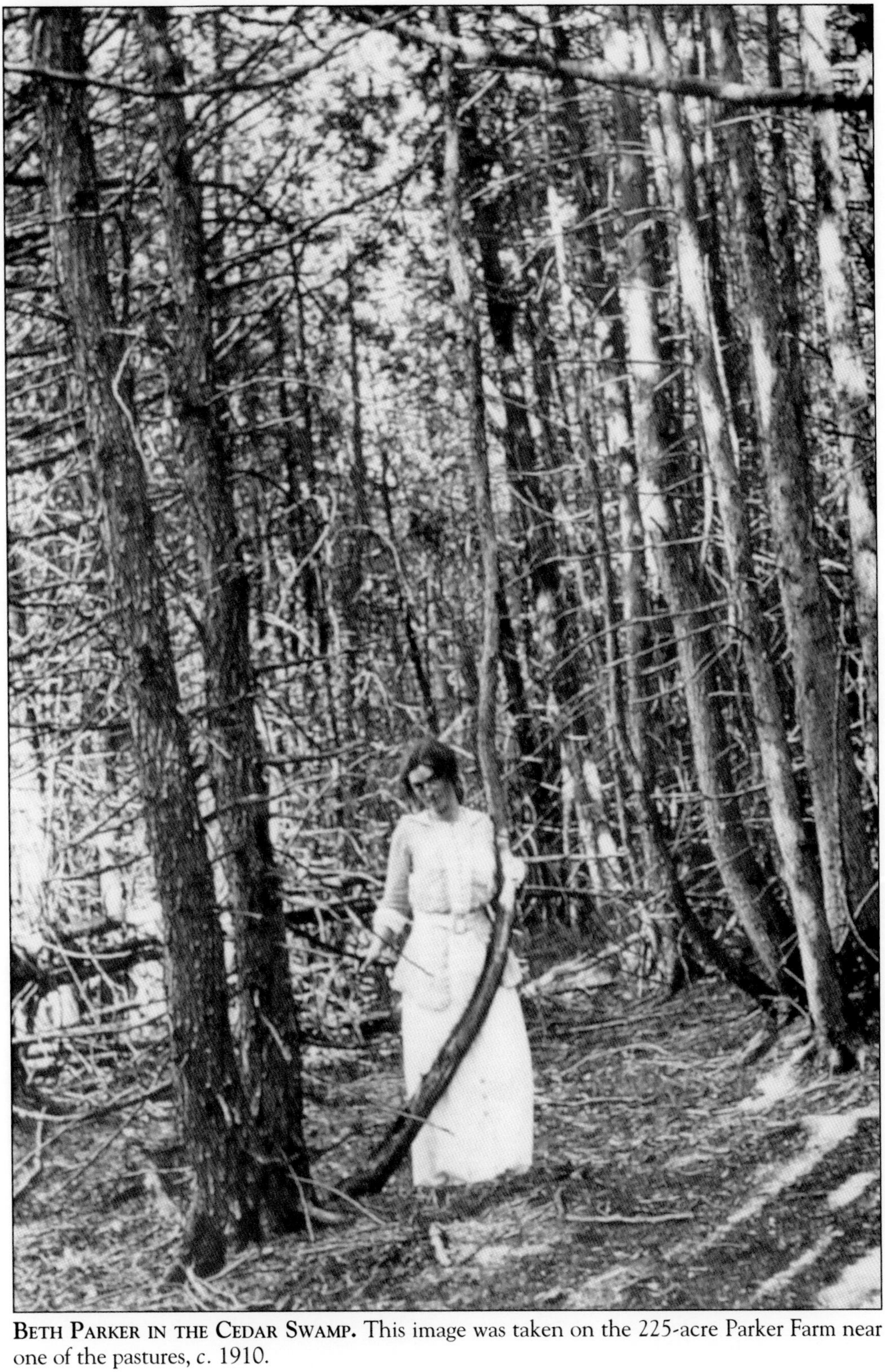

BETH PARKER IN THE CEDAR SWAMP. This image was taken on the 225-acre Parker Farm near one of the pastures, *c.* 1910.

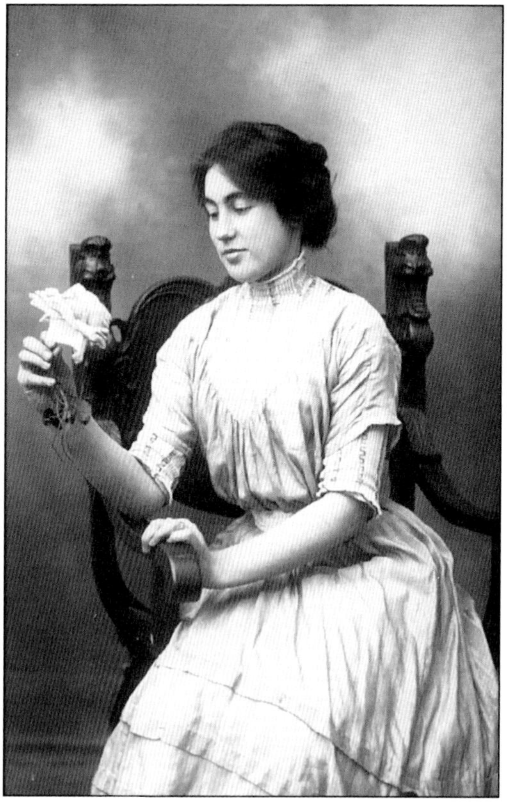

FLORENCE PARKER BARSTOW IN 1916.

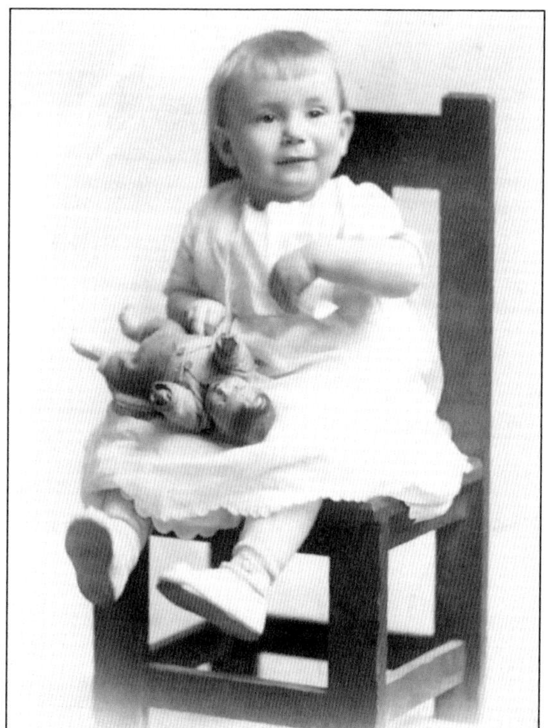

RICHARD PARKER BARSTOW, TWO YEARS OLD, C. 1914. Dick became a civil engineer working for the state of Maine, the town of Norridgewock, and W.H. Hinman Co.

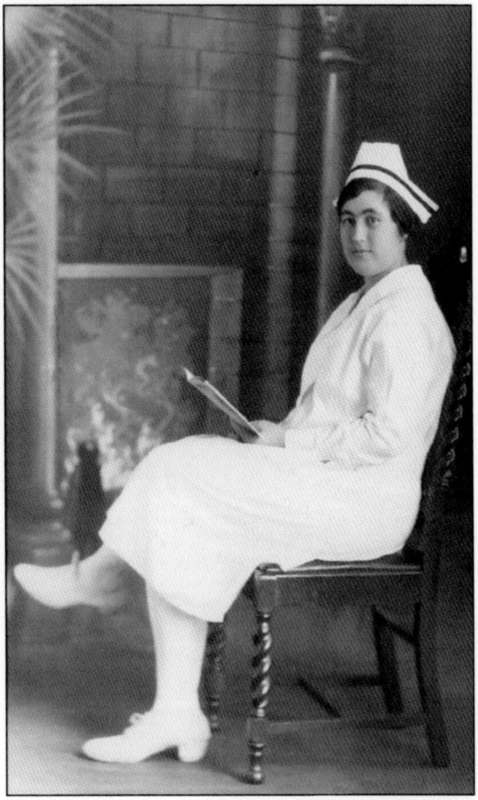

Florence Parker Barstow, Registered Nurse, in 1923. Florence served all over Somerset County. She had trained at the Kennebec Valley Hospital in Skowhegan.

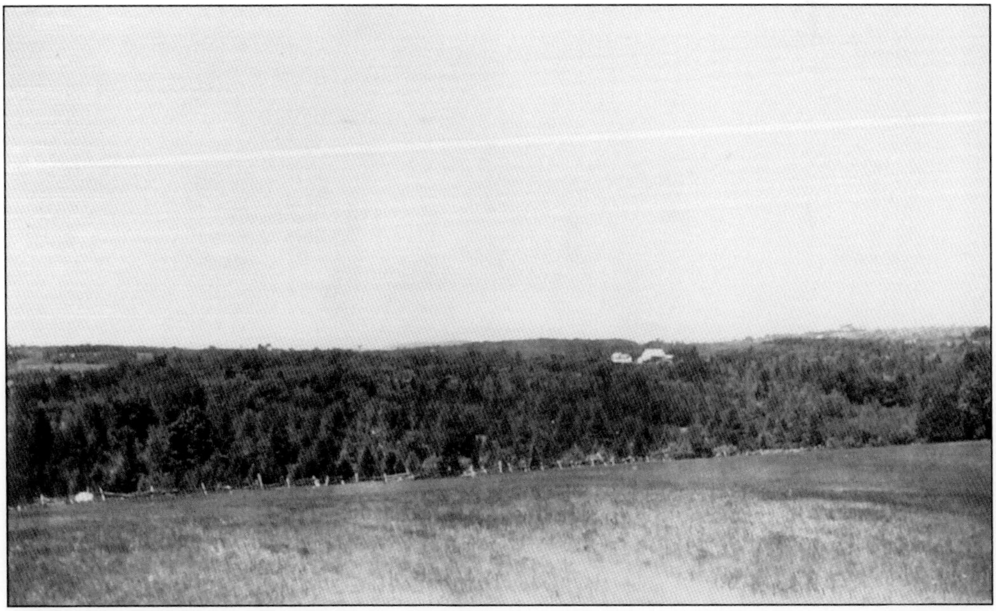

View from the Giant Elm Tree on the Parker Farm in Norridgewock. The neighboring St. Peter dairy farm is at the middle rear.

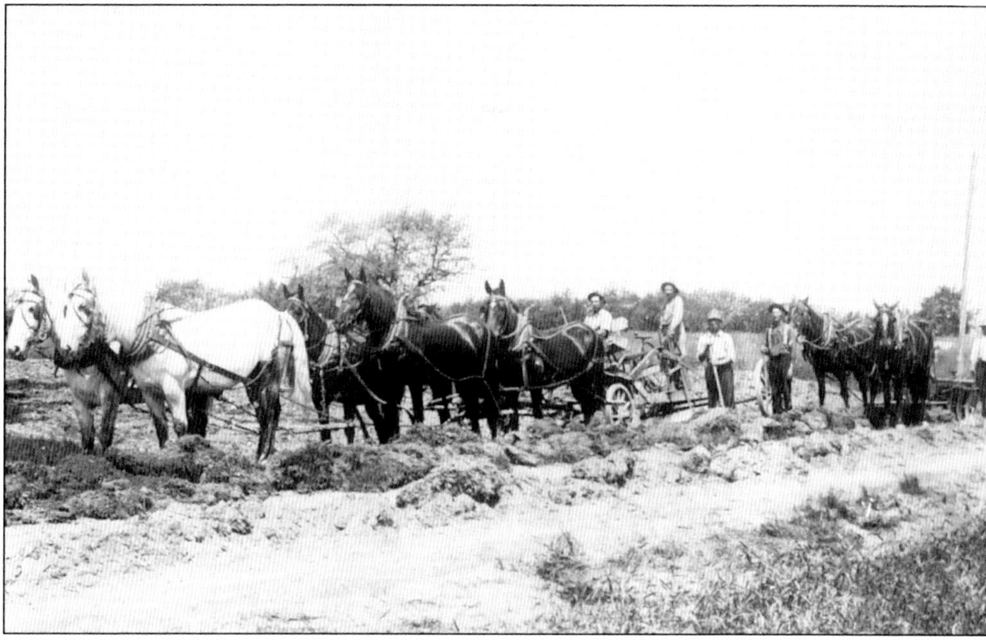

A NORRIDGEWOCK ROAD IN THE SPRING. Here a town crew is machining the road to get the rocks and ruts out. Neighbors helped the crew, and the crew stayed overnight at different homes, c. 1910s.

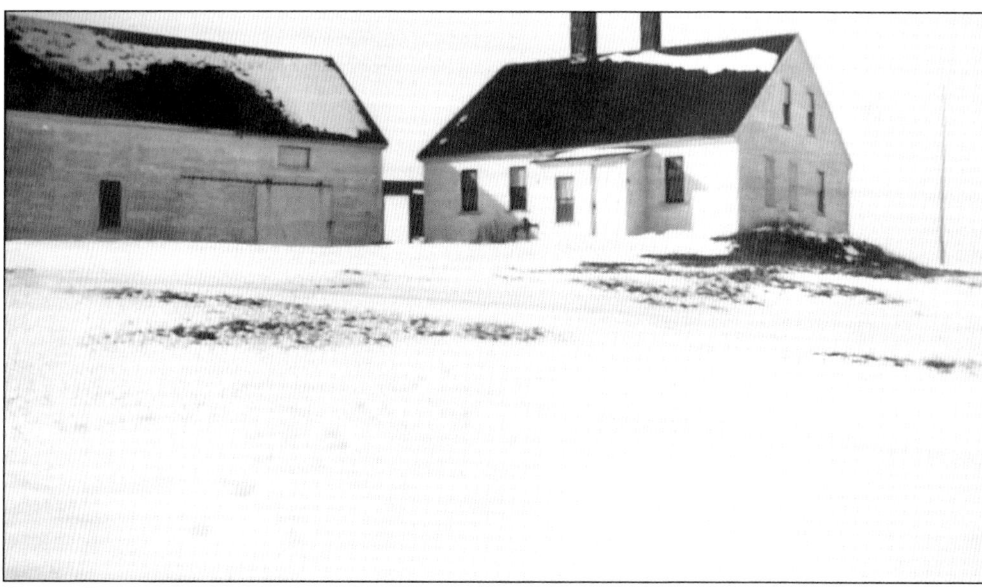

ADAMS PLACE, ACROSS THE ROAD FROM THE PARKER FARM IN NORRIDGEWOCK IN 1925. Hired men from the Parker Farm lived there. Later, Richard Barstow lived there also.

George Parker in the 1920s. This image depicts George changing a tire.

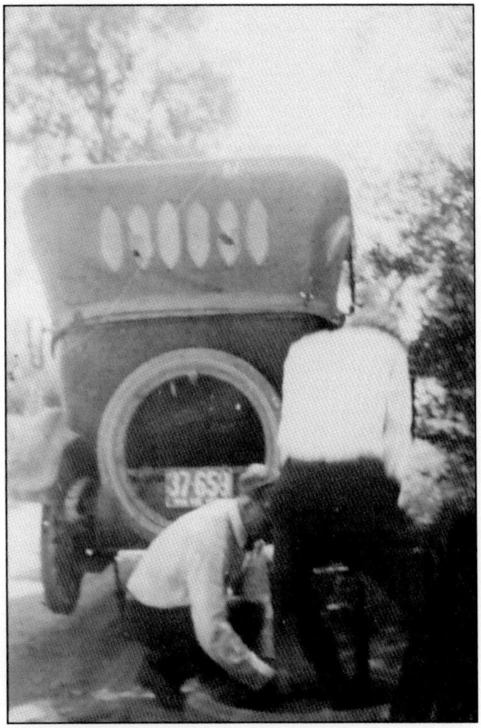

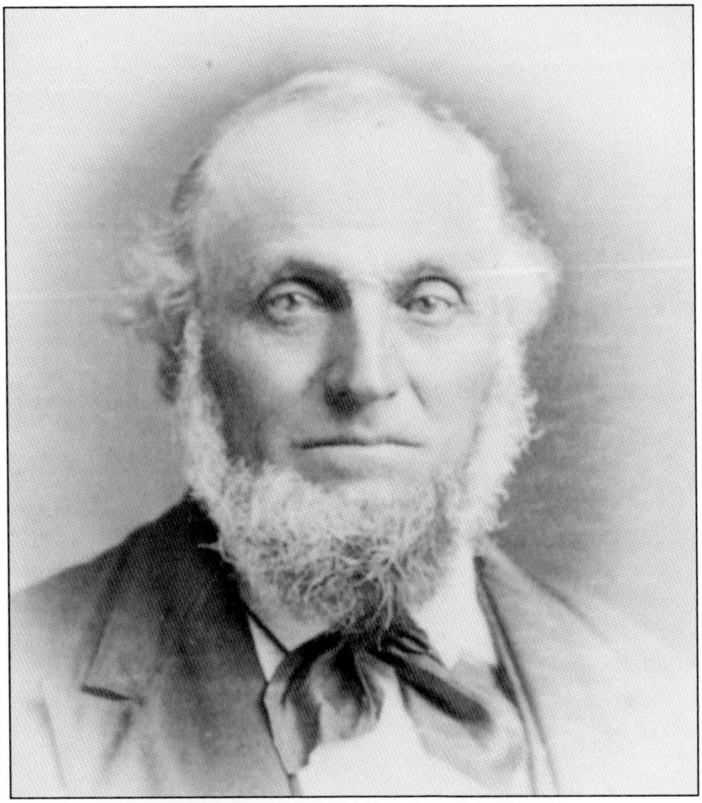

Jonas Parker in the late 1800s. Jonas was of the third generation of Parkers to live on the farm. He was born December 27, 1819, and died May 13, 1906.

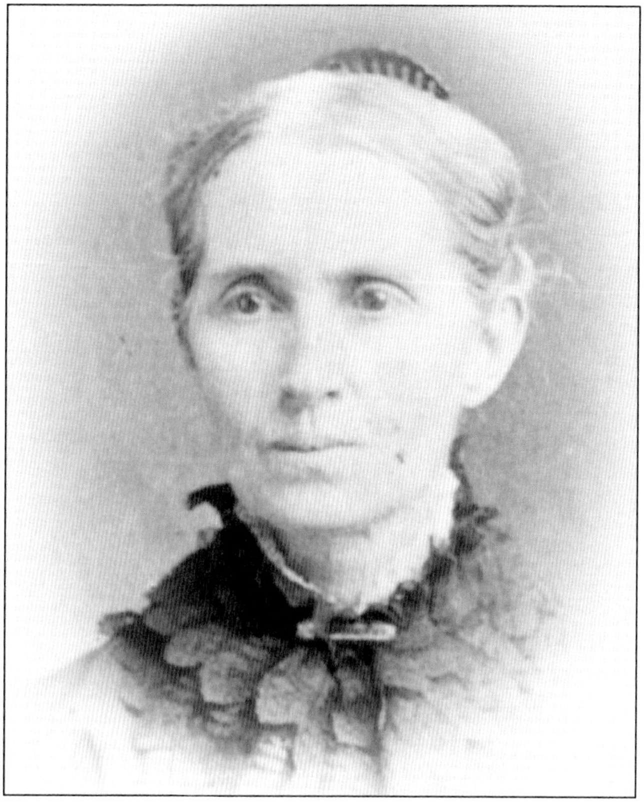

Hannah Stewart Varney Parker, Jonas's Wife, c. late 1890s.

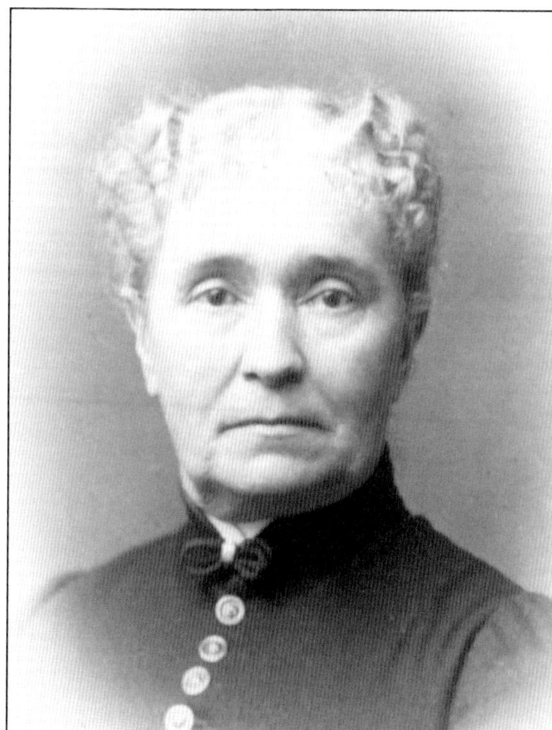

Martha Parker Robbins, Sister of Jonas Parker and Wife of Dr. John Robbins, c. 1890s.

Six

Harris-Everett Family

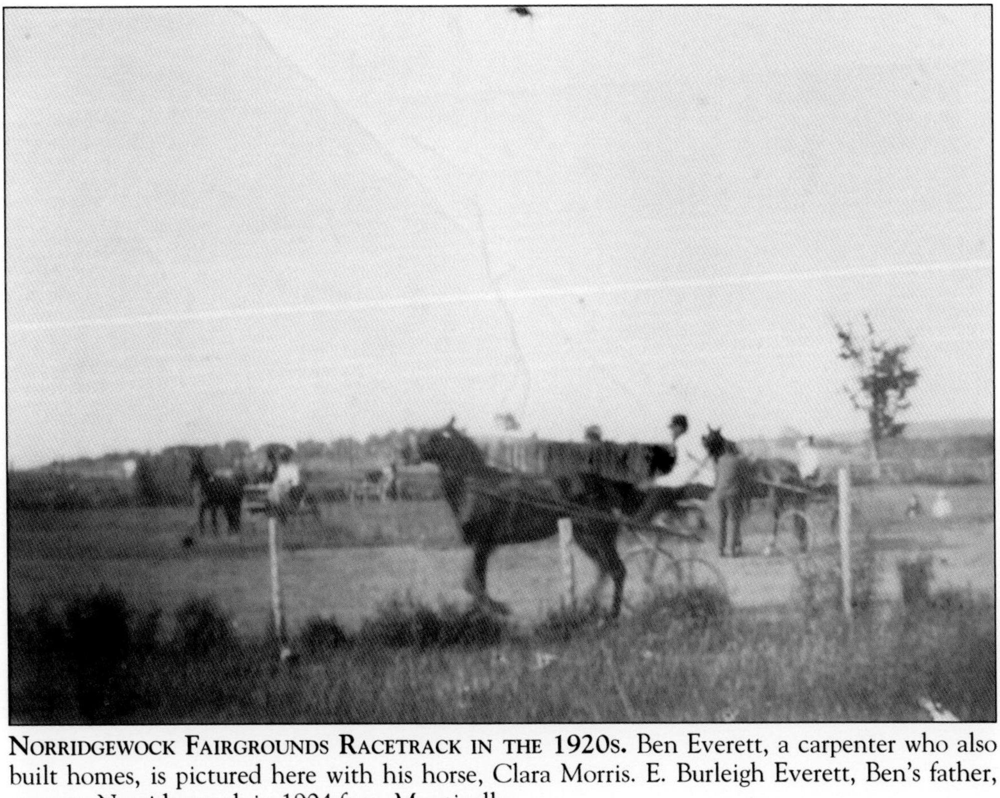

NORRIDGEWOCK FAIRGROUNDS RACETRACK IN THE 1920S. Ben Everett, a carpenter who also built homes, is pictured here with his horse, Clara Morris. E. Burleigh Everett, Ben's father, came to Norridgewock in 1904 from Monticello.

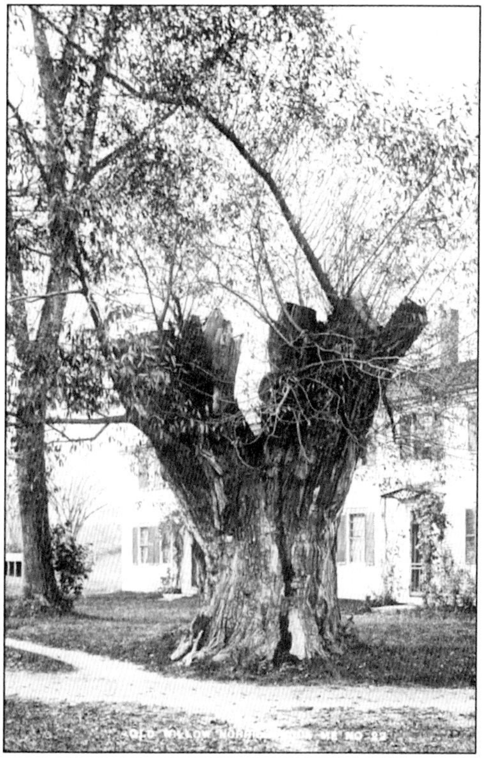

The Huge Willow Tree in Norridgewock, after It Was Cut, c. 1920s. This tree was considered by some to be the largest tree in Maine.

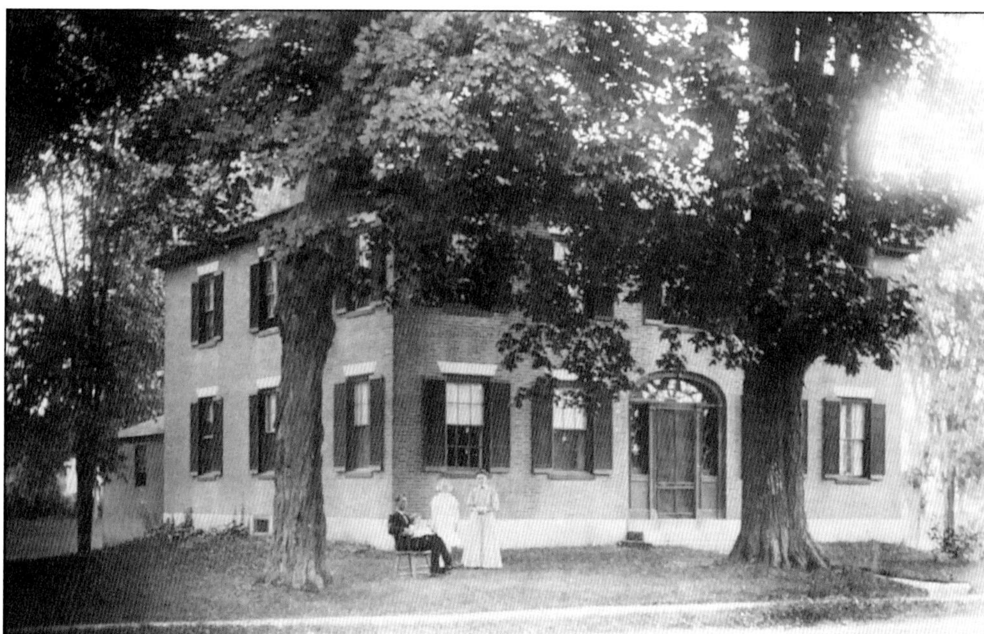

Home of Wilfred G. Everett, Left Front with Baby Wilfred in His Lap, c. 1910s. Standing in front are Rita and Ada Everett. Wilfred purchased the home from the Dole family on the condition that Madame Caroline Dole could live with the Everetts until her death.

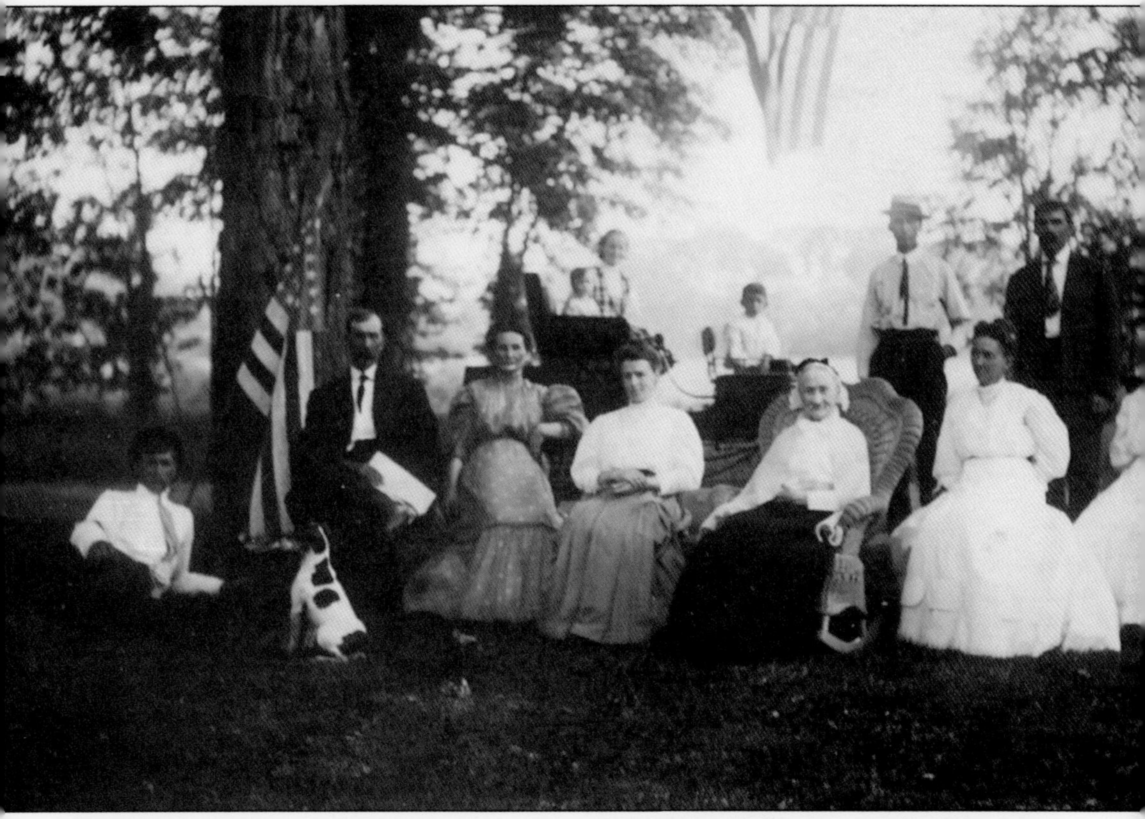

THE EVERETT FAMILY AT A FOURTH OF JULY GATHERING. Pictured from left to right at the former Dole house in the early 1900s were the following: Ben Everett and his dog "Bruce"; his father, E. Burleigh Everett; his mother, Mrs. Susan Briggs Everett; Aunt Ada Everett; Mrs. Caroline Dole, then 100 years old; Mrs. Hamlin Hale with her husband behind her; and Maybelle Jones Everett. Uncle Wilfred "Fred" Everett is the man wearing the straw hat. In the Stanley Steamer at the rear were, from left to right, the following: Wilfred, Rita, and Charles Everett. One of Mrs. Dole's grandsons started the Dole pineapple empire in Hawaii.

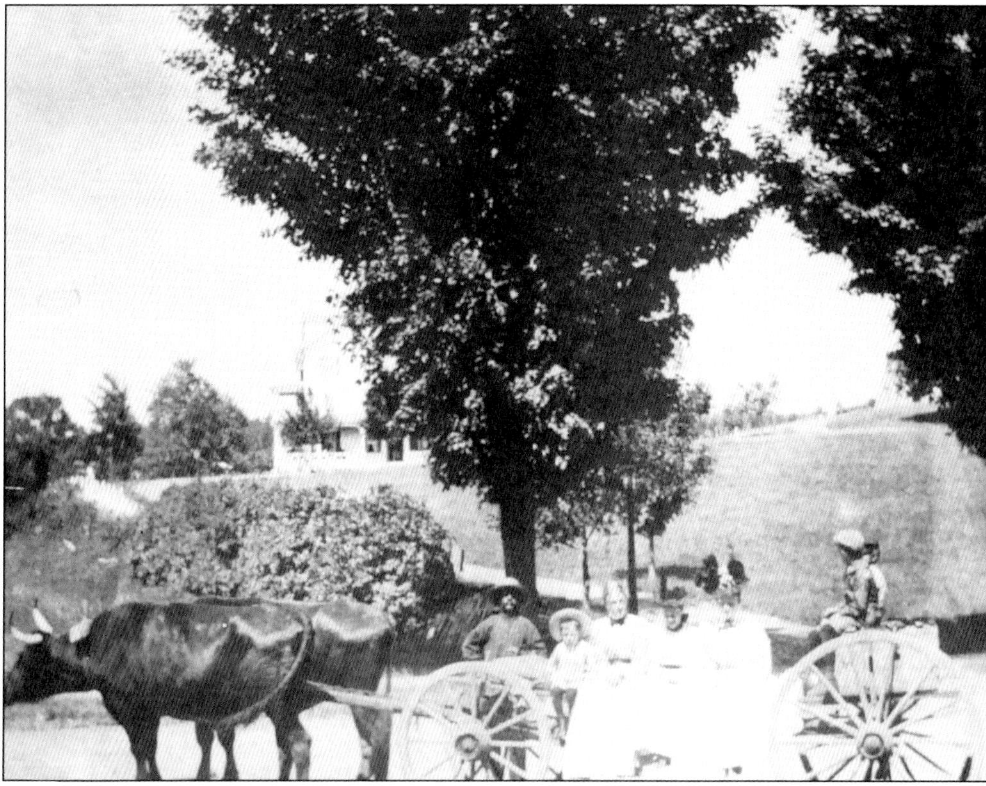

SUMMER IN NORRIDGEWOCK FOR VISITORS FROM NEW BRUNSWICK, NEW JERSEY, ON FERNSIDE FARM, OWNED BY SELDON AND SUSIE HARRIS FULLER. Harry Harris came to Norridgewock in 1906 from New Brunswick. The Fullers had come to Norridgewock just before the turn of the century. Seldon Fuller purchased the home owned by the Frye family. The area where the ox cart was is now under water. The water came when Central Maine Power put in a dam at Skowhegan.

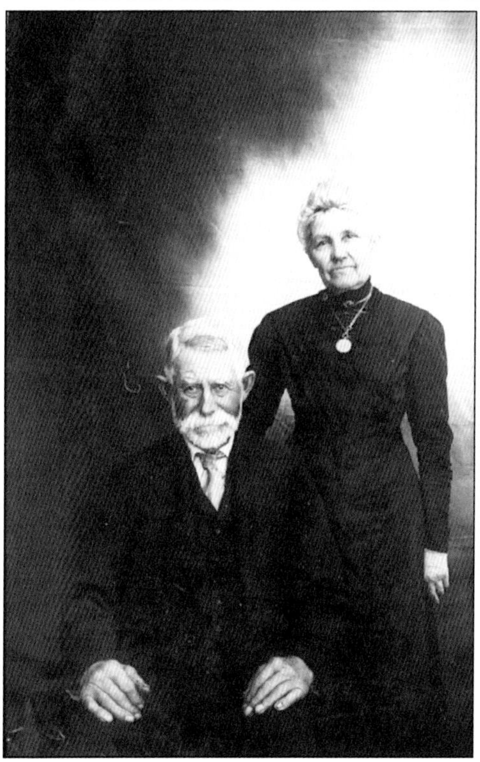

SELDON AND SUSIE HARRIS FULLER, C. EARLY 1900S. The Fullers were the owners of Fernside dairy farm in Norridgewock.

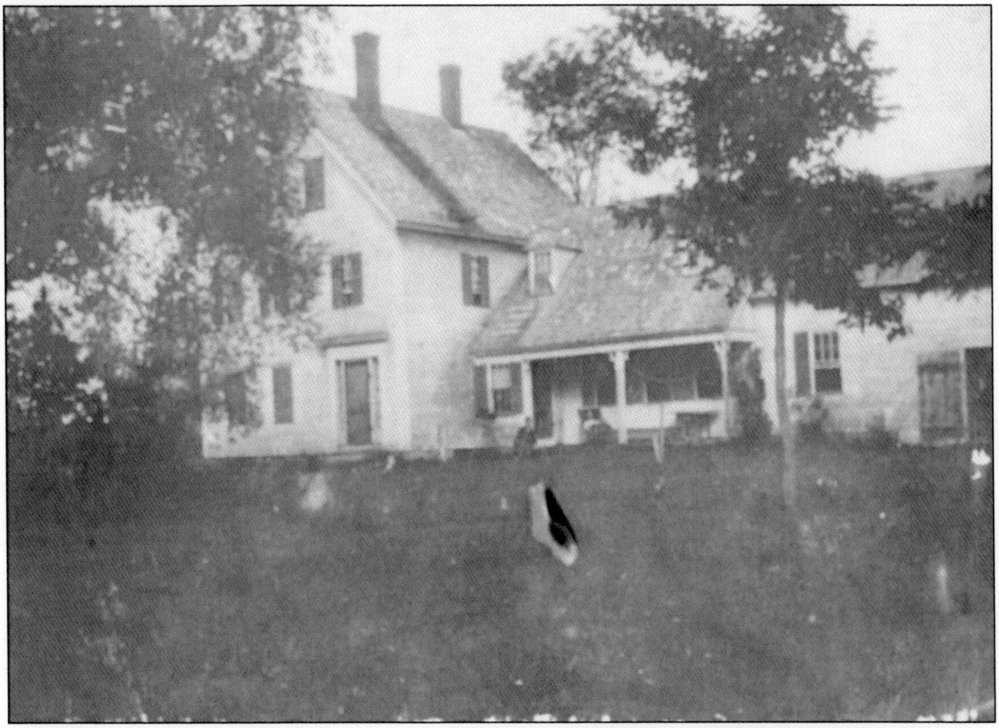

FERNSIDE, C. EARLY 1900S. This is the Fuller home, where John N. Harris was born.

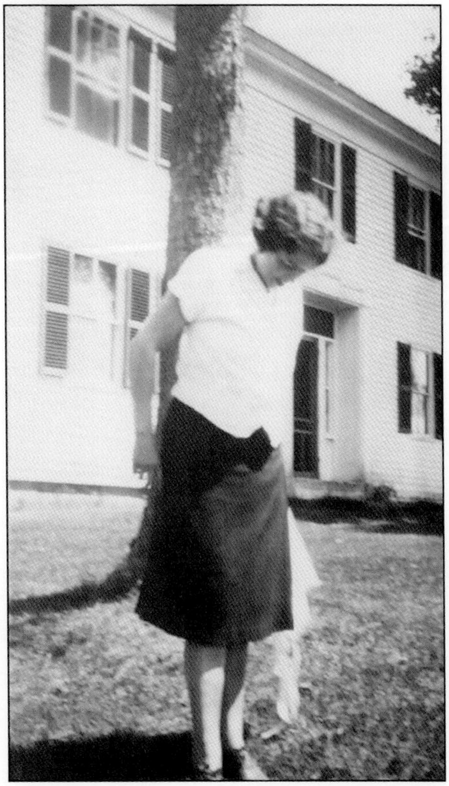

FLORENCE EVERETT HARRIS, AT THE ELMS, C. 1929. Florence came to Norridgewock at the age of 15 from Monticello. The Elms was the former home of Professor Hamlin Eaton, founder of the Eaton School. The house burned shortly thereafter.

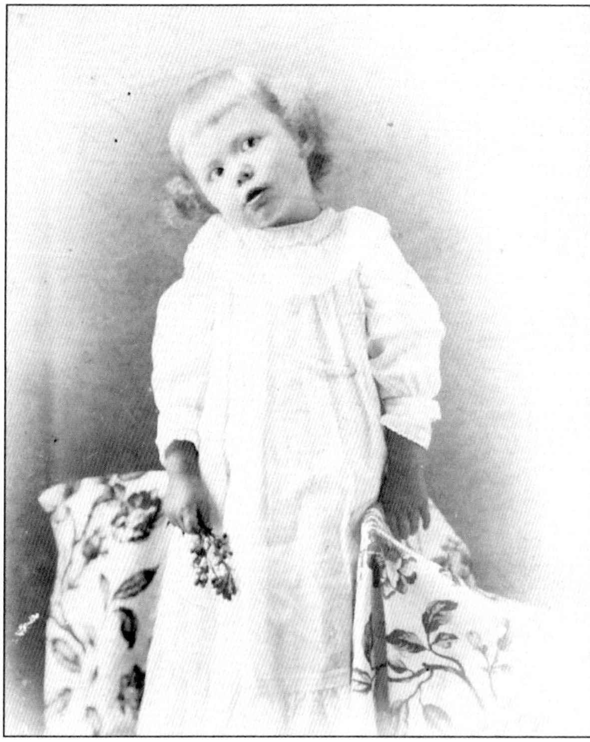

Linnion "Linnie" Irene Brown. Linnie was a cousin of the Harris family. She is pictured here at age four in her night dress.

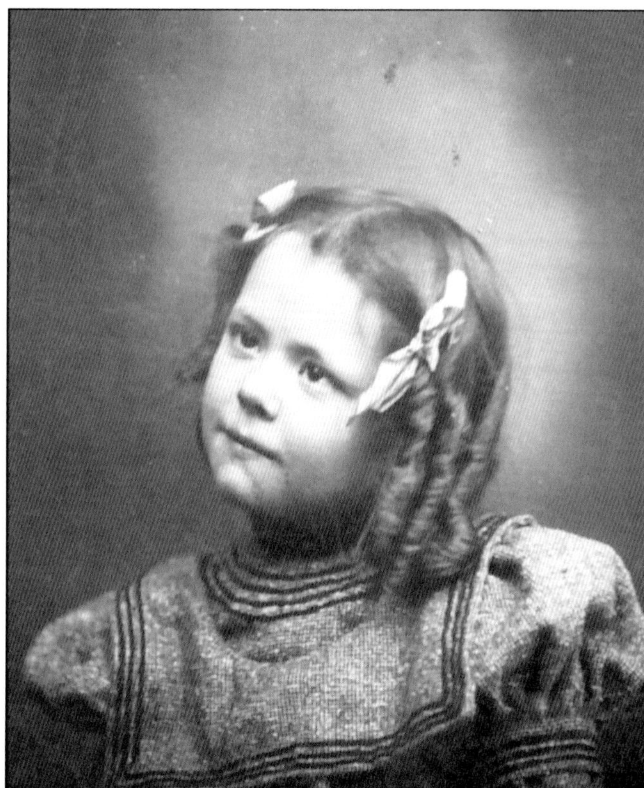

Another Portrait of Linnie. Daughter of Dr. Walter and Louise Brown, Linnie smiles at age five with her curly hair in ribbons.

Linnie, with Angora Tam, Somewhere between the Ages of 10 and 12 in 1905. Note the fashions in this series of photographs of the girl and woman. Dr. Brown was a dentist who moved to Norridgewock in the late 1890s from Morrill, where he had been a selectman.

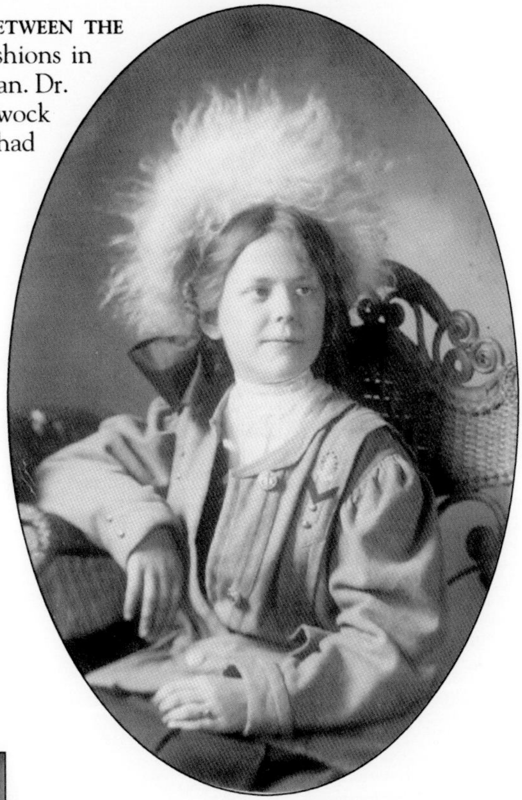

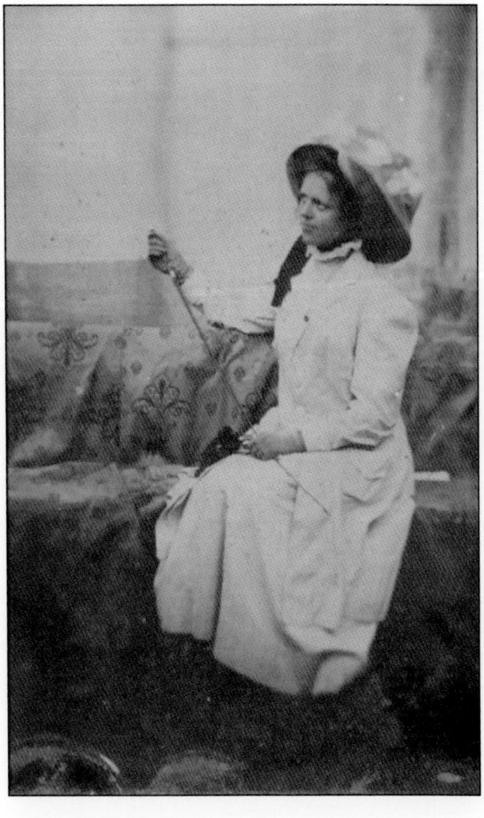

A Tintype Photograph. Linnie shows off a new dress and hat while holding what appears to be a riding crop in her hands. This may have been a riding outfit.

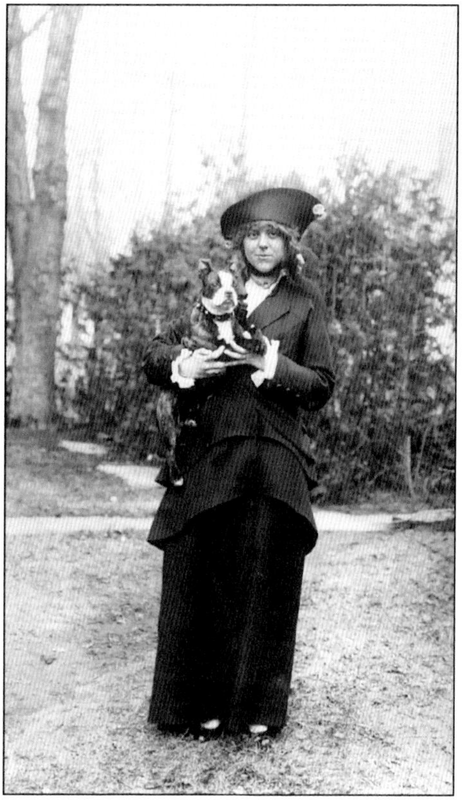

Linnie Brown. Visiting Norridgewock after she became a cashier at the Bank of Boston in Boston, Linnie shows off the latest style. This image was probably taken during World War I.

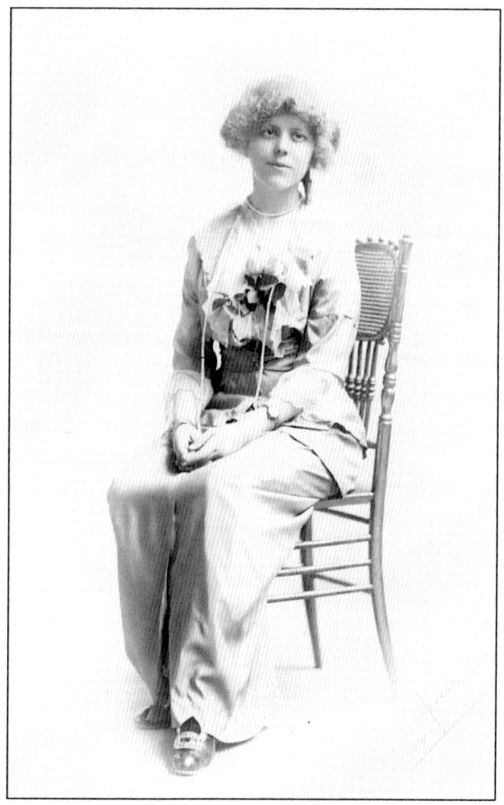

Linnie in 1920. At this time, she was still working in Boston.

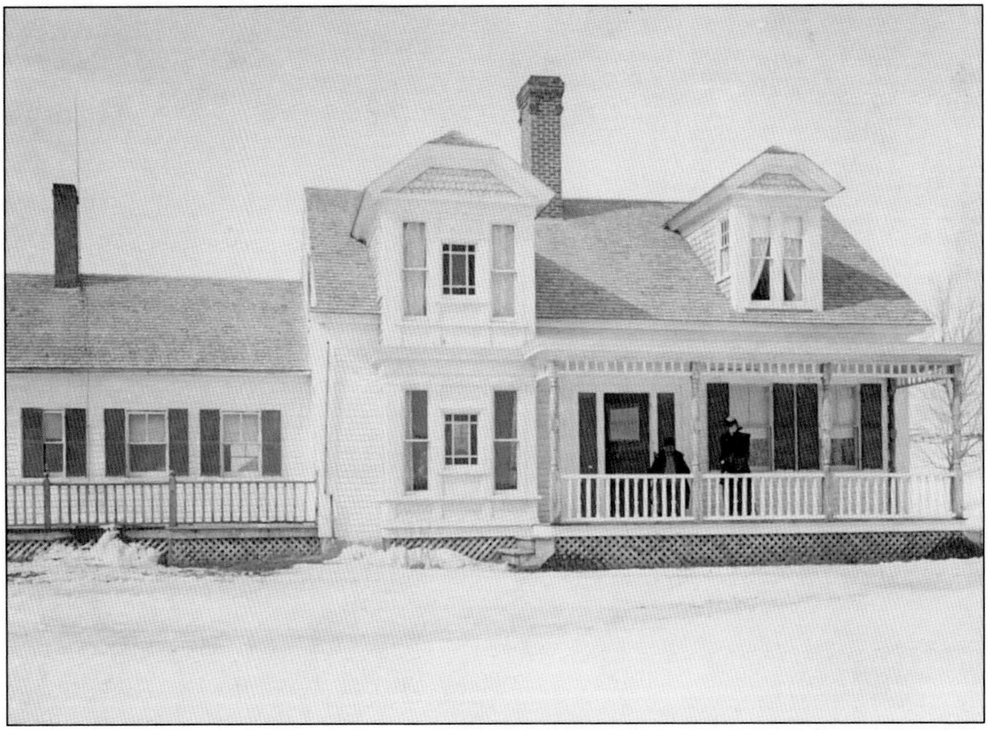

SARAH HARRIS FRYE AND JOHN FRYE. Here they sit on the porch of their Norridgewock home in the 1910s. They were Quakers and came to Norridgewock from Bangor, where he had been a top official at Bangor State Hospital. The house was sold by Sarah to Harry Harris in 1919. It's one lot above the home of author Sophie Mae Clark, who wrote under the pen name of "Pen Shirley."

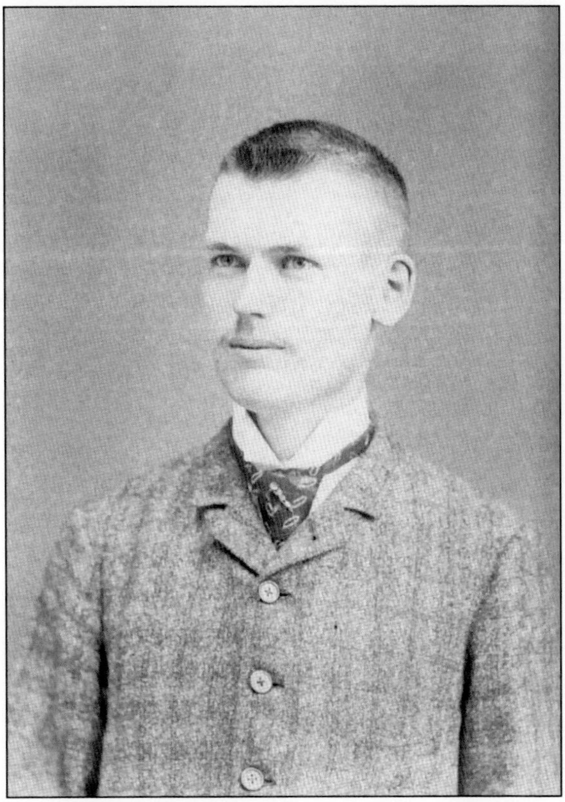

DR. WALTER BROWN IN THE 1880S.

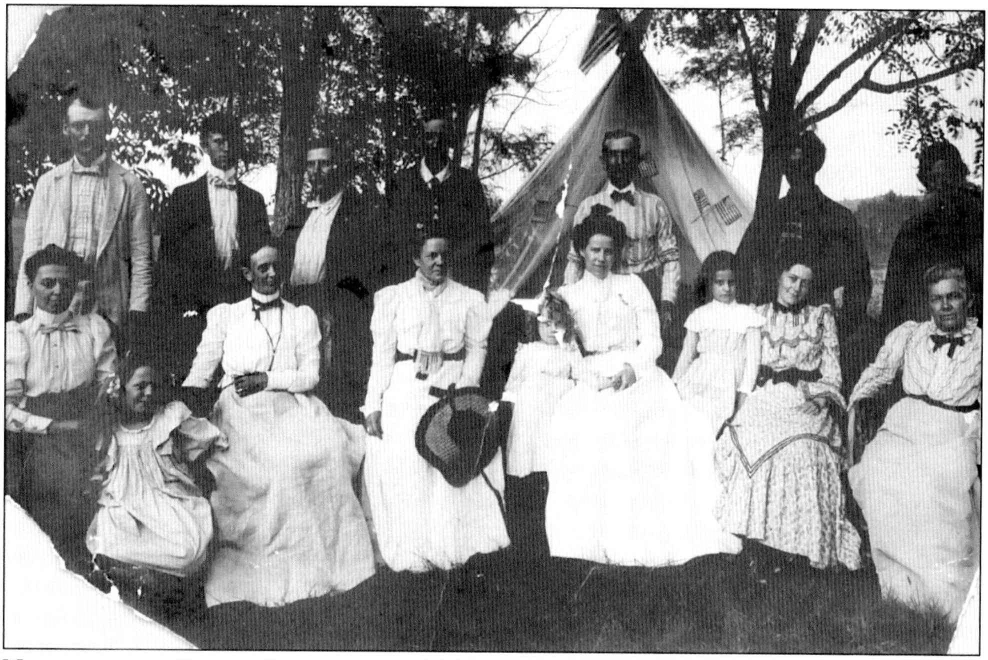

Norridgewock Family Scene in the 1900s. Pictured from left to right are the following: (front row) Aunt Lou Brown; Linnion (the young girl in front); Anna Greenwood Harris (very prominent in Baptist church work); Sarah Frye; Mrs. Will (Harriet) Harris with daughters Hazel and Violet; Esther Fuller; and Susie Fuller; (back row) Dr. Walter Brown, Harry Harris, Dr. John Harris, Mr. Gilman, Will Harris, Charles Fuller, and Seldon Fuller.

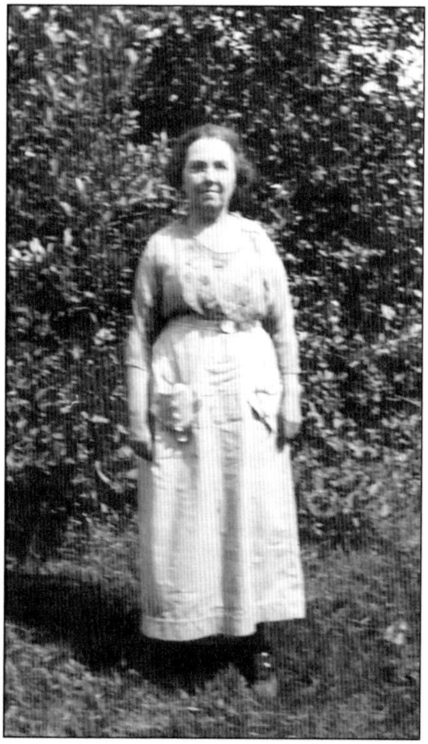

Lou Brown in Her Thirties, c. 1920s. She was the wife of Dr. Walter Brown and a half-sister of Susie Fuller and Sarah Frye.

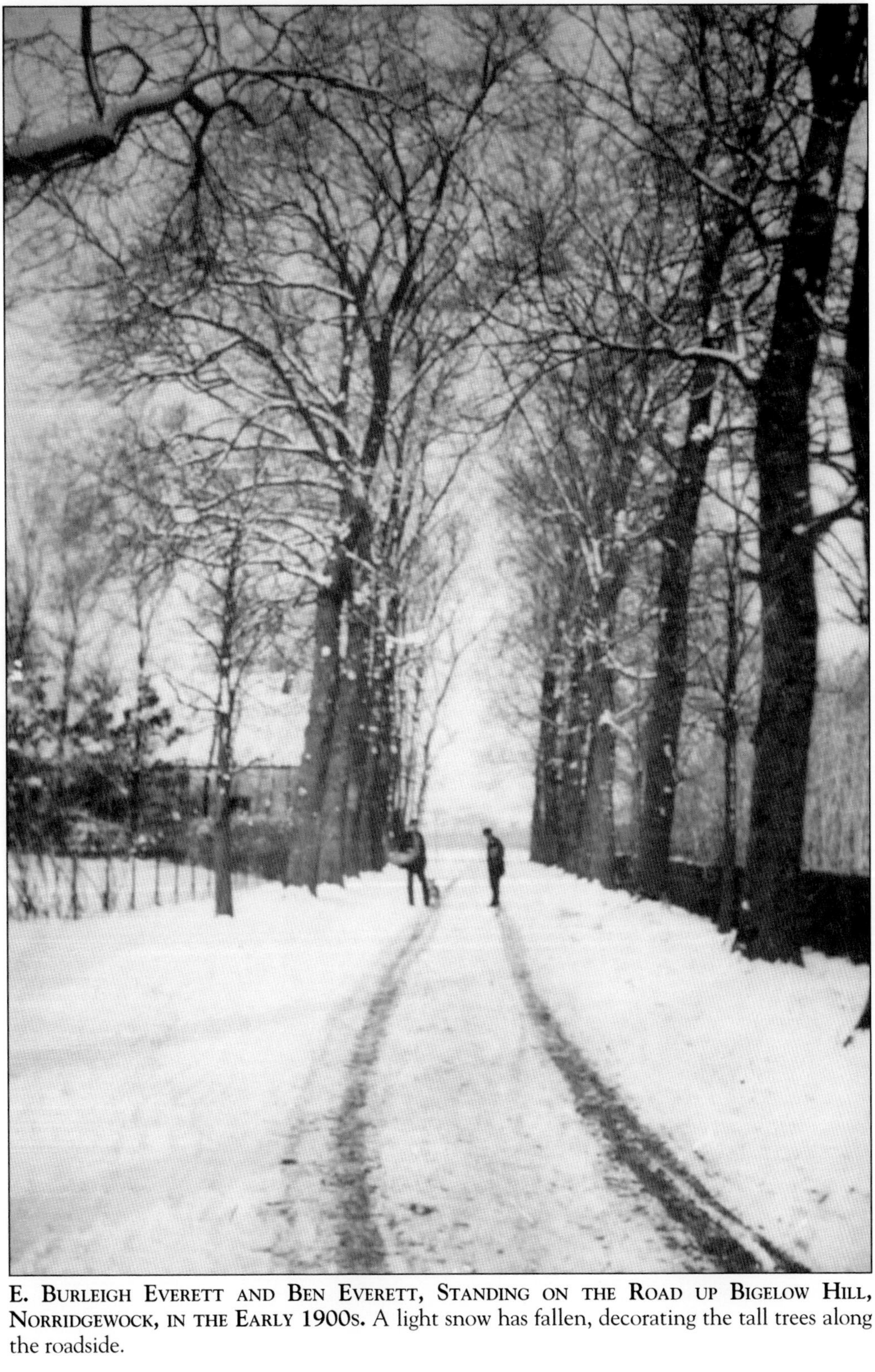

E. Burleigh Everett and Ben Everett, Standing on the Road up Bigelow Hill, Norridgewock, in the Early 1900s. A light snow has fallen, decorating the tall trees along the roadside.

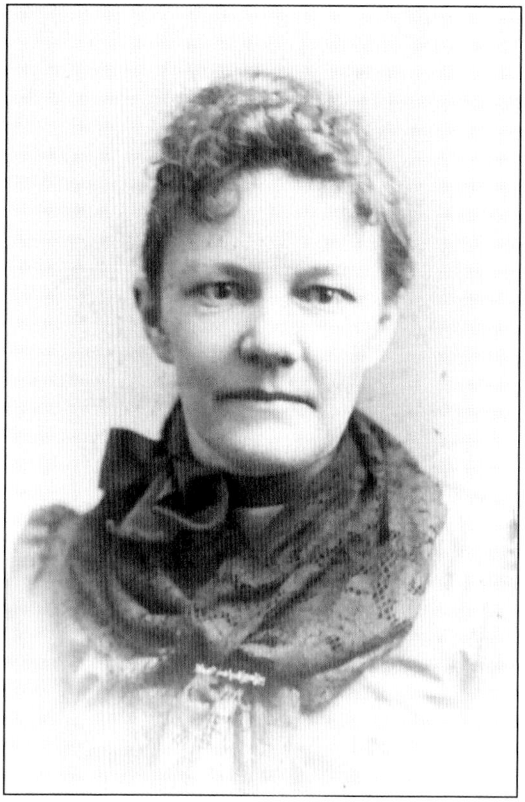

SARAH HARRIS FRYE (BORN ON MARCH 27, 1845), C. 1880.

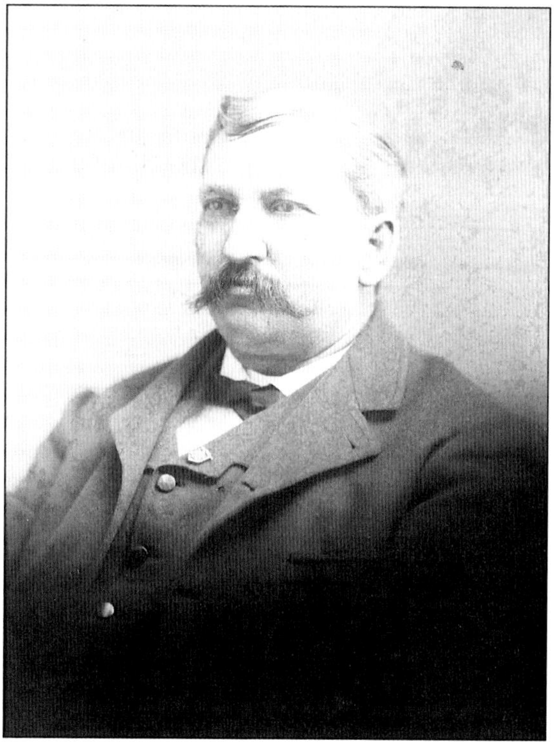

JOHN FRYE, SARAH FRYE'S HUSBAND, IN NORRIDGEWOCK, C. 1880S. The Quaker couple had much to do with Oak Grove Seminary in Vassalboro.

Ebenezer Frye on His 90th Birthday, c. 1880s. He was Sarah Harris Frye's father-in-law.

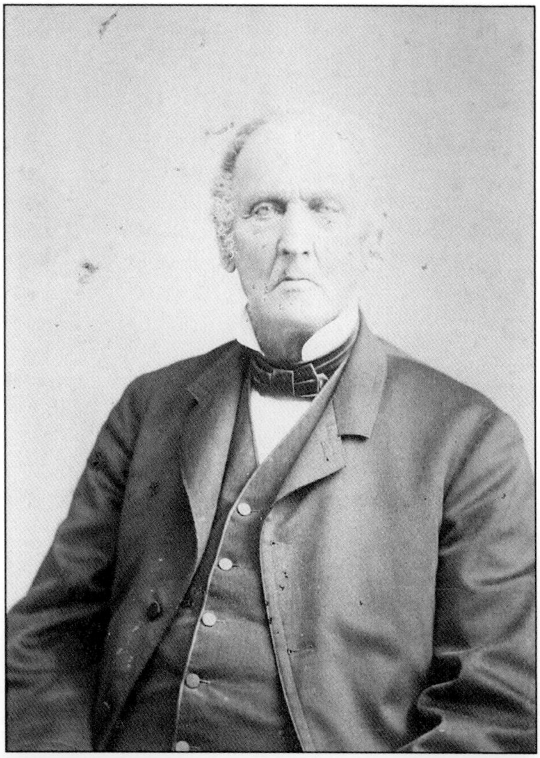

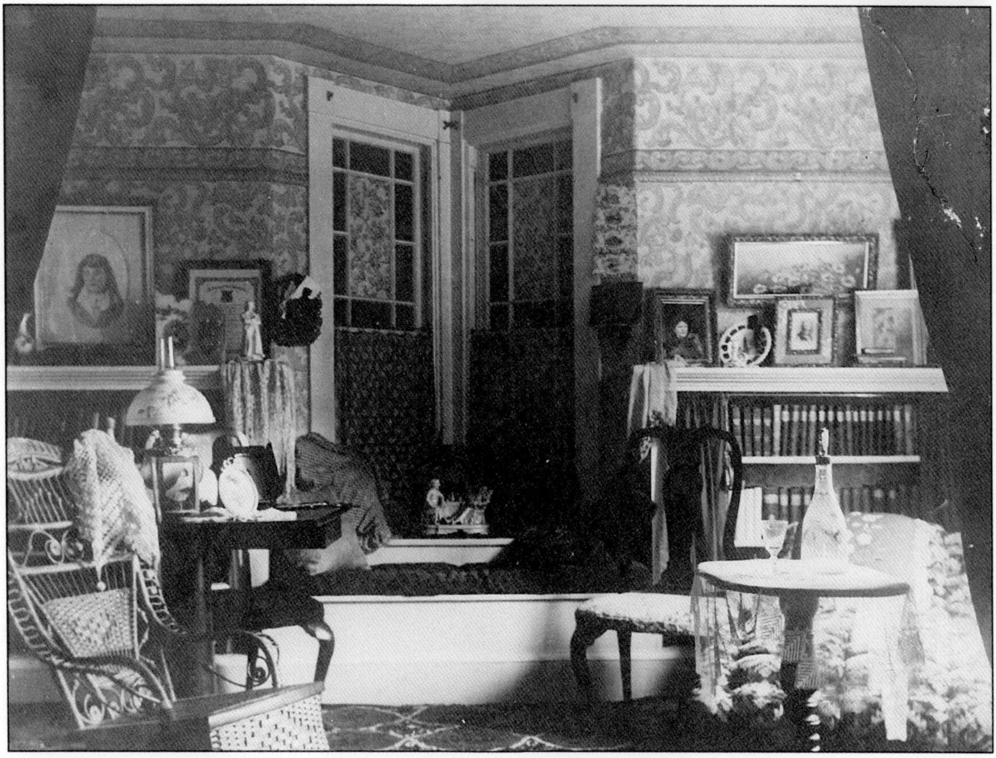

Interior of the Sarah Frye Farm in Norridgewock, c. 1890s.

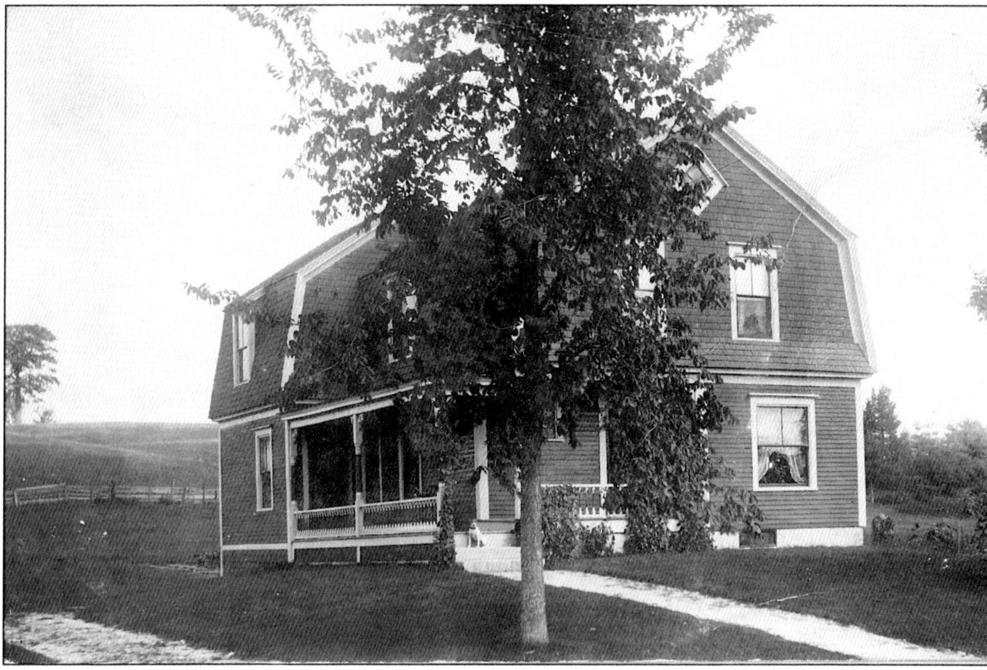

Home of Ben E. Everett in Norridgewock in the 1900s.

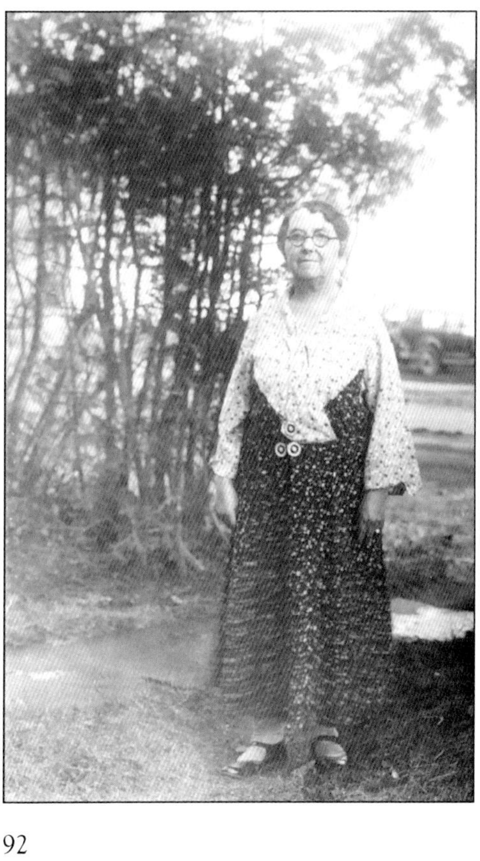

Mrs. Lou (Walter) Brown in the 1920s.

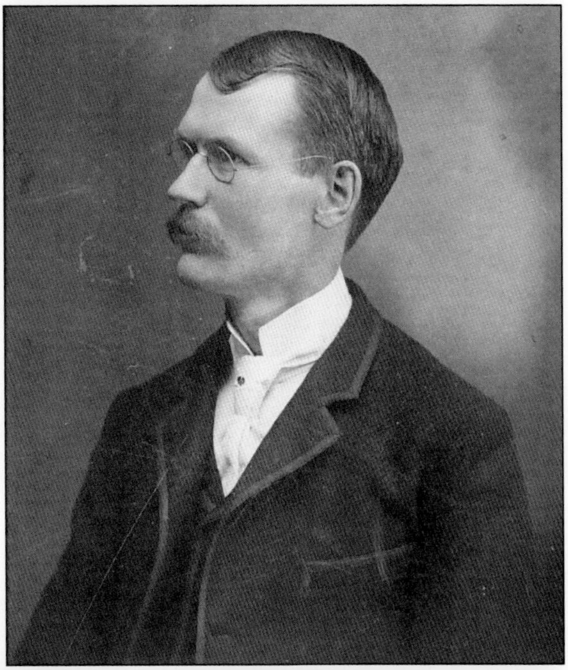

Dr. Walter Brown, Possibly in the 1890s.

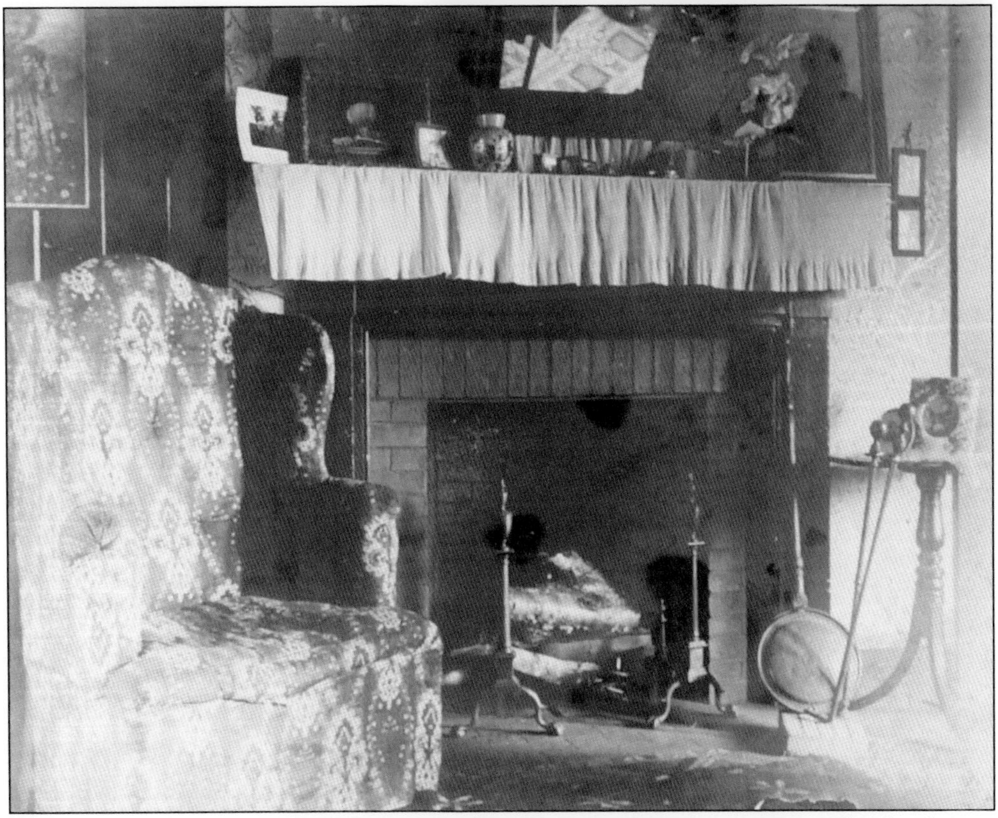

Fireplace at Dr. Walter Brown Home in Norridgewock, c. 1900s. The fireplace is complete with bellows, tongs, and a warming pad.

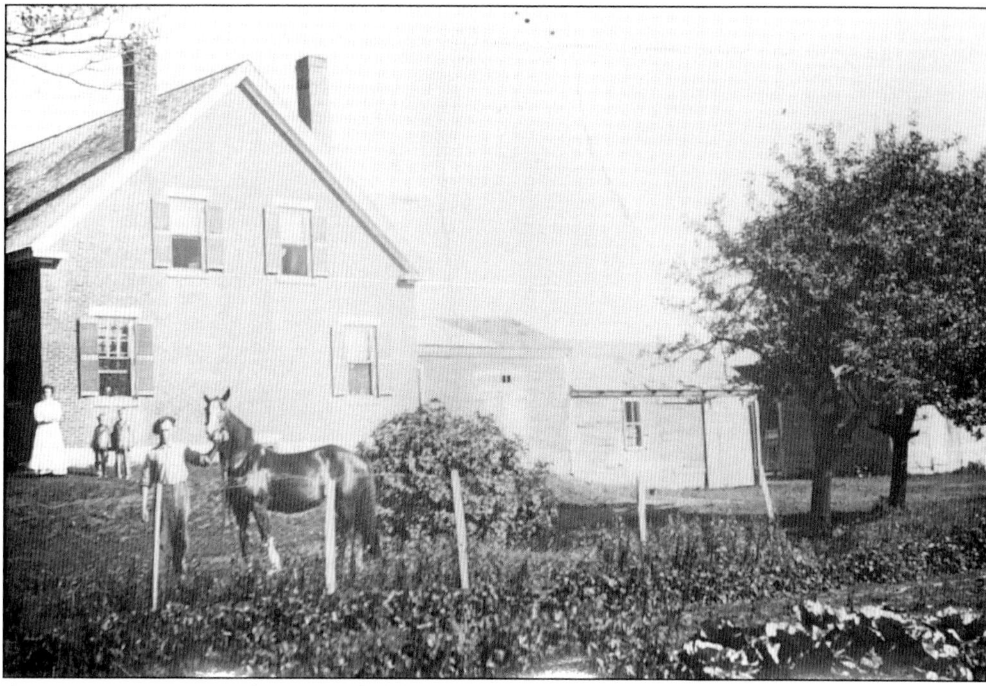

ALFRED EVERETT. Here he is seen holding a horse on his Norridgewock farm in the late 1890s. His wife, Lillian, is visible in the background with their two sons, Donald (left) and Roland.

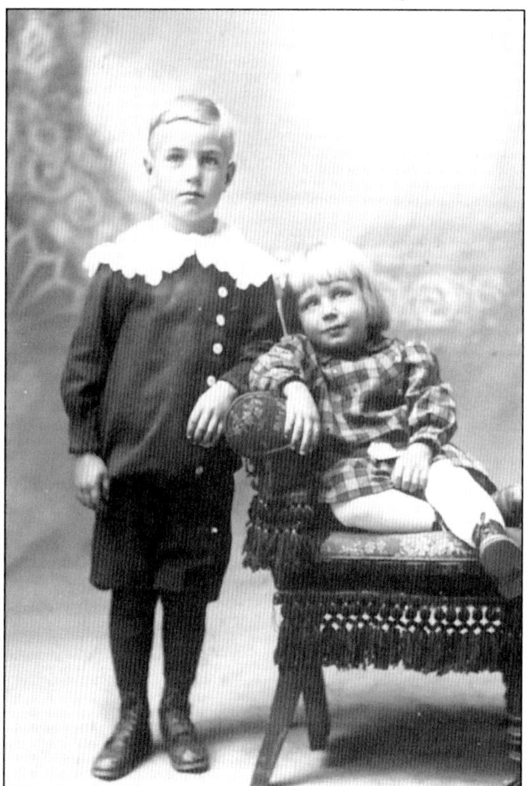

ROLAND (LEFT) AND DONALD EVERETT IN THE LATE 1880S OR EARLY 1890S. Roland looks very dapper in his Little Lord Fauntleroy suit.

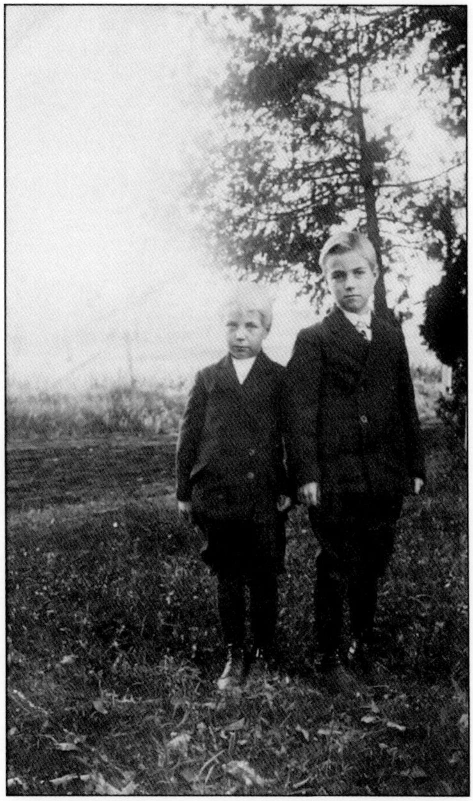

Donald and Roland Everett a Few Years Later, but Still in the 1890s.

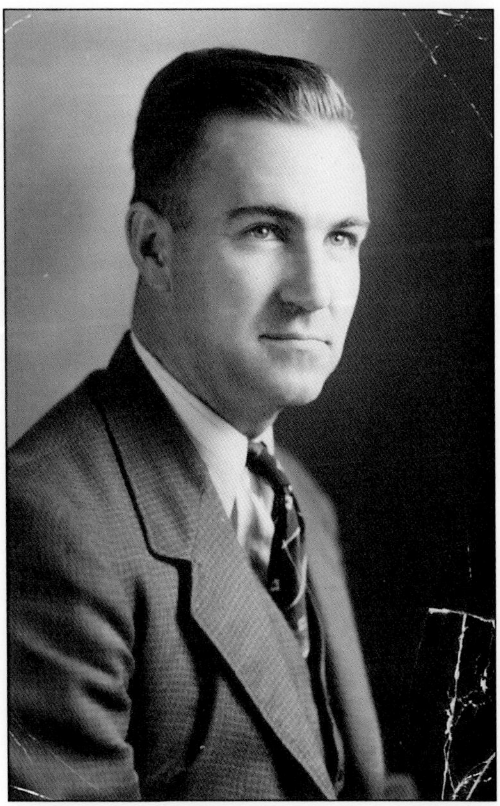

Roland Everett in the 1950s. He was a legislator and builder of homes in Norridgewock. Everett Street in Norridgewock is named after him. Roland married the daughter of a Norridgewock druggist. Roland died in 1967.

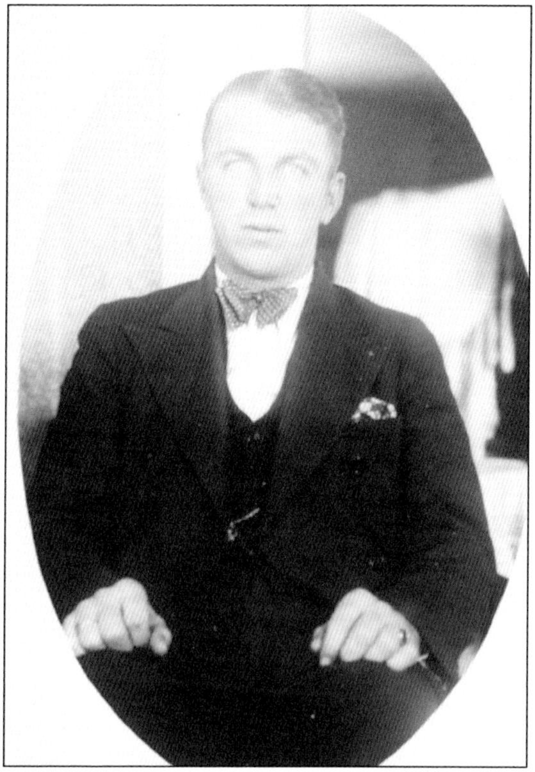

DONALD EVERETT AT EVERETT'S VARIETY STORE IN NORRIDGEWOCK. His wife was Della, and his daughter, Joan, still lives in the town.

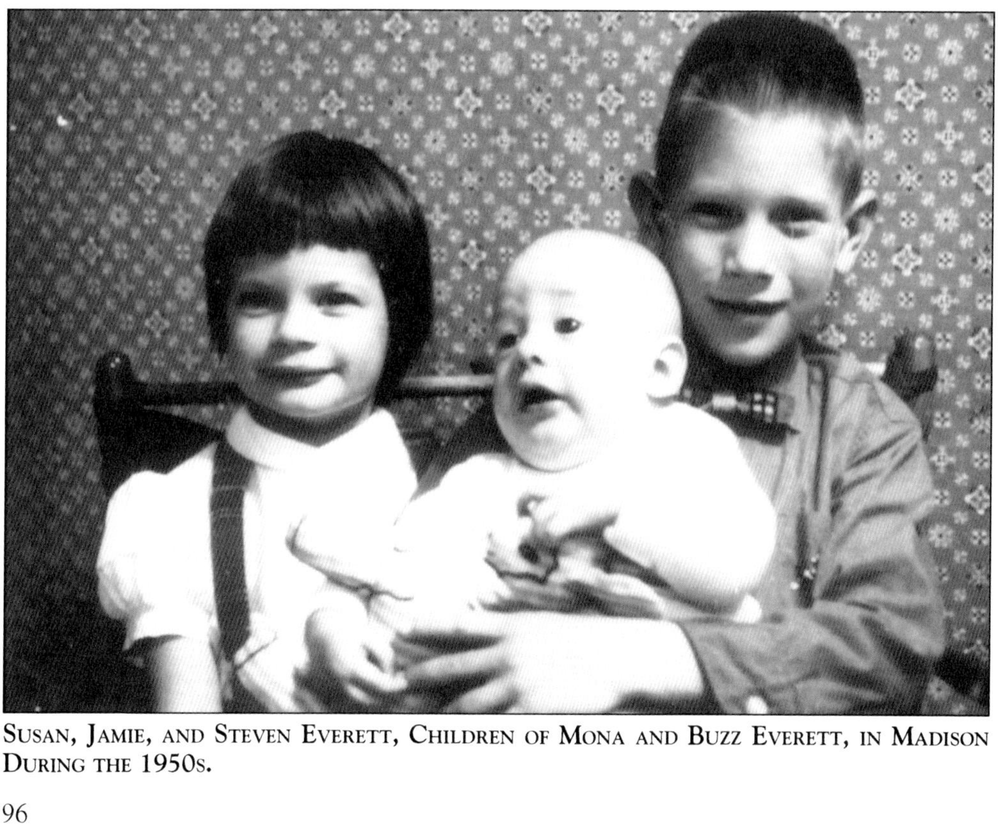

SUSAN, JAMIE, AND STEVEN EVERETT, CHILDREN OF MONA AND BUZZ EVERETT, IN MADISON DURING THE 1950S.

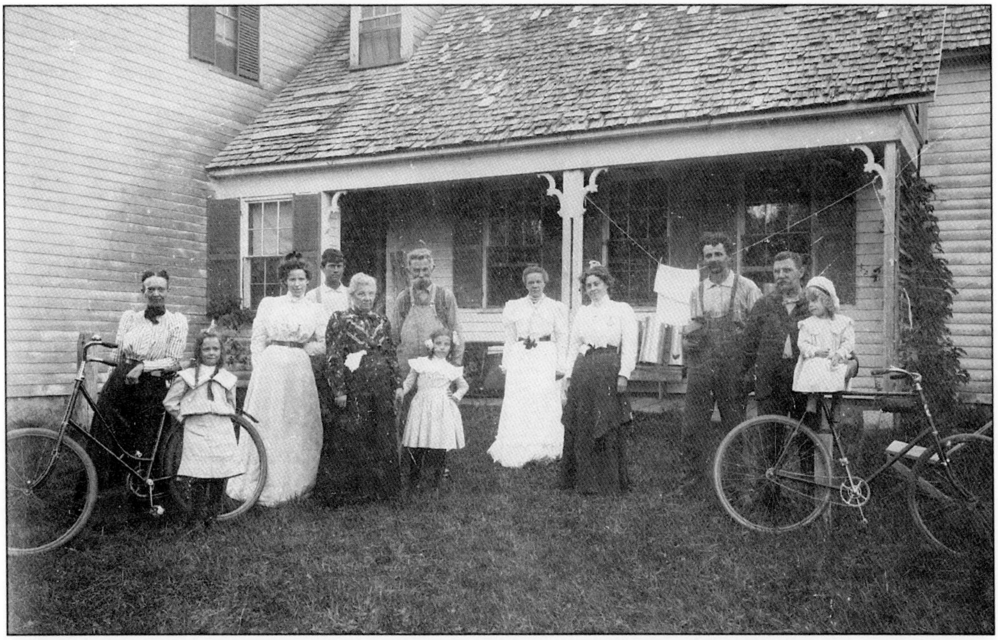

HARRIS FAMILY AT FERNWOOD DAIRY FARM, SKOWHEGAN ROAD, NORRIDGEWOCK, ABOUT THE TURN OF THE CENTURY. Pictured from left to right were the following: Anna Greenwood Harris, Linnie Brown, Hattie Hudson Harris (Mrs. William), Harry Lloyd Harris, Susannah "Susie" Harris Fuller, Seldon Fuller (owner of the farm), Violet Hudson Harris, Sarah Harris Frye, Mrs. Charles Fuller, Charles Fuller, Dr. John Niles Harris, and Hazel Harris.

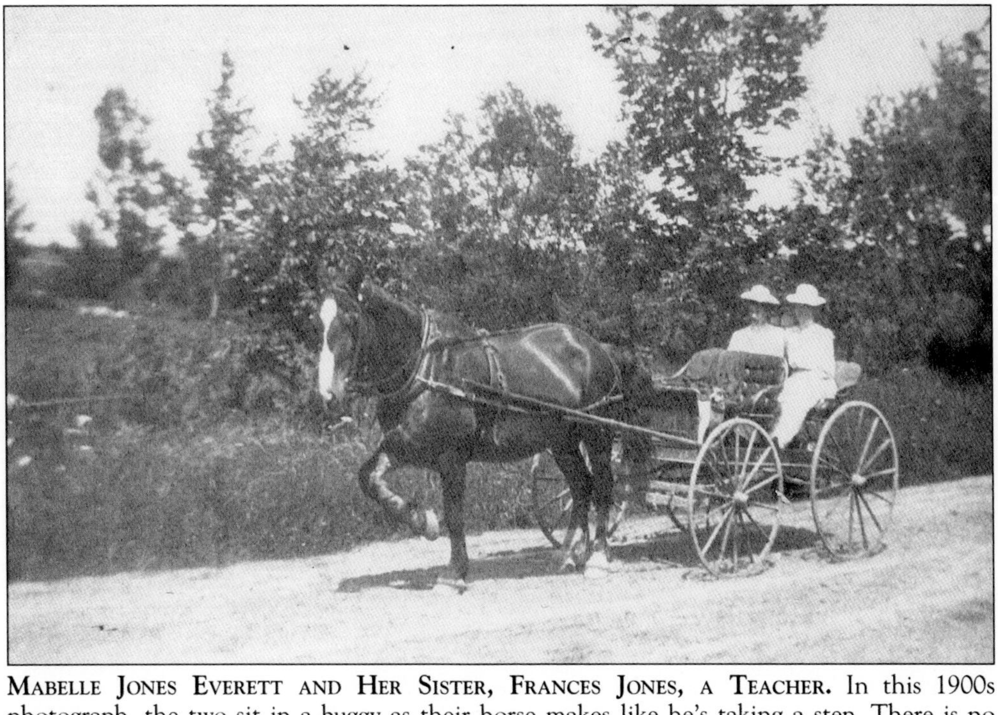

MABELLE JONES EVERETT AND HER SISTER, FRANCES JONES, A TEACHER. In this 1900s photograph, the two sit in a buggy as their horse makes like he's taking a step. There is no driver. The driver probably took the photograph.

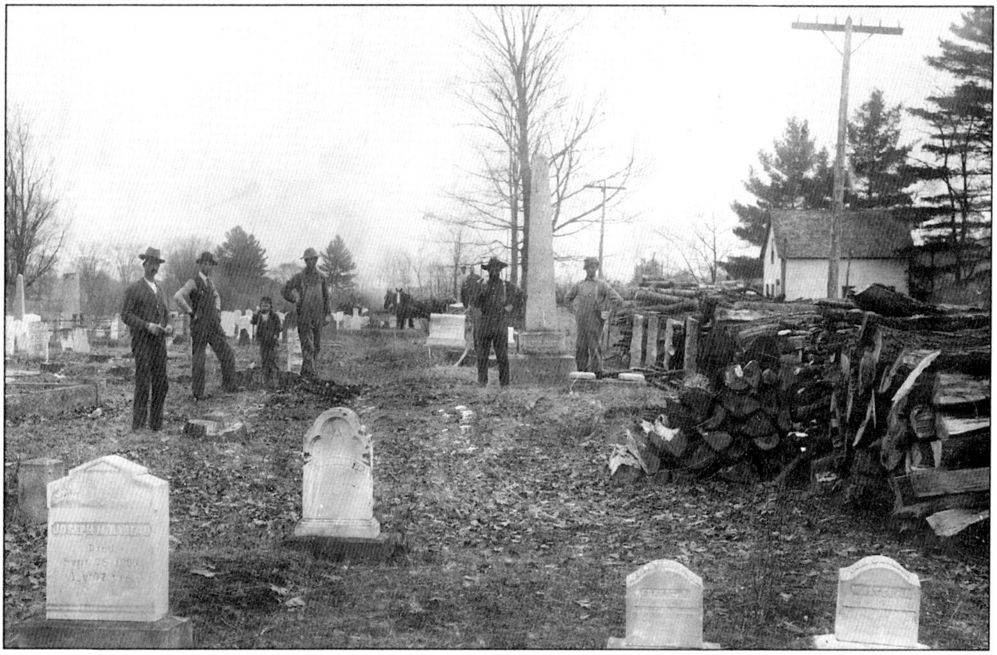

A NORRIDGEWOCK CEMETERY. Fred Everett and Harry Harris were among those cutting down trees at one of the town's cemeteries in the 1900s.

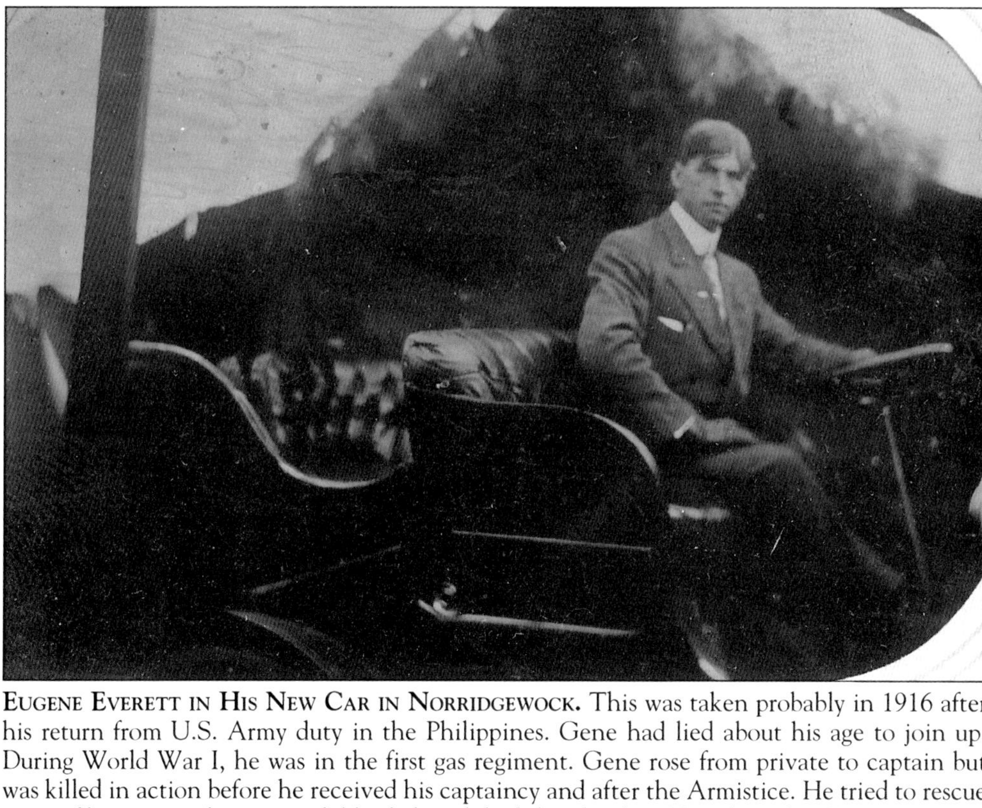

EUGENE EVERETT IN HIS NEW CAR IN NORRIDGEWOCK. This was taken probably in 1916 after his return from U.S. Army duty in the Philippines. Gene had lied about his age to join up. During World War I, he was in the first gas regiment. Gene rose from private to captain but was killed in action before he received his captaincy and after the Armistice. He tried to rescue some of his men and was gassed, blinded, and died shortly after. He is buried in France.

Seven

The River

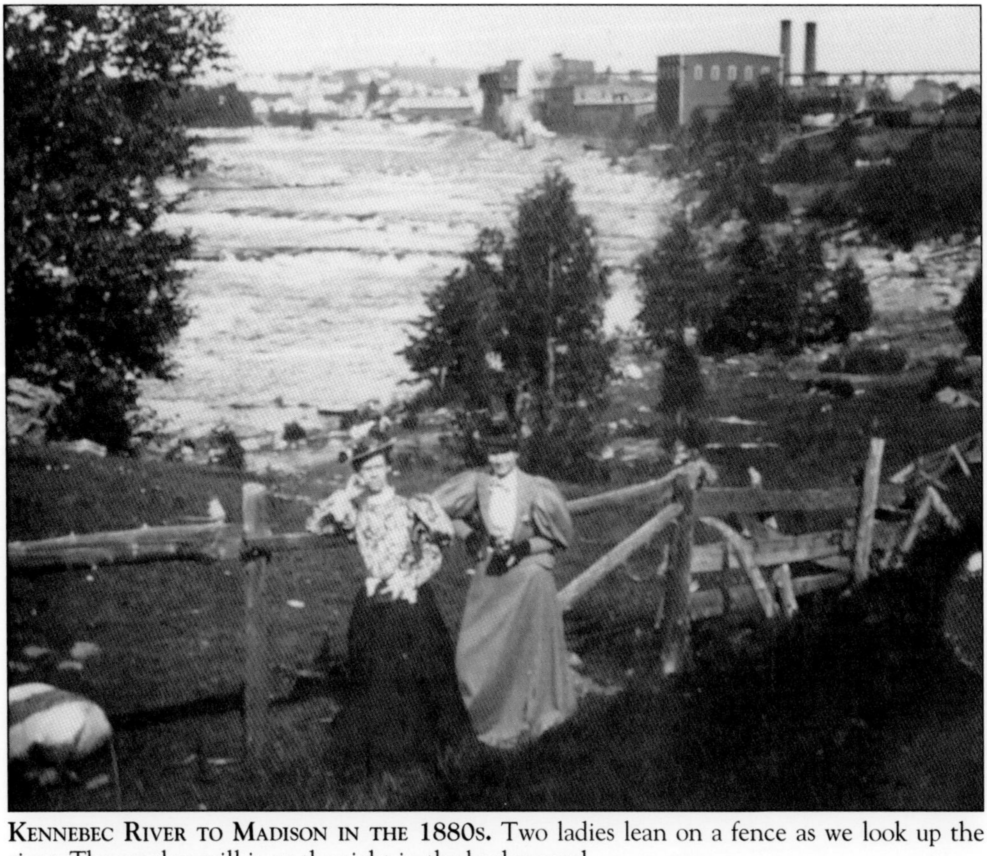

Kennebec River to Madison in the 1880s. Two ladies lean on a fence as we look up the river. The woolen mill is on the right in the background.

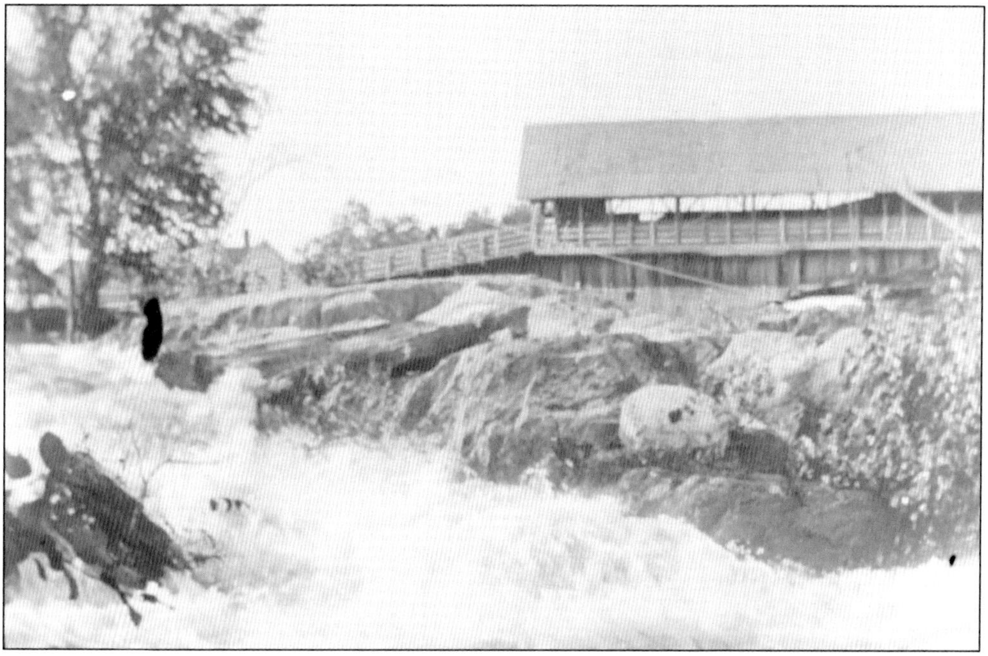

THE KENNEBEC AT MADISON WITH WHAT LOOKS LIKE A COVERED WALKWAY ON THE RIGHT, C. 1890S.

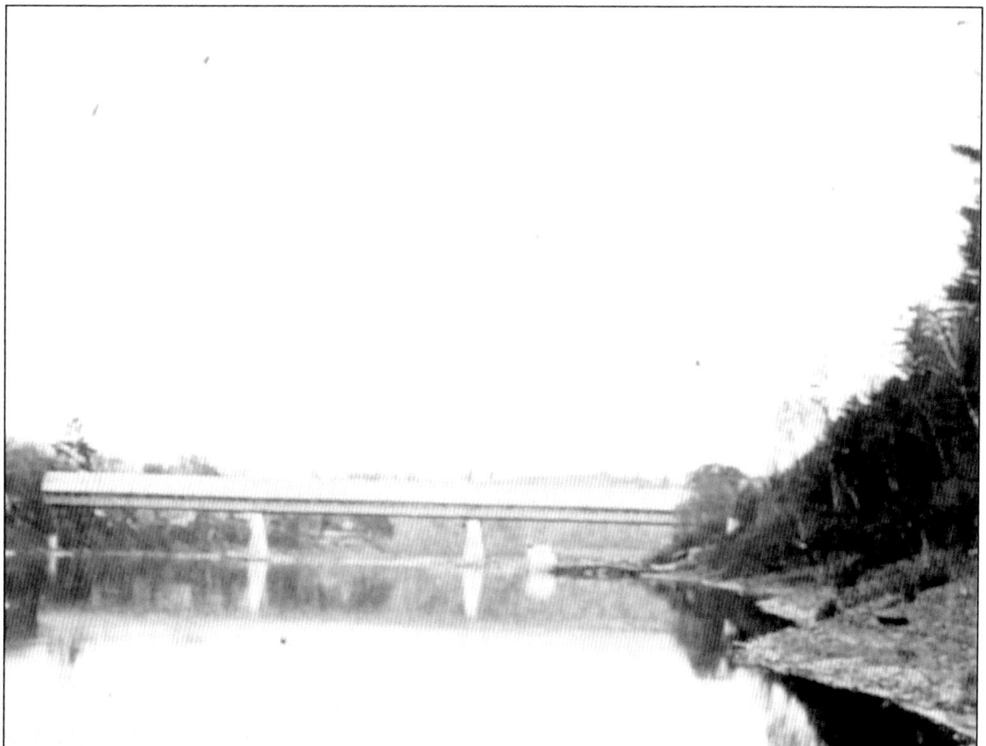

OVER THE KENNEBEC RIVER AT NORRIDGEWOCK. This covered railroad bridge was 680 feet long and 70 feet high.

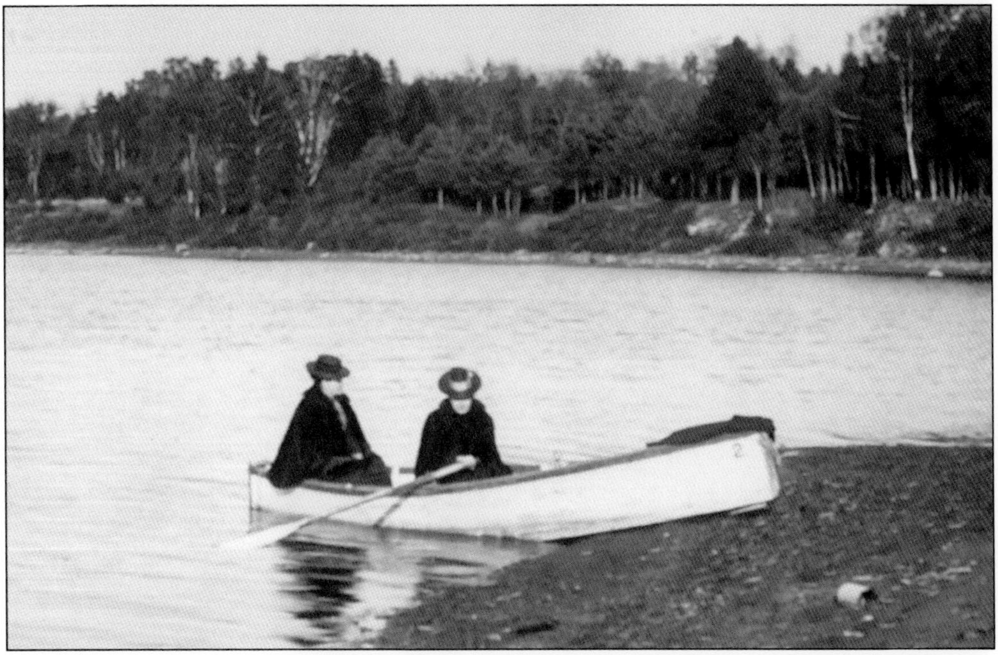

THE "PINES" DURING AUGUST 1897. These two women are posing in a rowboat by the Pines in South Norridgewock.

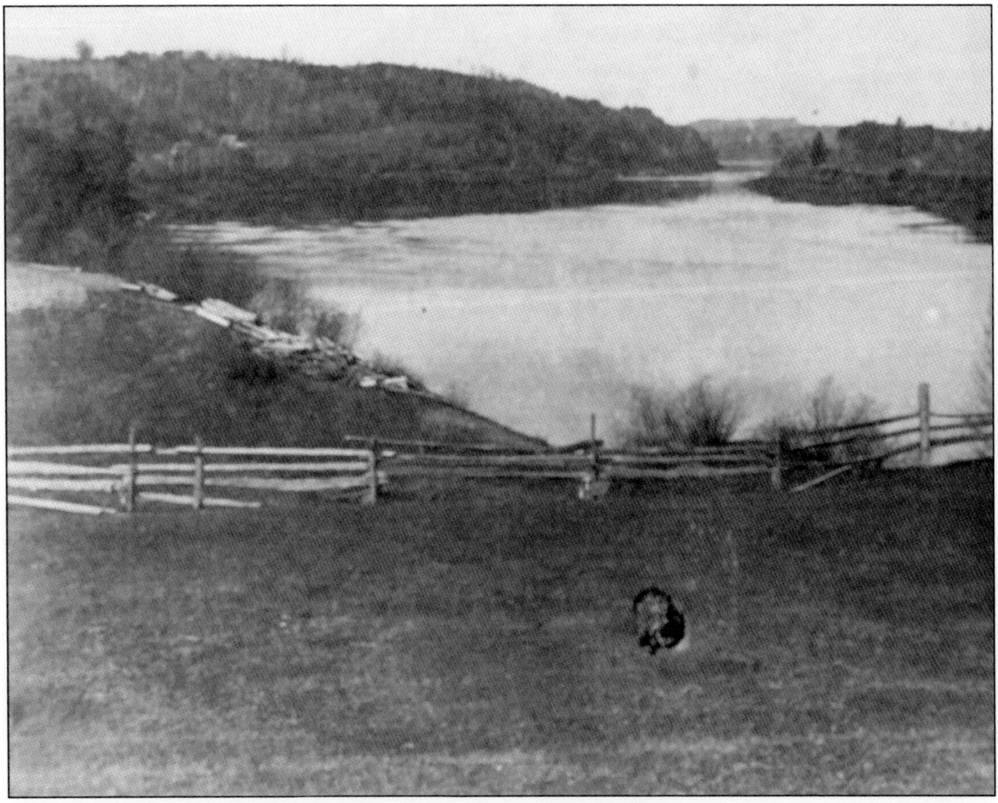

UP THE KENNEBEC FROM SOUTH NORRIDGEWOCK IN THE 1890s.

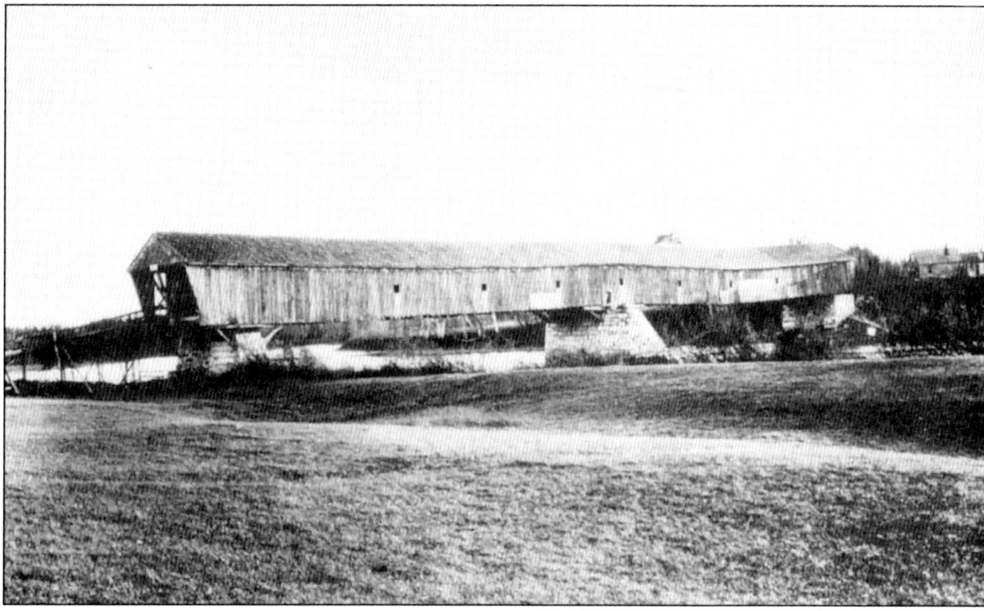

Patterson Bridge, a Long Covered Bridge in Madison. In the first part of the nineteenth century, bridges on this part of the Kennebec came and went with a great frequency. That pace slowed a bit in the second half of that century and fell off considerably through the twentieth century.

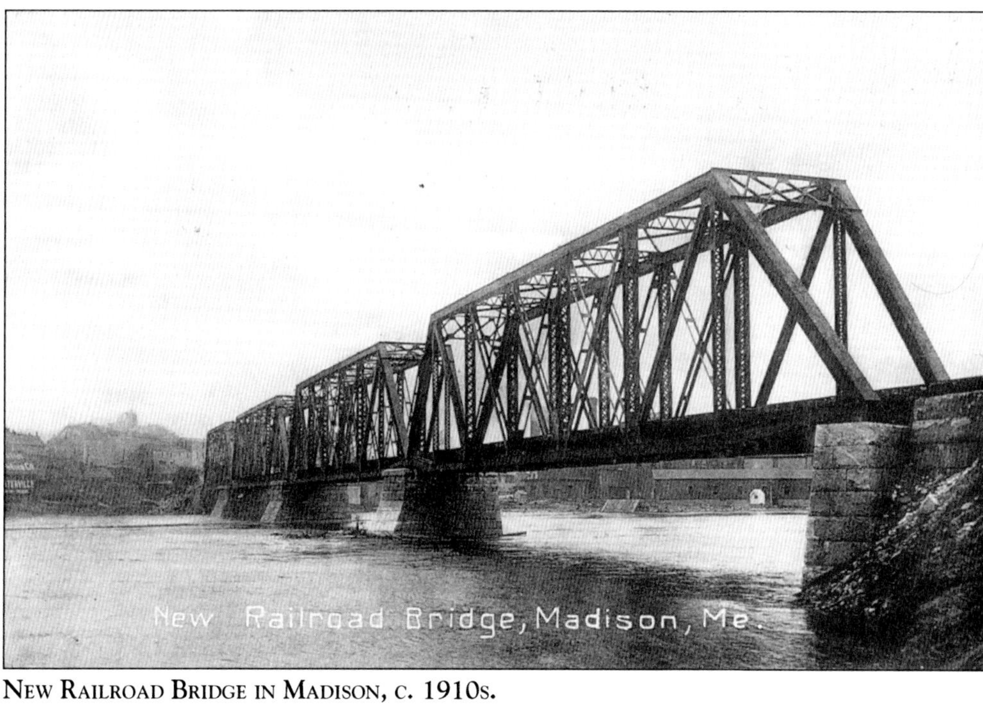

New Railroad Bridge in Madison, c. 1910s.

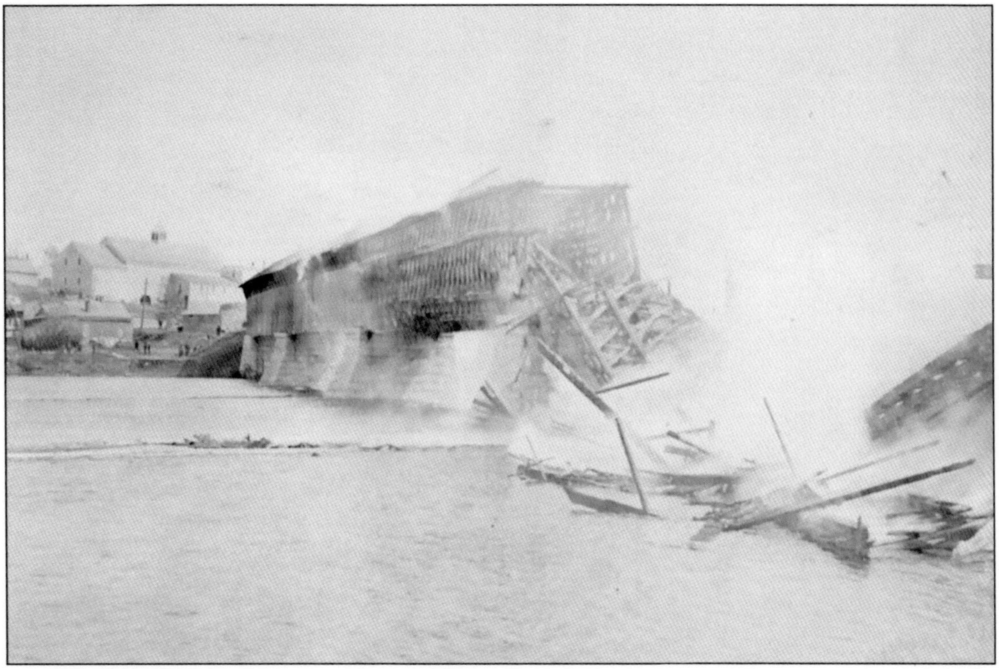

Covered Bridge on Memorial Day, 1906. This burning bridge is falling into the Kennebec River at Madison.

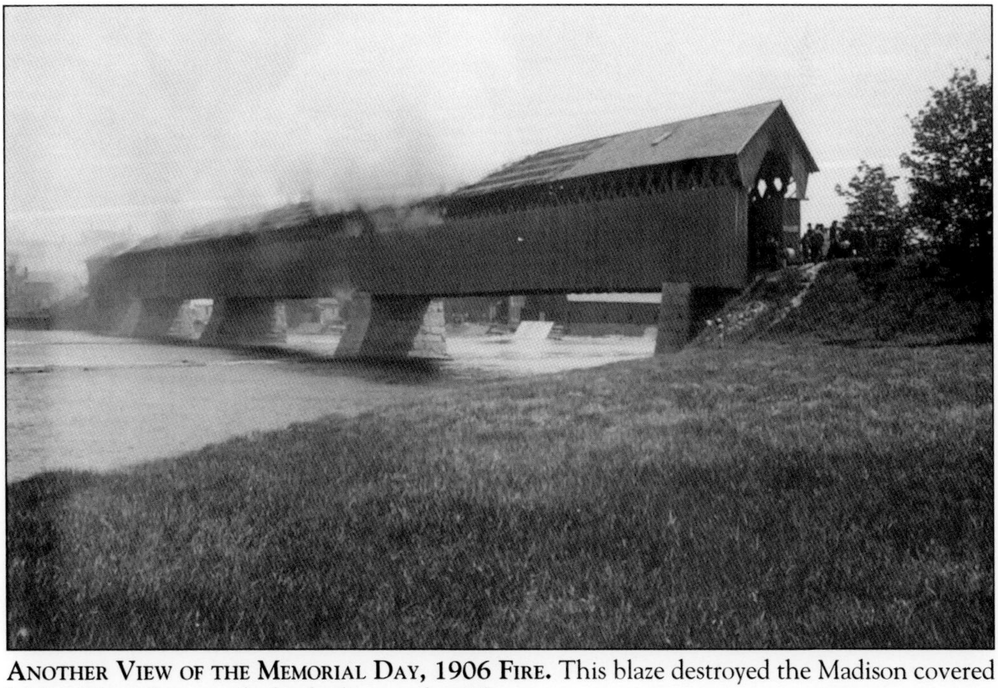

Another View of the Memorial Day, 1906 Fire. This blaze destroyed the Madison covered bridge. Note the crowd of onlookers at the right.

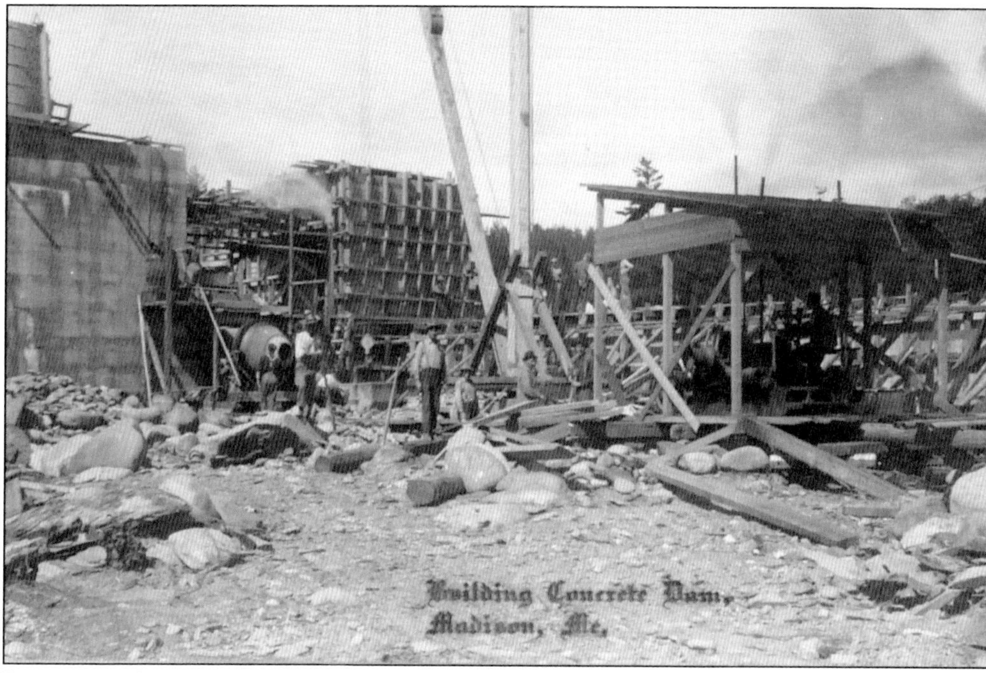

BUILDING A CONCRETE DAM ON THE KENNEBEC AT MADISON, C. 1900S.

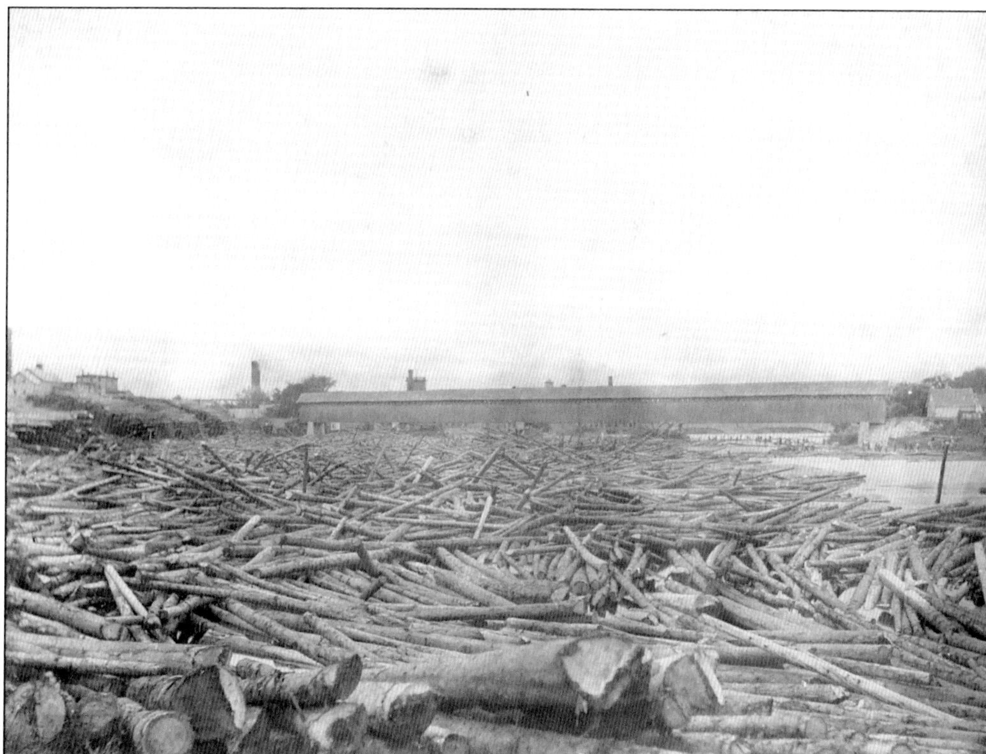

LOGS ON THE KENNEBEC RIVER AT MADISON IN THE 1890S OR EARLY 1900S BY THE RAILROAD COVERED BRIDGE.

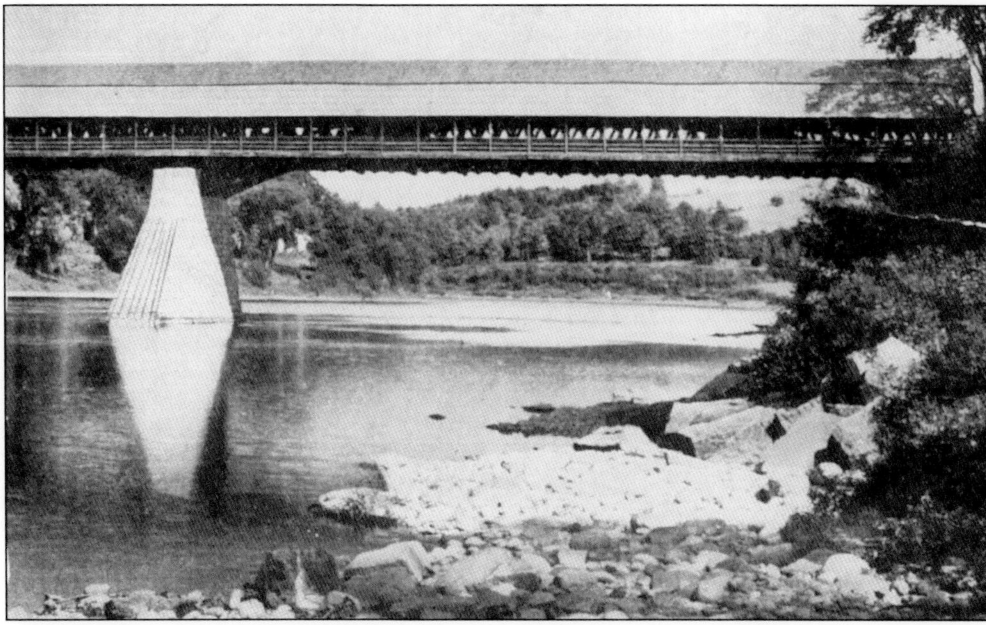

NORRIDGEWOCK TOLL COVERED BRIDGE OVER THE KENNEBEC IN THE 1890S.

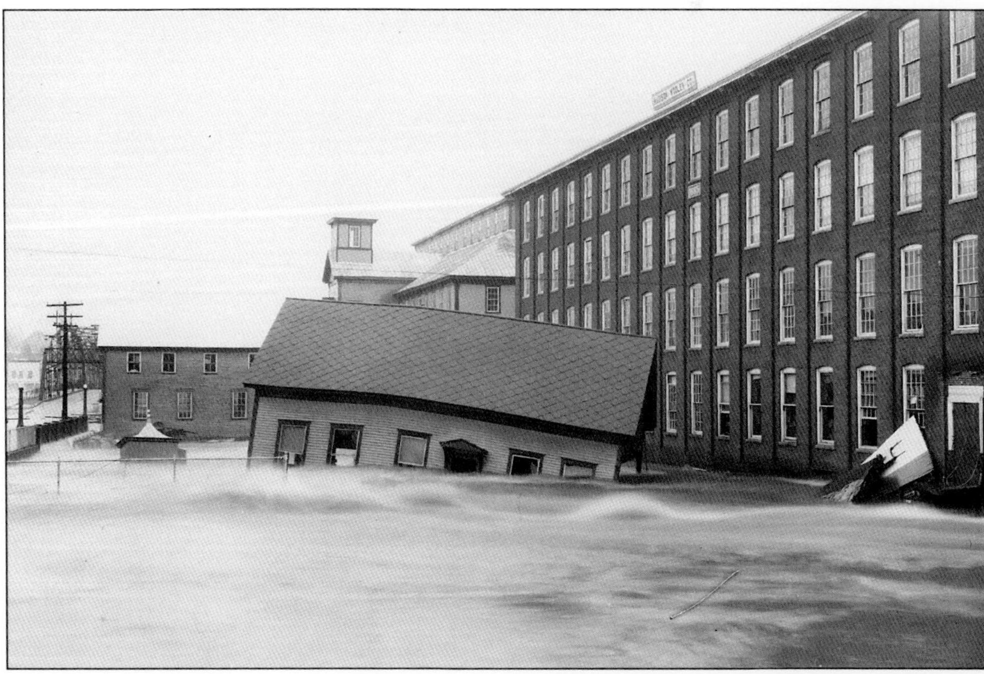

THE GREAT 1936 FLOOD OF THE KENNEBEC. In this photograph, we see the water striking the Madison Woolen Company. A small building by the mill is being swept away.

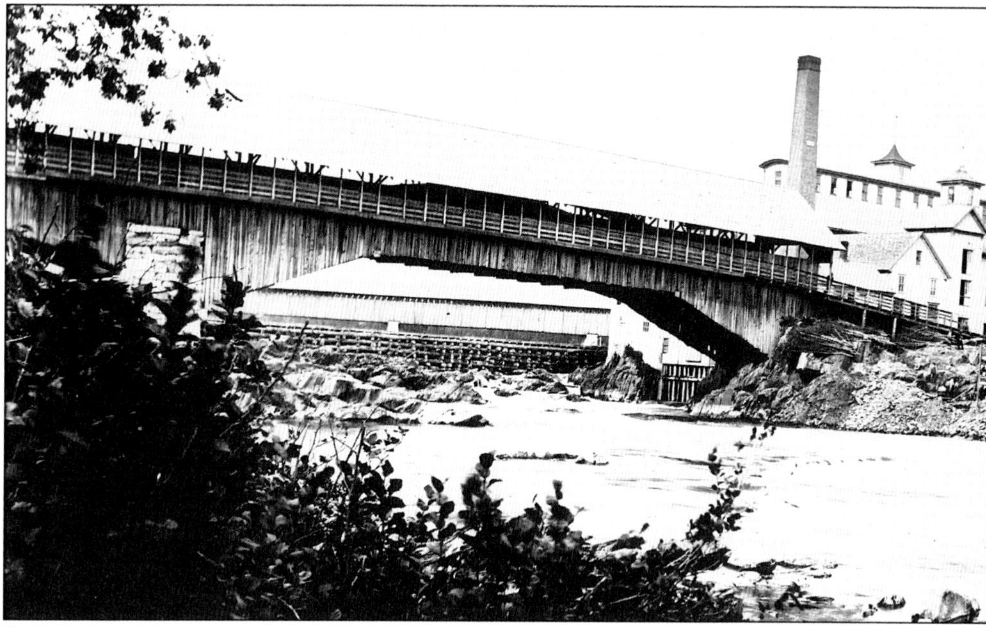

COVERED BRIDGE OVER THE KENNEBEC BETWEEN MADISON AND ANSON, C. 1910S.

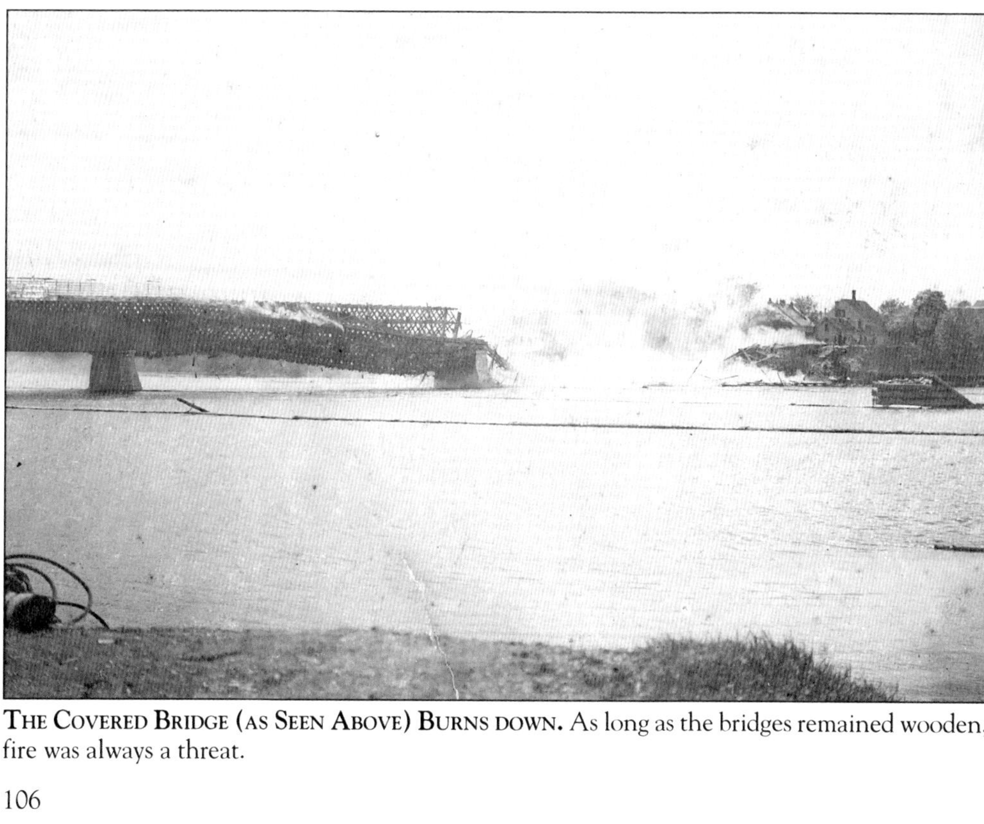

THE COVERED BRIDGE (AS SEEN ABOVE) BURNS DOWN. As long as the bridges remained wooden, fire was always a threat.

Eight

Leisure Time and Recreation

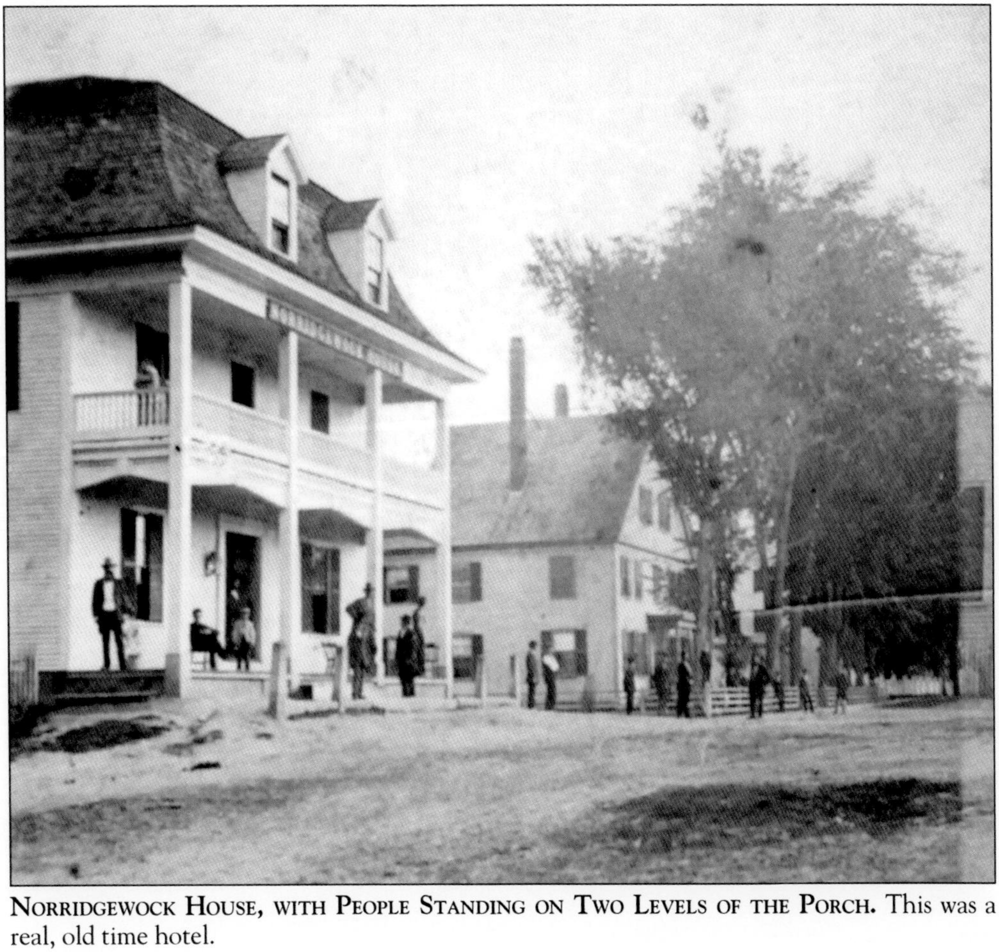

Norridgewock House, with People Standing on Two Levels of the Porch. This was a real, old time hotel.

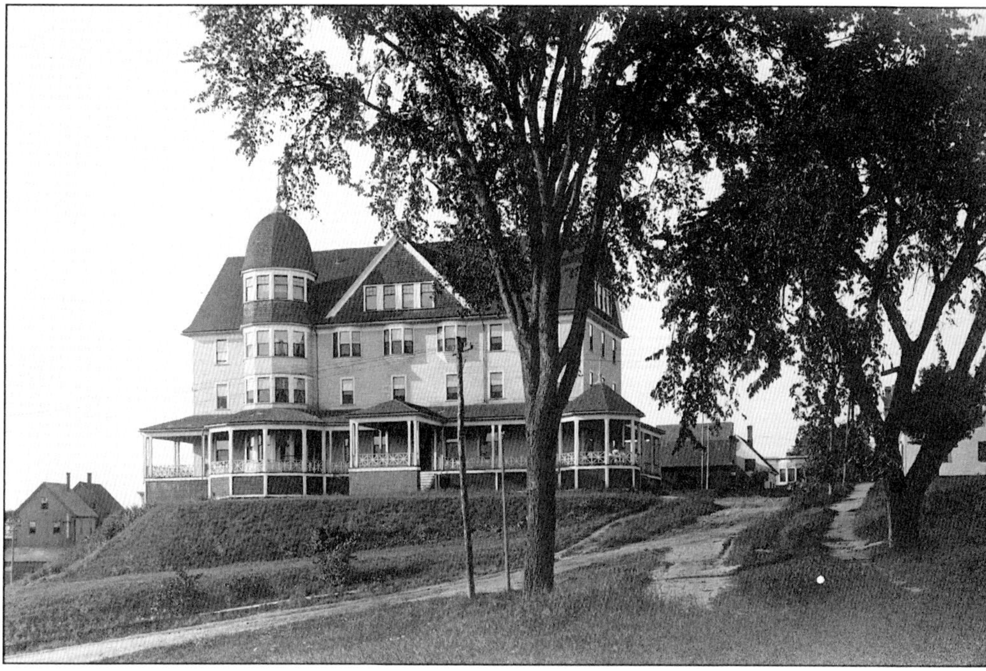

Hilton House in Madison, c. 1900s.

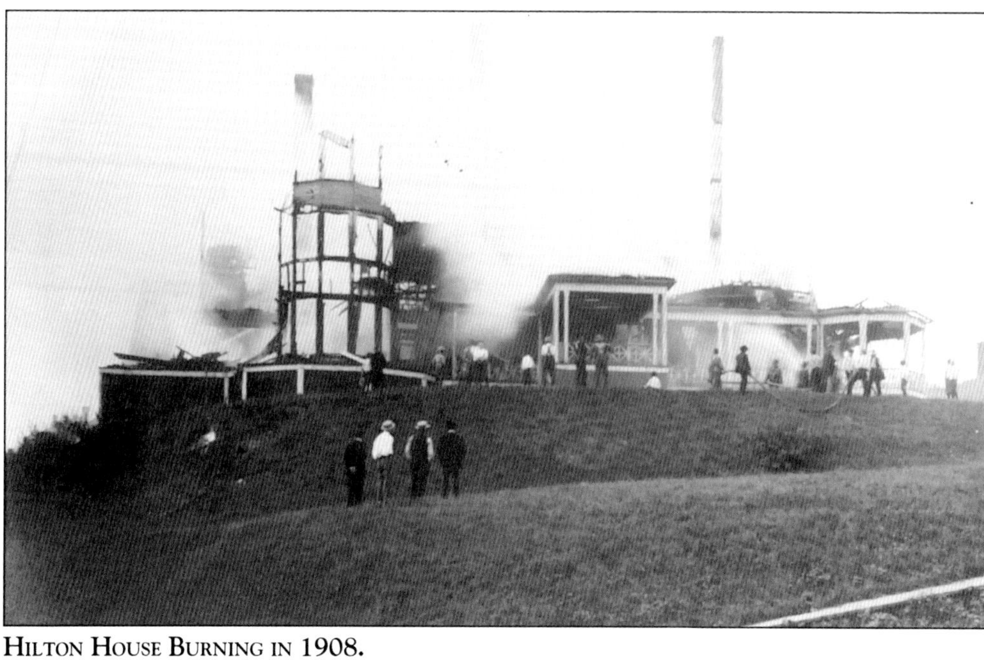

Hilton House Burning in 1908.

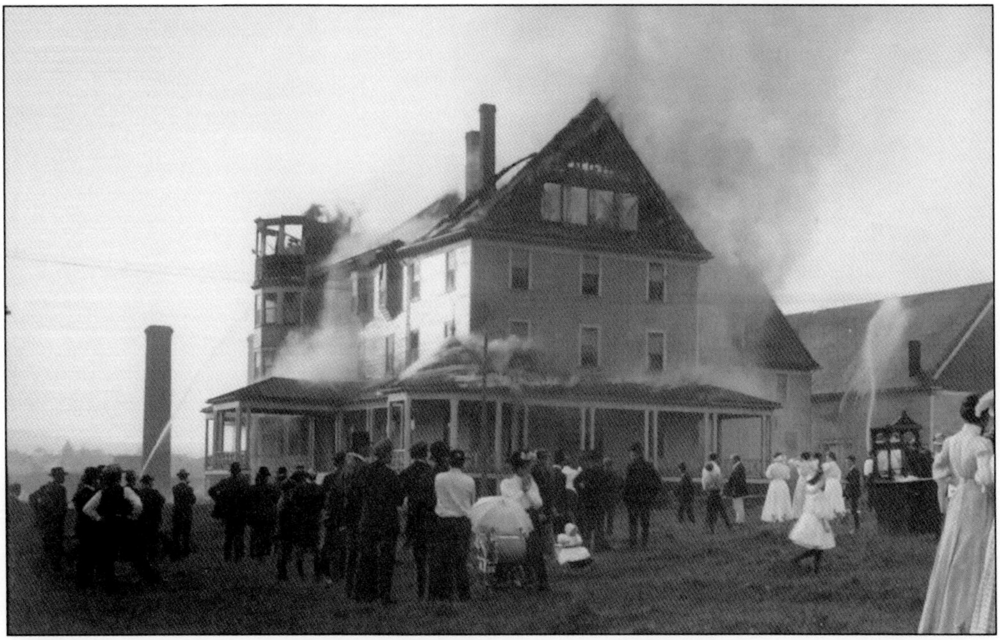

A Different View of the Hilton House Fire.

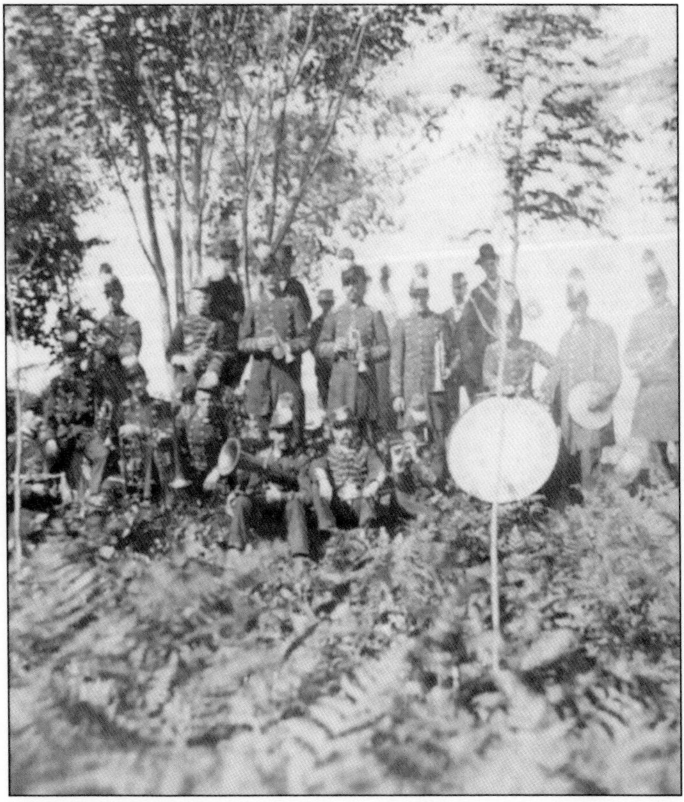

Norridgewock Cornet Band, c. 1890s.

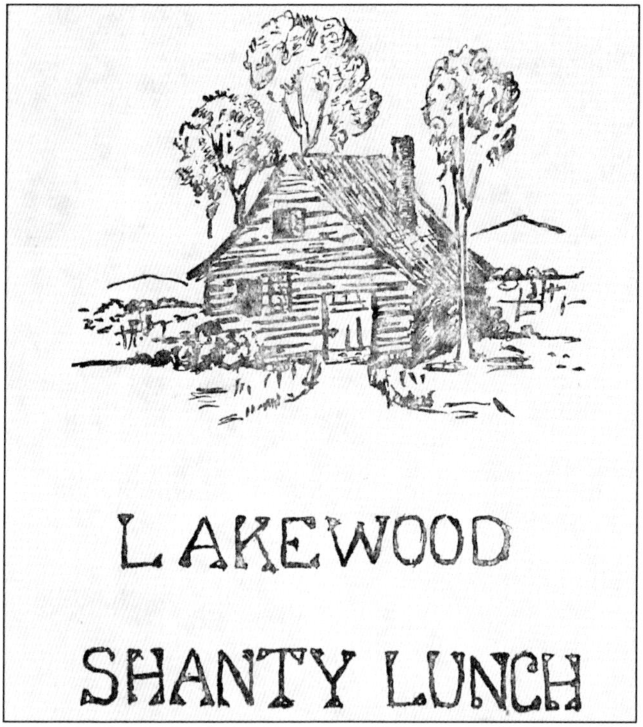

JUNIOR CLASS OUTING OF MADISON HIGH SCHOOL. The outing was held at Lakewood Shanty Inn on June 3, 1935. A lettuce and tomato sandwich cost 15¢.

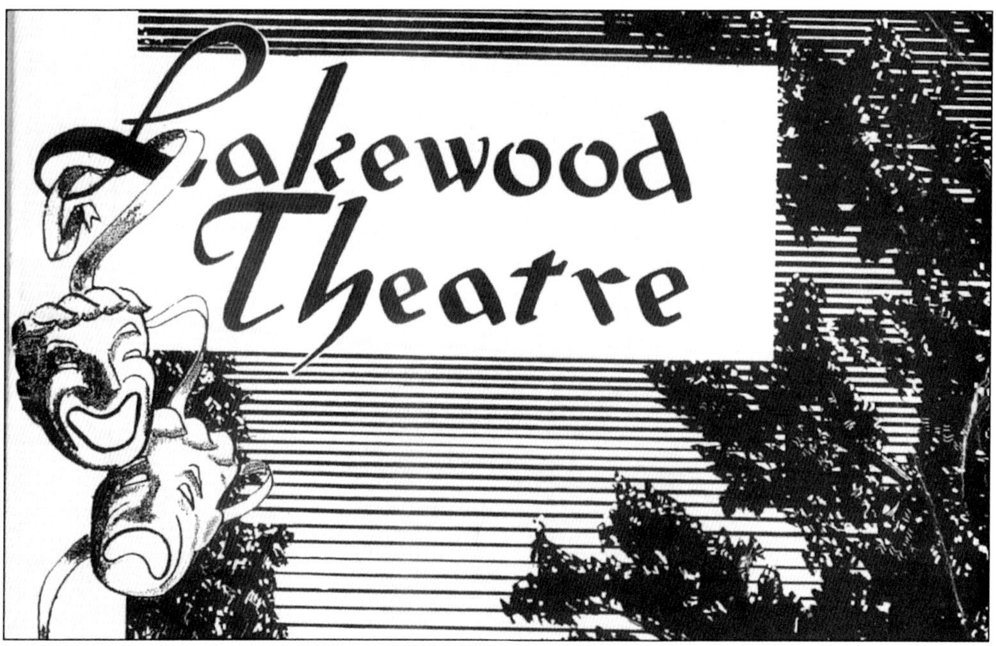

LAKEWOOD THEATRE. The theater is located a few miles from Madison Center but still in the town. This is a program for the showing of *Let Us Be Gay* during the opening week of June 4, 1949. It was Lakewood's 49th year. There was usually a resident company, but the best play I ever saw there was *The Four Poster* with that great acting husband-and-wife team of Hume Cronyn and Jessica Tandy. Lakewood had much more than just theater. There was an inn, a gift shop, bungalows, and a golf course.

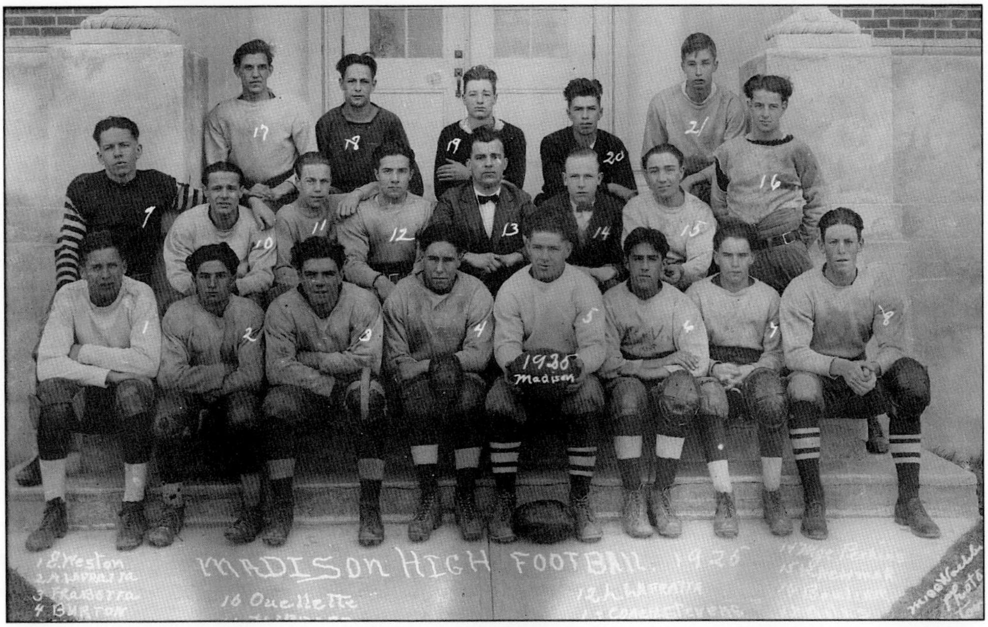

THE 1926 MADISON HIGH SCHOOL FOOTBALL TEAM. The members of the team are listed by number: l. Erlon Weston, 2. A. LaFratta, 3. Kicky Frabotta, 4. Burton, 5. Captain Andy Strang, 6. Venziano, 7. Snell, 8. Renier, 9. Giro, 10. Dom Ouellette, 11. Punky Hibbard, 12. L. LaFratta, 13. Coach Stevenson, 14. Manager Perkins, 15. Ratchrnar, 16. Beaulier, 17. Niles, 18. Leavitt, 19. Prey, 20. Lloyd "Bulldog" Harris, and 21. Weston.

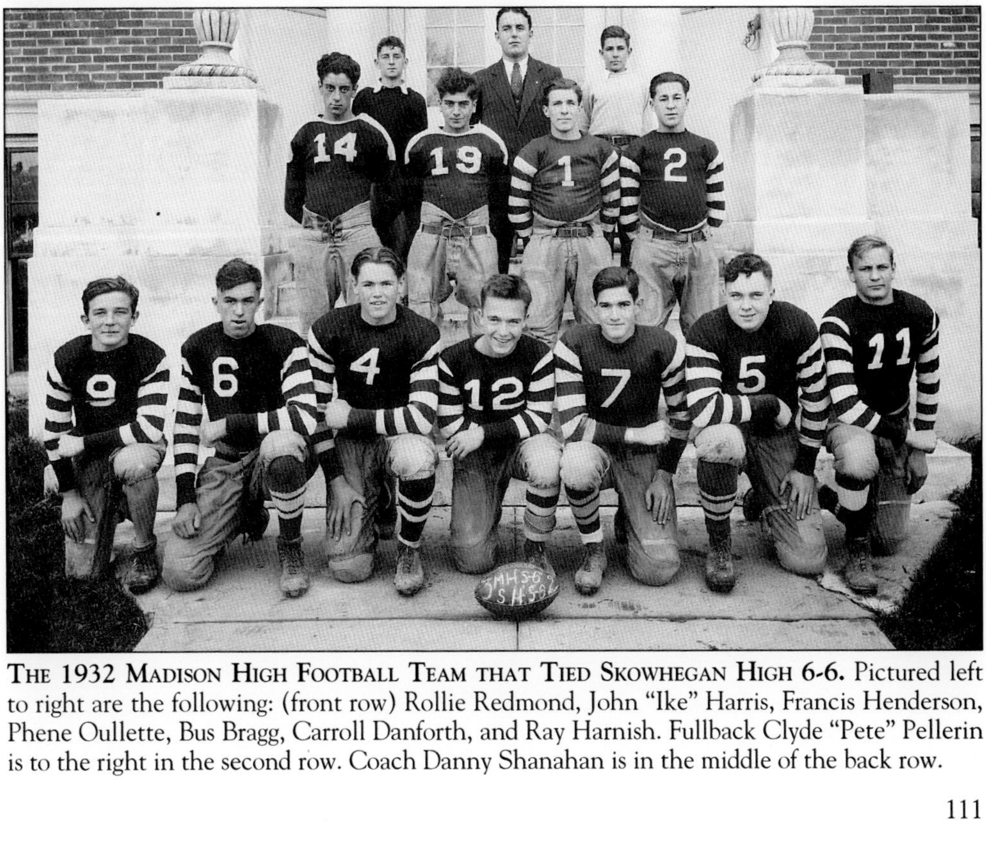

THE 1932 MADISON HIGH FOOTBALL TEAM THAT TIED SKOWHEGAN HIGH 6-6. Pictured left to right are the following: (front row) Rollie Redmond, John "Ike" Harris, Francis Henderson, Phene Oullette, Bus Bragg, Carroll Danforth, and Ray Harnish. Fullback Clyde "Pete" Pellerin is to the right in the second row. Coach Danny Shanahan is in the middle of the back row.

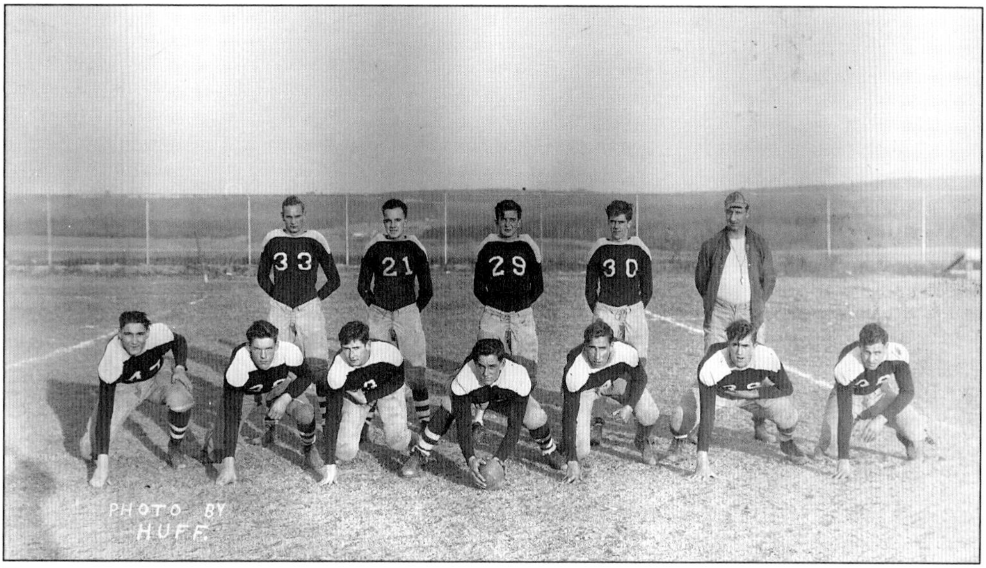

THE 1934 MADISON HIGH FOOTBALL TEAM. The school's team pictures were all destroyed in the recent fire there. Ike Harris is on the right in the front row, next to the end. Hal Harnish is on the right end in the front row, while Ray Harnish is on the left in the back row. Bob Savoie is second from left on the back row, and Rollie Redmond is third from left on the back row. The coach was Mose Nanigan.

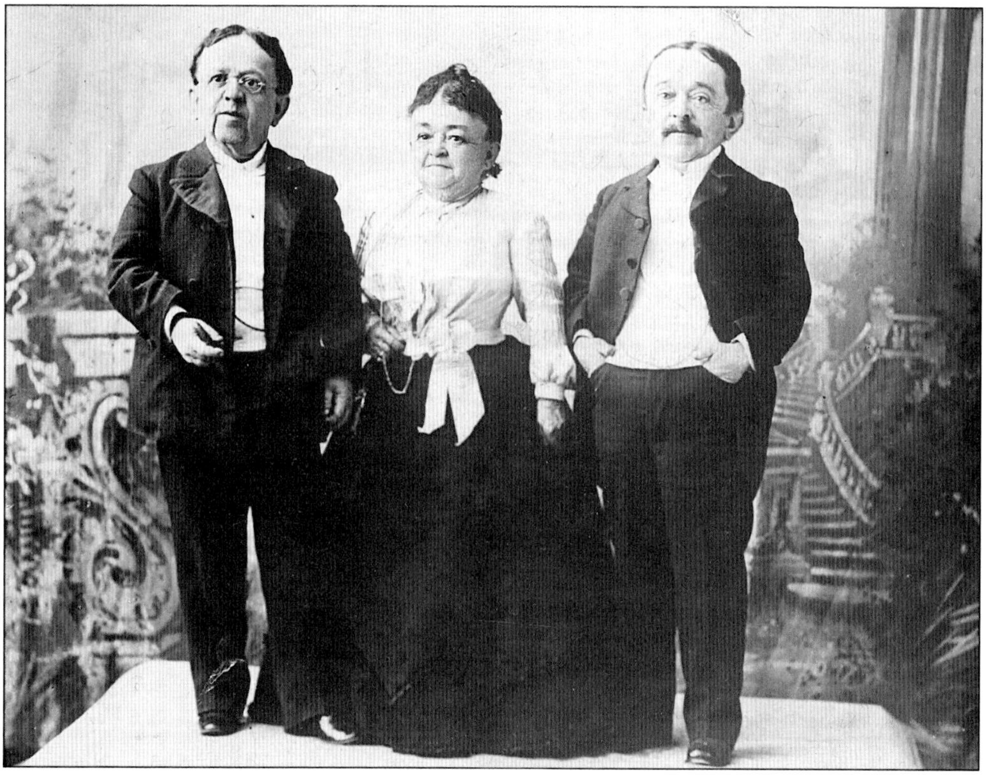

COUNT MAGRI AND MRS. TOM THUMB IN UNION HALL, MADISON. Here they are standing on a table about 1900. As far as is known, Phineas T. Barnum was not around.

PRIVATE TUTOR PLAY PROGRAM AT MADISON HIGH SCHOOL, C. 1913. The characters and those students who played them are as follows: Fred Spencer, who believes experience is the best teacher (played by Mayland Morse, Class of 1914); George Carothers, a chum who also seeks experience (Roy Heywood, '13); Mr. Spencer, Fred's father, who owned an oil well (Carold Brown, '13); Hans Dinklederfer, the private tutor (Merle Tinkham, '15); Richard, servant at the Spencers (Frank Cookson, '13); Mrs. Spencer, Fred's mother, who has social aspirations (Minnie L. Lister, '13); Dolly Spencer, Fred's sister, who has a mind of her own (Doris Carpenter, '13); and Miss Snap, a detective (Marian Shaw, '14). The Madison High School Dramatic Club put on the play.

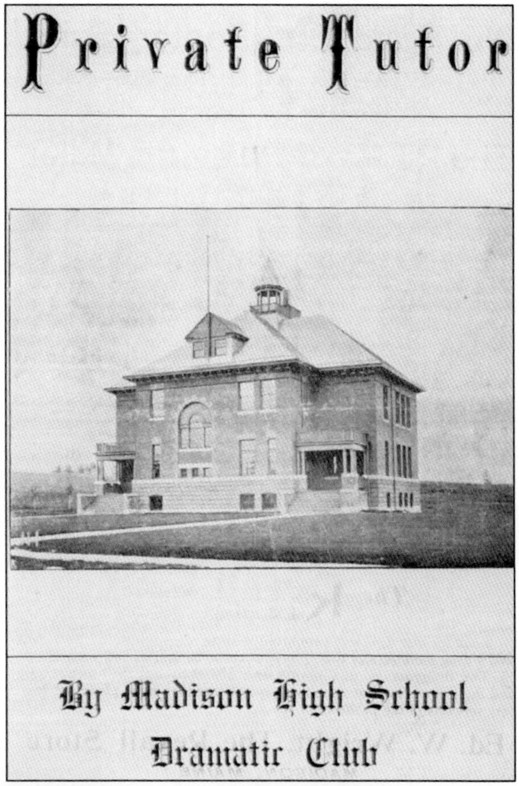

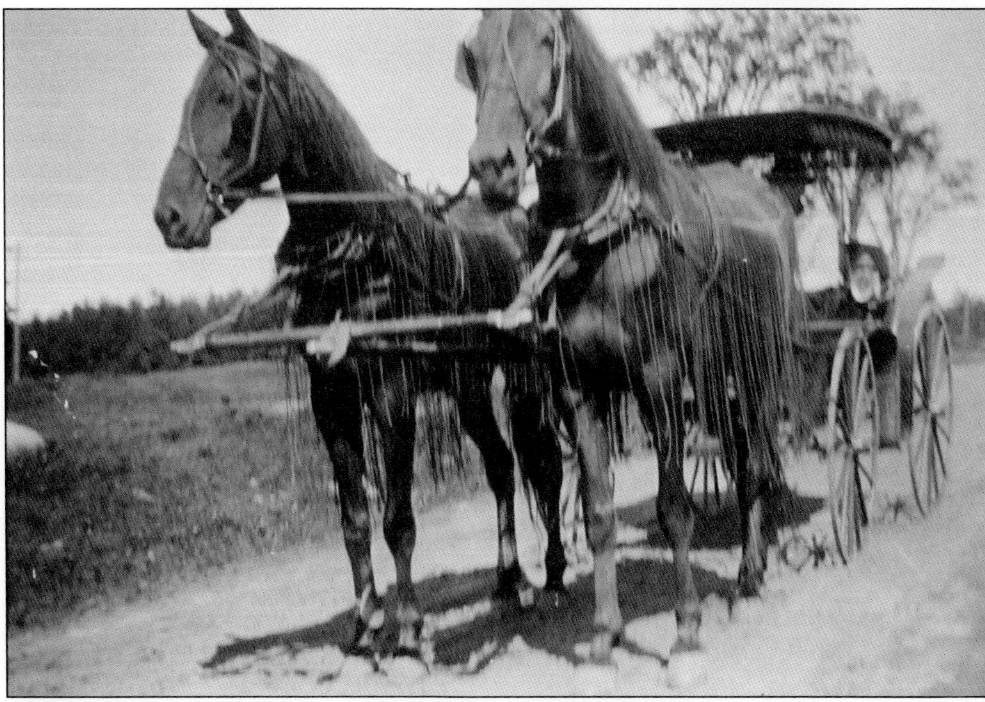

CHARLES WILBER'S FAMILY ON ITS WAY TO COPLIN PLANTATION INSIDE STRATTON, A 4-MILE TRIP. See the streamers on the harness holding the horses to the buggy?

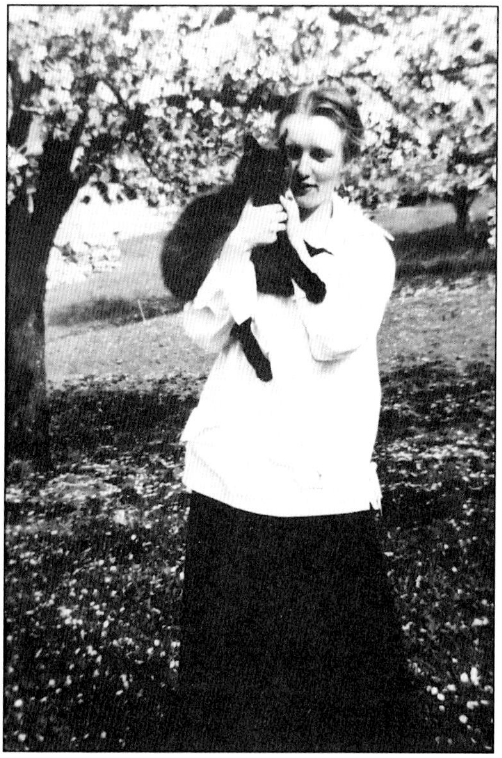

Erma Wilber of Madison and Her Black Cat. Is that a flowering apple tree?

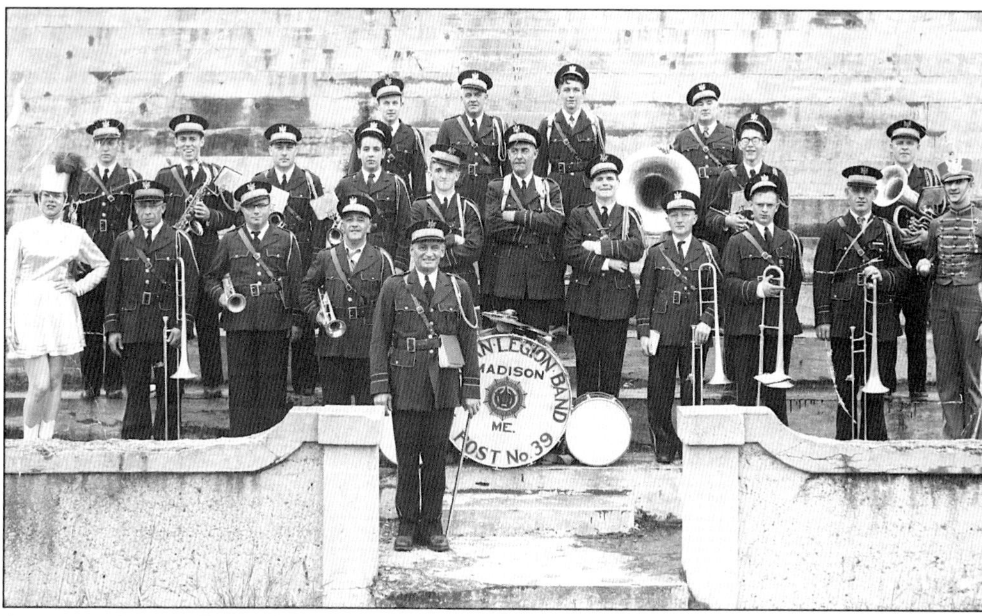

American Legion Band, Post 39, Madison, c. 1930s. The band leader, Wilfred Deschenes, is in front. Pictured from left to right are the following: (first row) Kay Turcotte (majorette), Lester Starbird, Nunzie LaFratta, Julian Venziano, Frank Foster, Robert Starbird, Edgar Strang, and Elwood Bearor (drum major); (second row) Paul Murray, Robert Savage, Merealden Corson, Leo Poirier Jr., Roger Snell Jr., Levi Sawyer, Roger Snell Sr., Peter Brown, and Wilmot Strang; (third row) Fred Taylor, Percy Houle, Donald Sawyer, and Elmer Russell.

FIREMEN'S MUSTER ON JULY 4, 1954, IN MADISON BY THE OLD WOOLEN MILL.

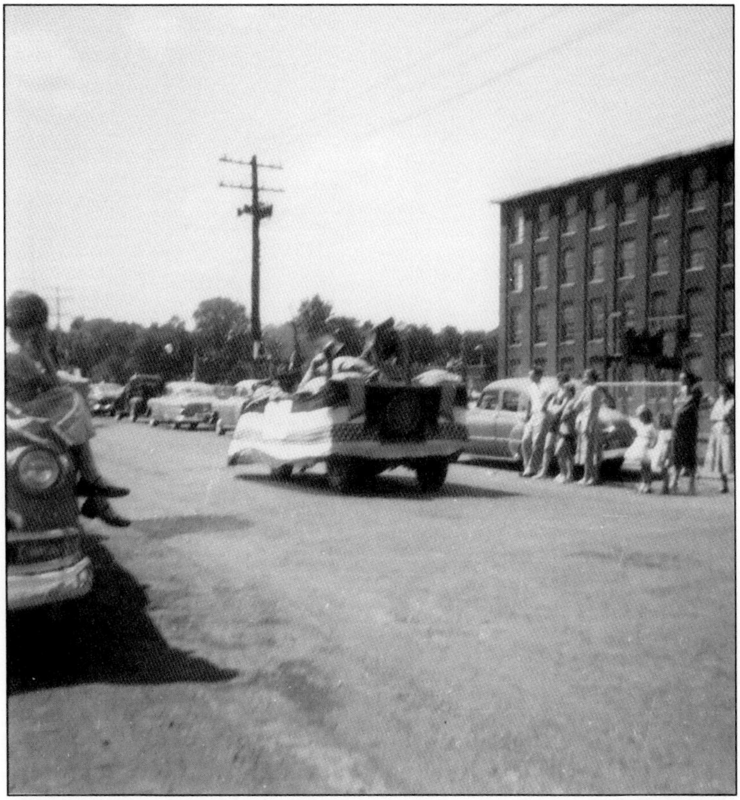

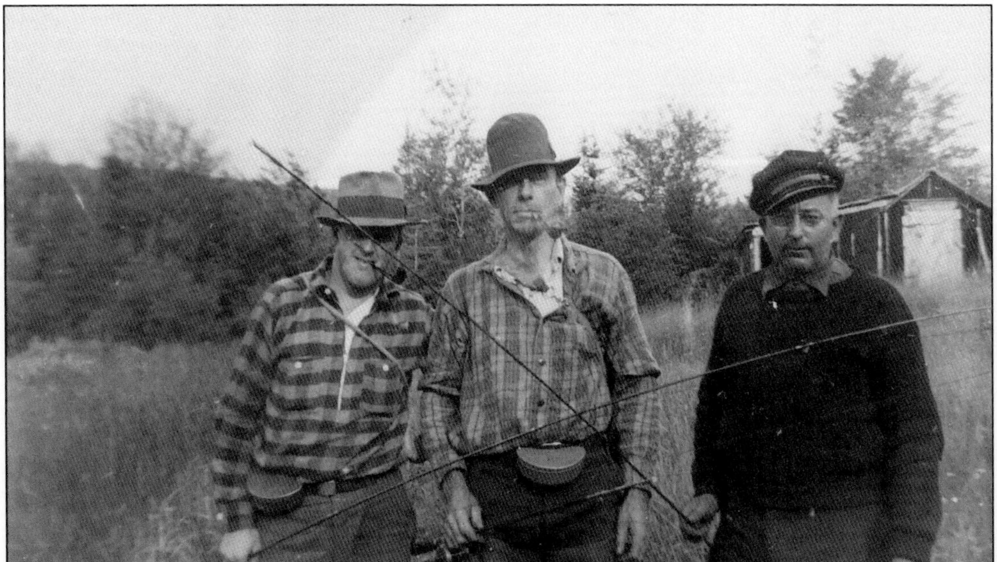

MEL FRAIN (WHO OWNED A GROCERY STORE), DON DYER, AND ULMONT STANLEY (WHO OWNED STANLEY'S GARAGE ON MAIN STREET, NORRIDGEWOCK). The trio have their fishing rods ready for a trip in 1945.

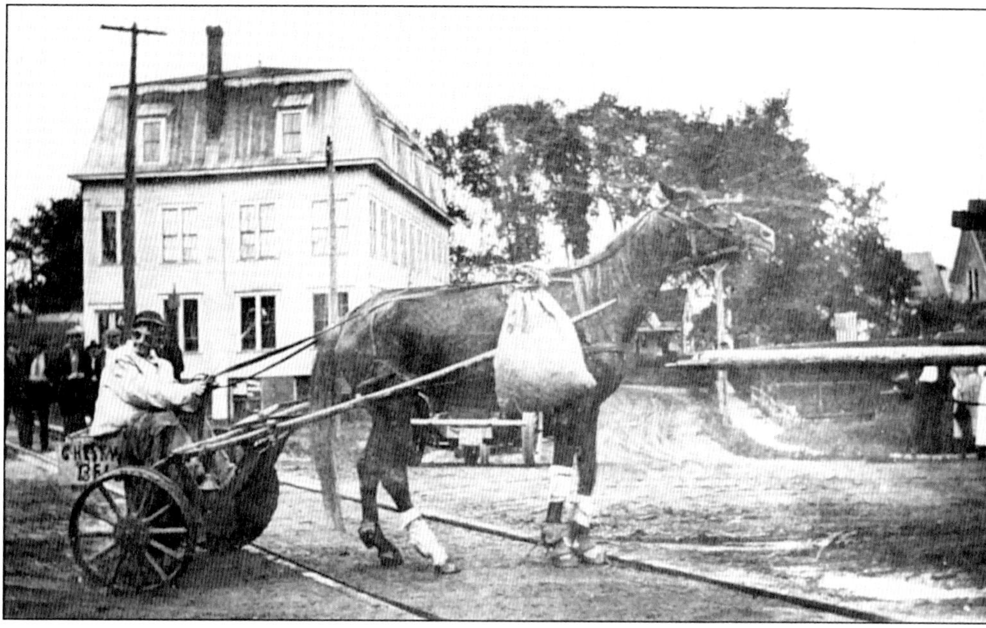

Norman Keene of Norridgewock. Keene is seen here driving his two-seater cart and was known to love horses.

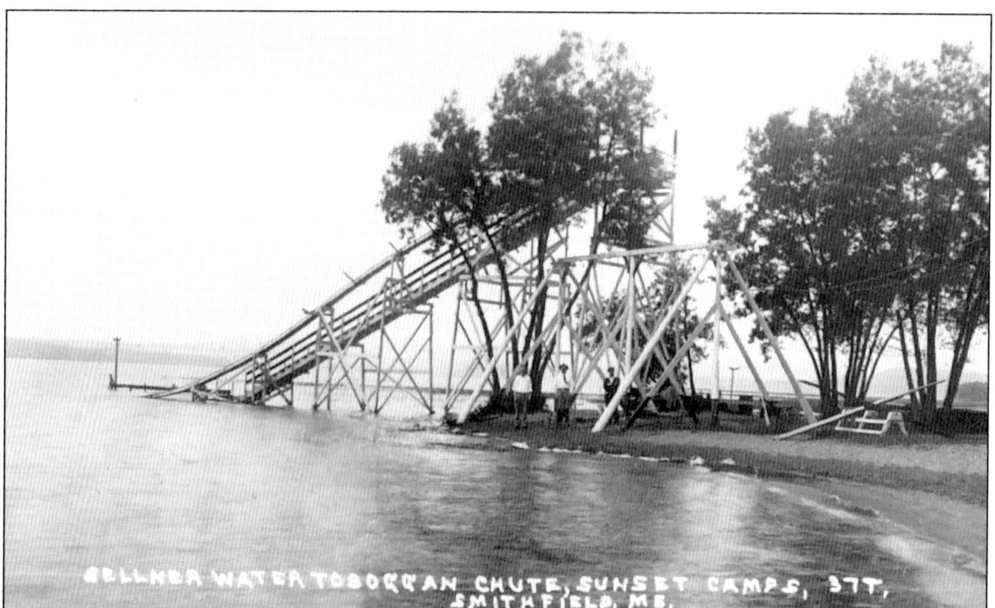

Sellner Water Toboggan Chute at Sunset Camps on North Pond in Smithfield, c. 1920s.

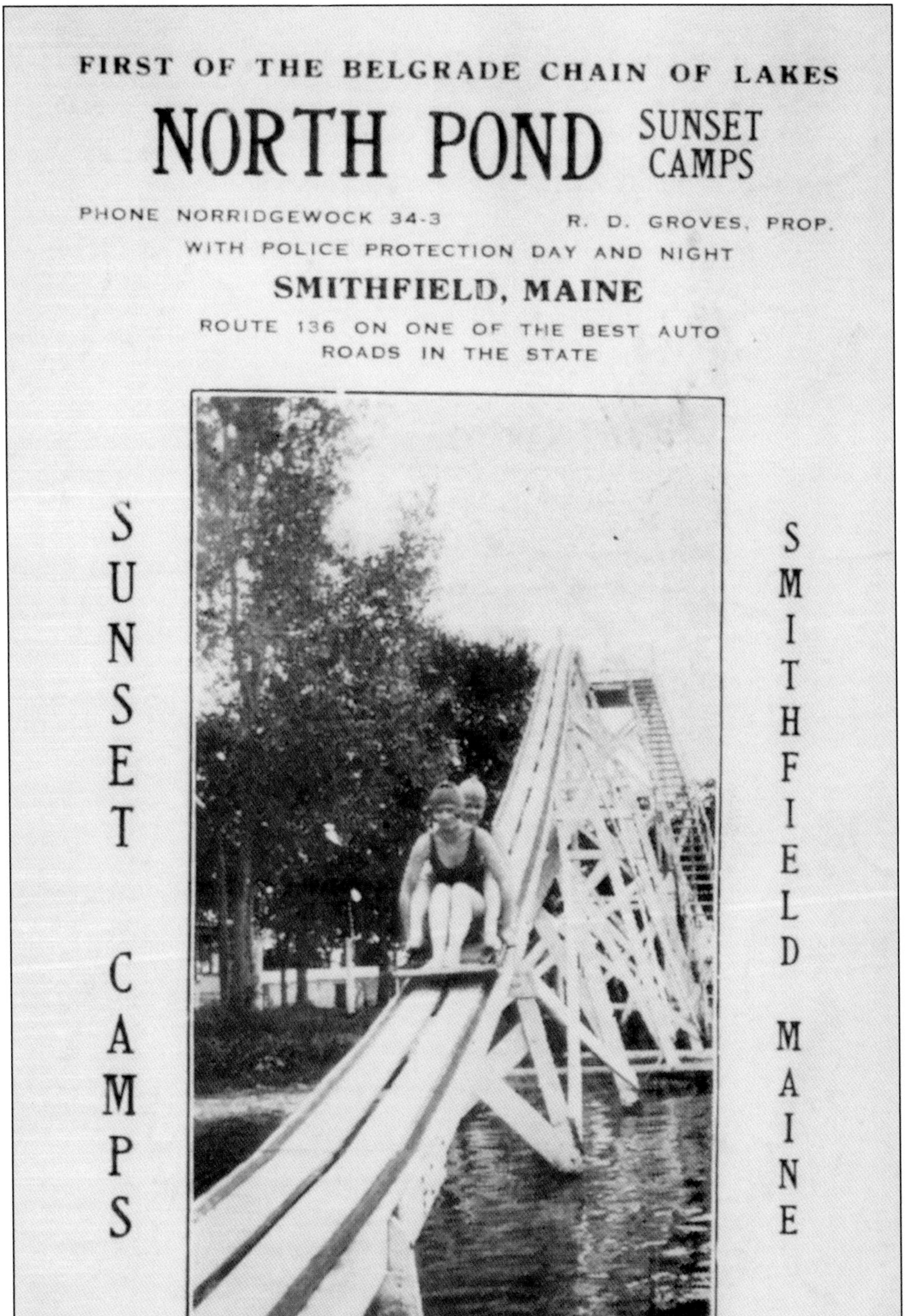

FRONT VIEW OF TWO ON THE CHUTE'S SLIDE, C. 1920S.

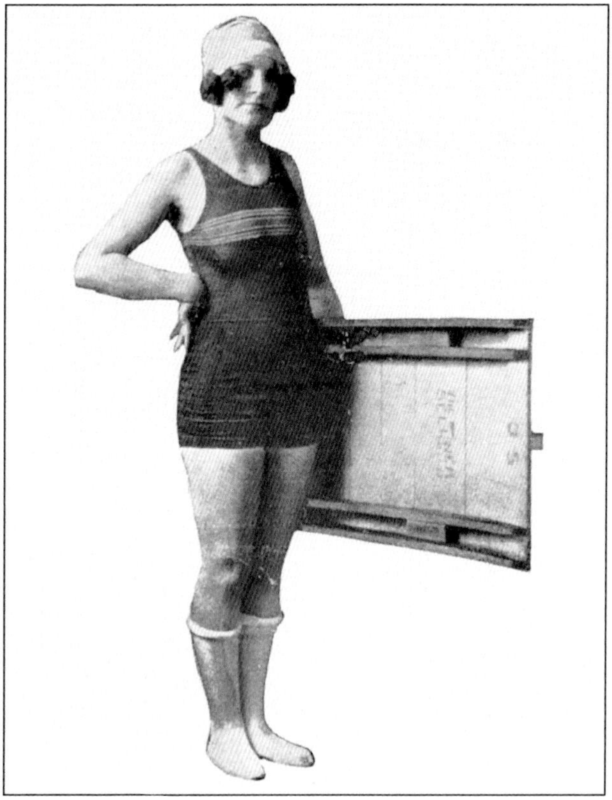

NORTH POND, SMITHFIELD. This is not the *Sports Illustrated* swimsuit issue. This style could be seen at Sunset Camps on North Pond, Smithfield, in the 1920s.

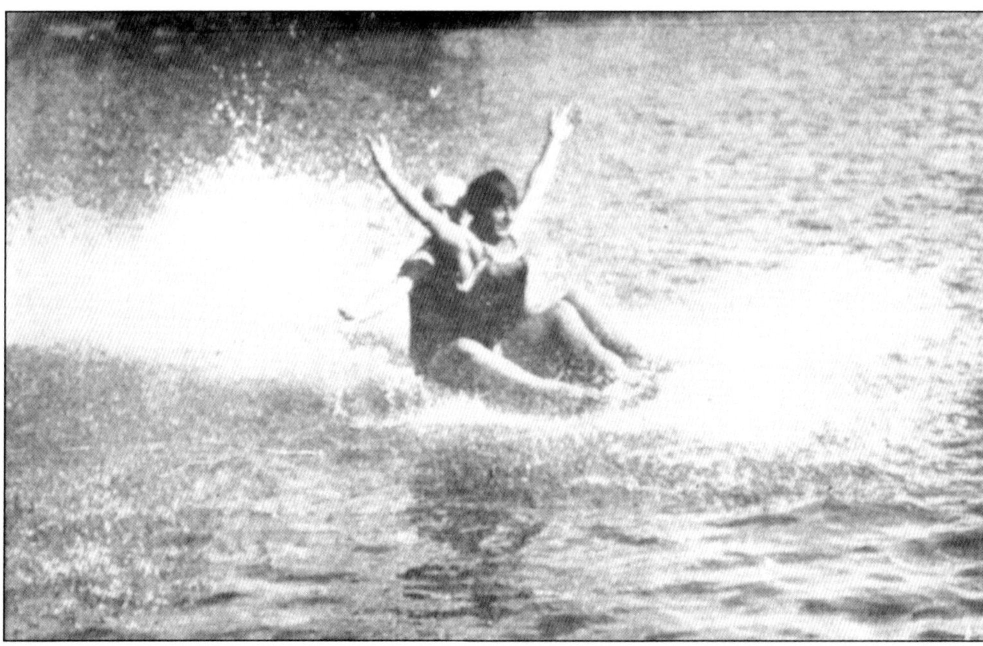

END OF THE RIDE FOR TWO WOMEN ON THE CHUTE IN THE 1920S.

Nine

Doers and Shakers

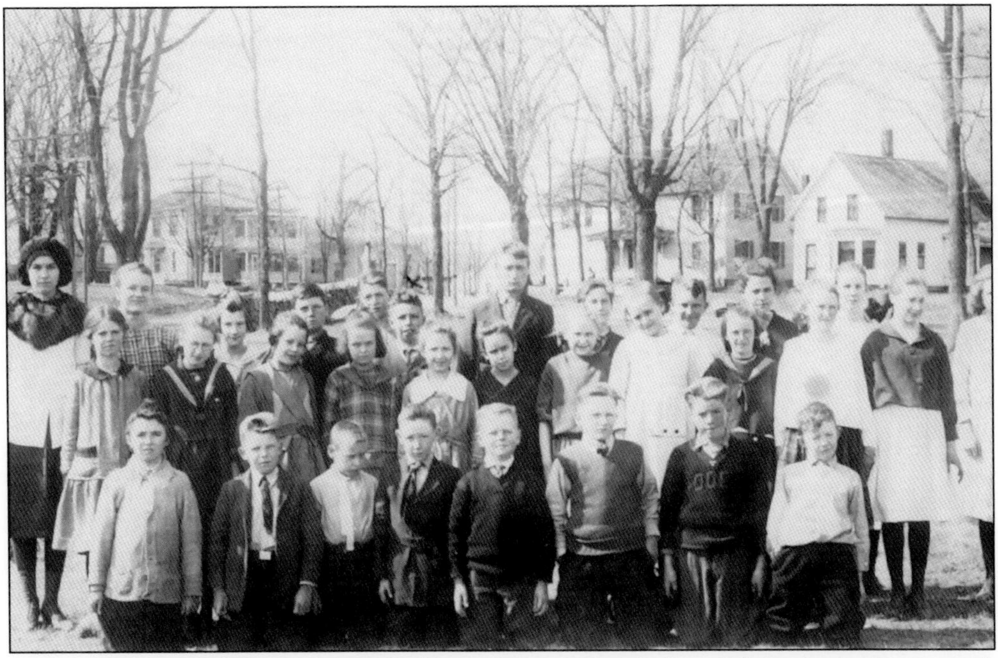

LLOYD "BULLDOG" HARRIS, C. 1920. Harris (pictured sixth from left in the back row, with the "x" over his head) went on to become a purchasing agent for Johnson and Johnson in New Brunswick, New Jersey.

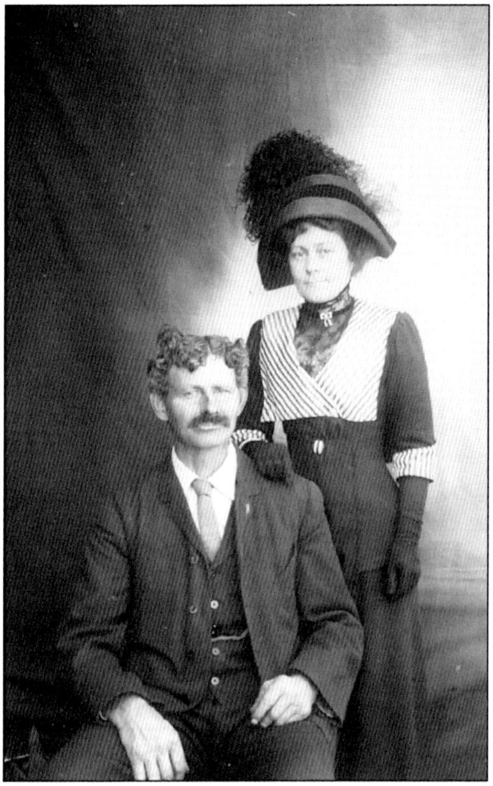

Charles Fuller of Norridgewock and His Wife, Esther, in the Early 1900s. Look at her ornate hat and his high, very curly hairdo.

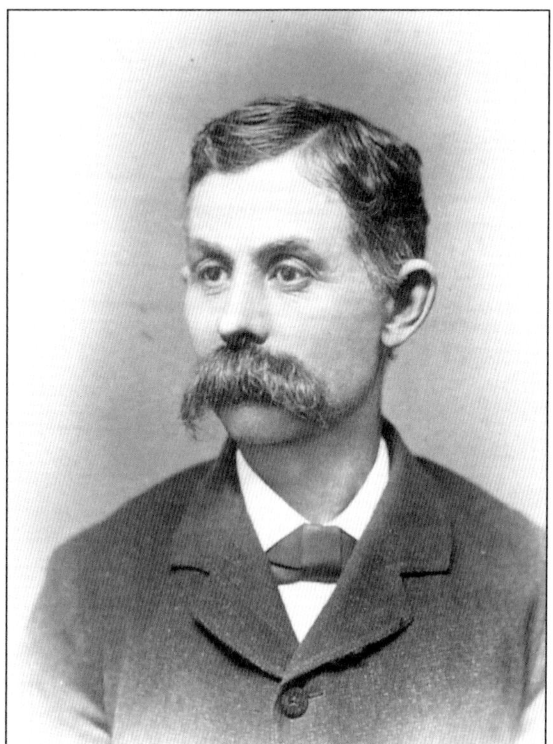

Charles Fuller of Norridgewock. He appears to be back on the straight and narrow with his hairdo.

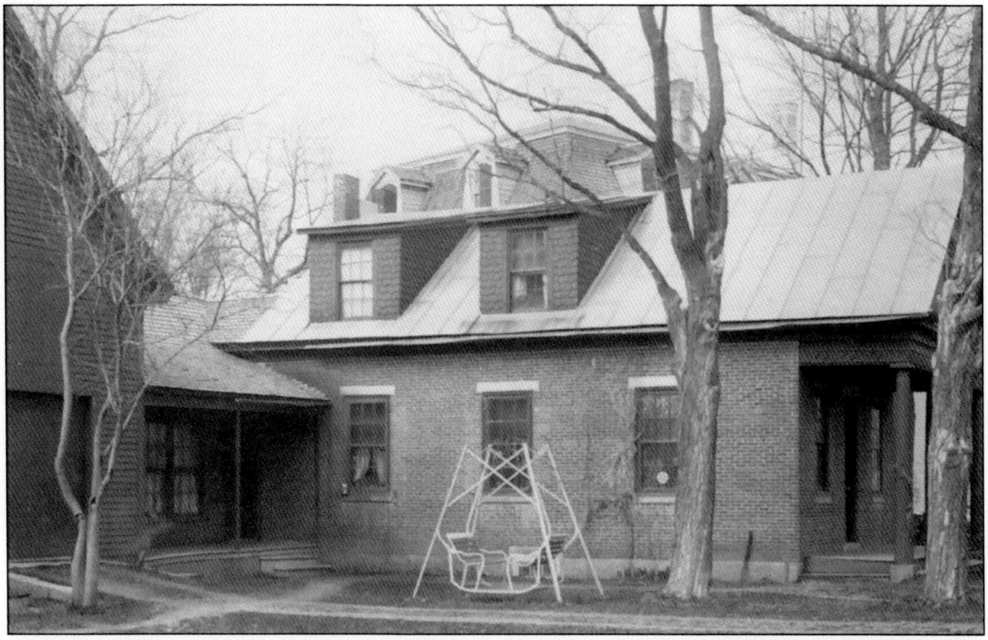

Dr. Walter Brown's Home in Norridgewock, c. Early 1900s. Eventually, the house was sold to the town for use by the Norridgewock Historical Society. The home was inherited by his only child, Linnie. Once, it had been the Female Academy. The building has very high ceilings in the living room, dining room, and kitchen. There is a twisted staircase with narrow treads.

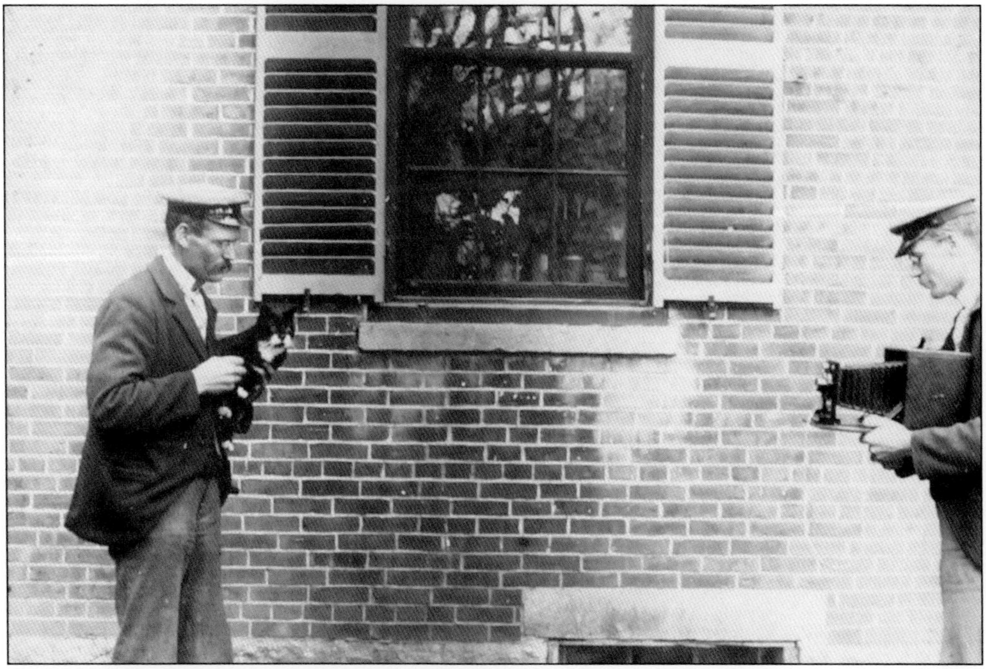

Dr. Brown, the Dentist. He was a talented fixer of almost everything. He could take trick photographs as this one shows. He interned with Dr. John Harris. Dr. Brown was the seventh son of a seventh son.

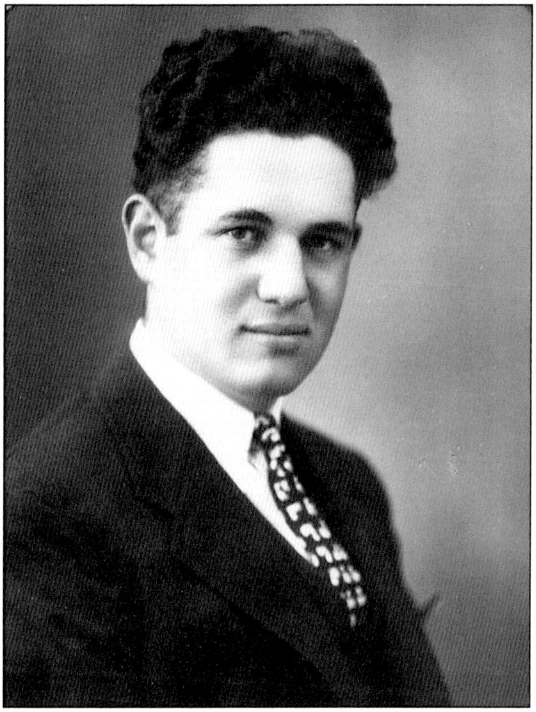

Ruel Blackwell of Madison. Blackwell's Hill, just outside Madison, was named after his family. There was also a Blackwell Block in Madison. Ruel was a University of Maine engineering graduate who worked many years for the state Department of Transportation.

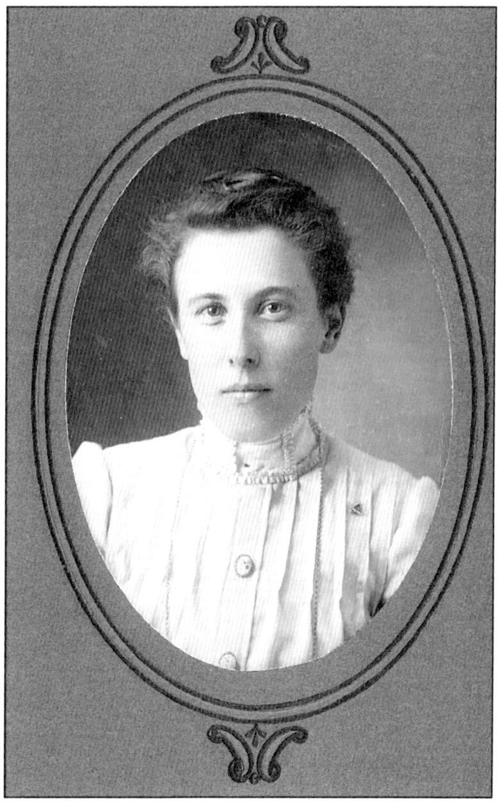

Blanche Wilber of the Prominent Wilber Family.

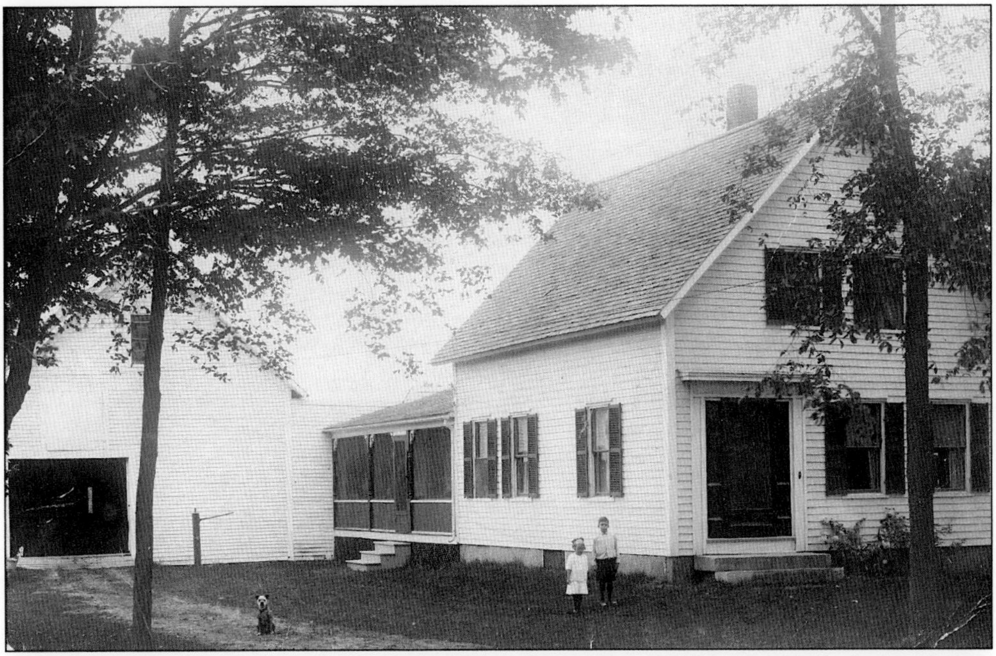

Philip and Esther Witham with Their Dog, Carl. Pictured here in 1916, the trio are in front of the Wallace Witham home on Mechanic Street in Norridgewock.

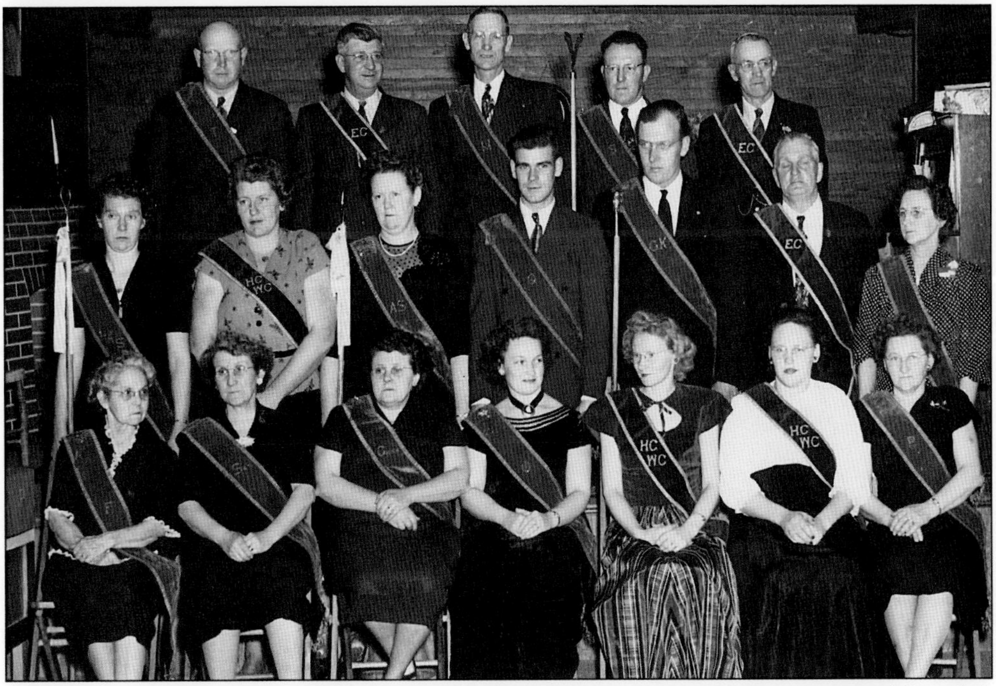

Members of the Smithfield Grange Drill Team in the 1940s. They are pictured from left to right as follows: (first row) Mabel Hartford, Bessie Hardy, Lillian Charles, unidentified, Doris Haines, unidentified, and Stella Stevens; (second row) three unidentified, Charles Haines, Cecil Jewett, Top Abbott, and Bessie Corson; (third row) Leon Witham, Robert Corson, Ernest Stevens, unidentified, and Luther Hartford.

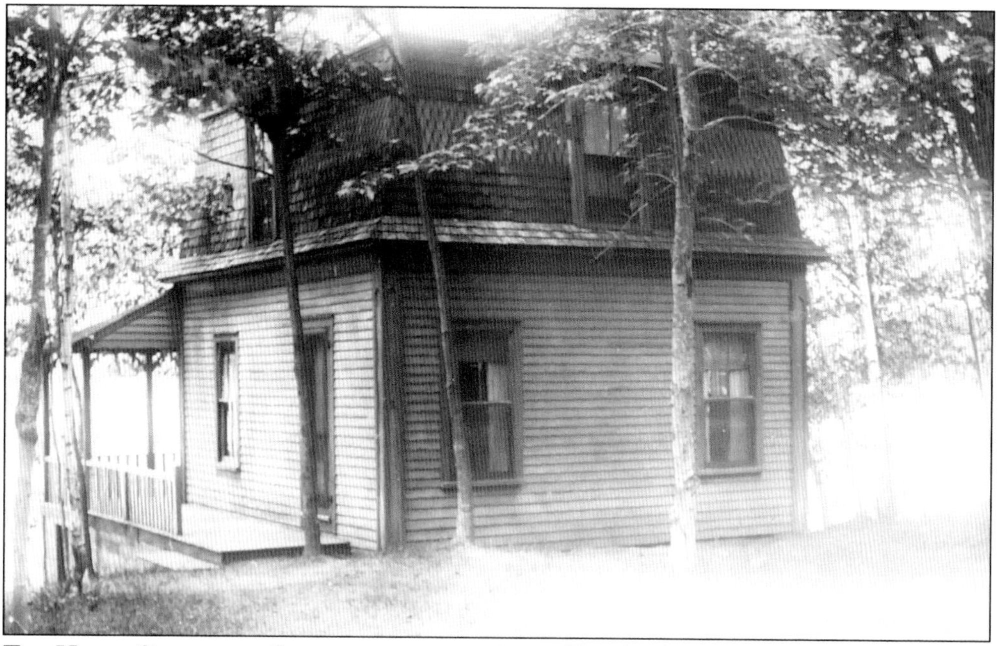

THE HIGHT COTTAGE IN SMITHFIELD IN THE 1920S. This family controlled several businesses in Skowhegan.

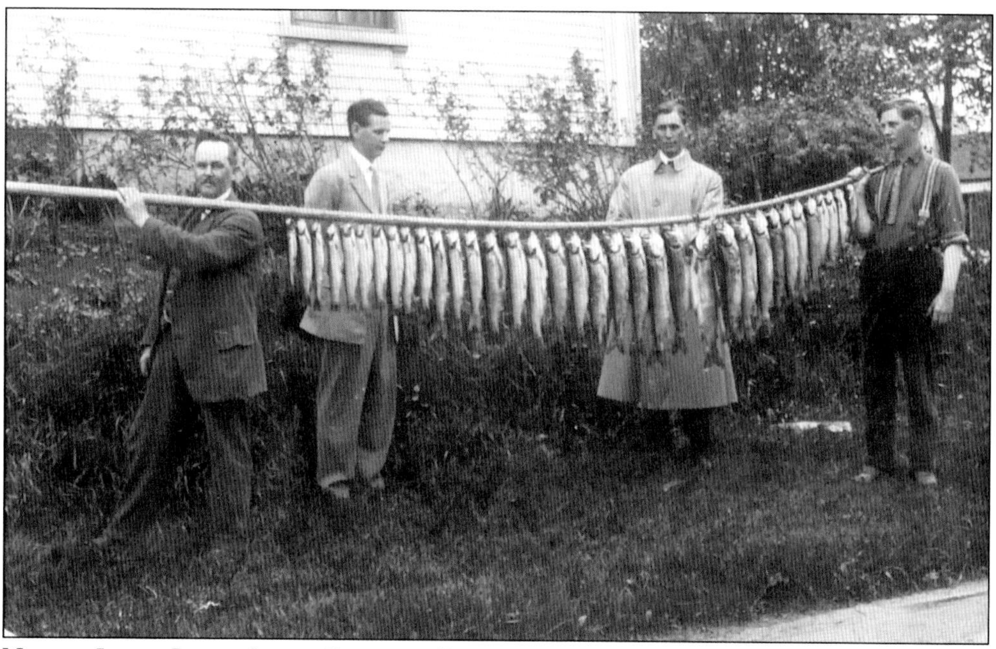

NELSON JONES, LEONE JONES, BENJAMIN EVERETT, AND CHESTER JONES ABOUT 1910. They have a catch of 35 fish, probably from North Pond. The four were from Norridgewock.

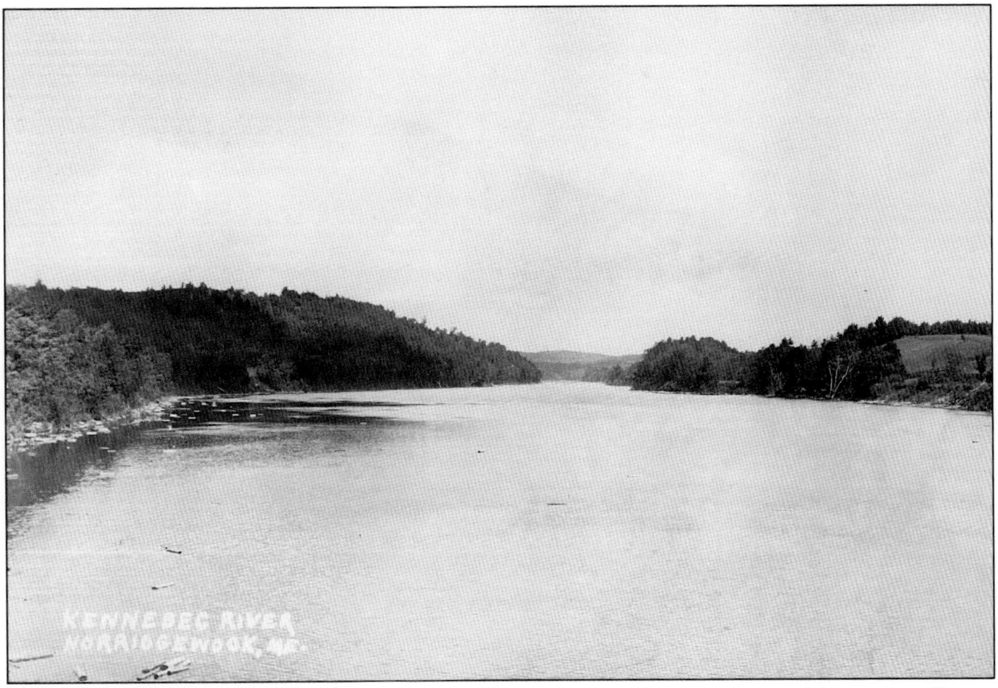

THE GREATEST ECONOMIC DOER AND SHAKER IN THE AREA—THE KENNEBEC RIVER AT NORRIDGEWOCK.

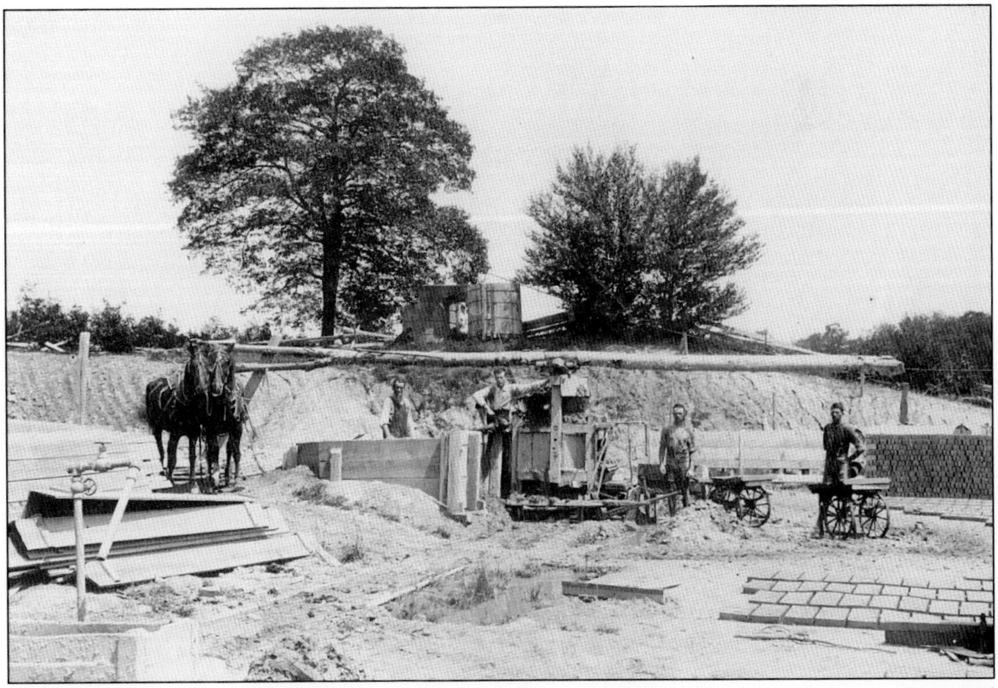

WINTHROP ROWELL'S BRICKYARD IN SMITHFIELD, C. 1900. There are horses, men, and machinery. You can almost feel the sweat on some of the workers.

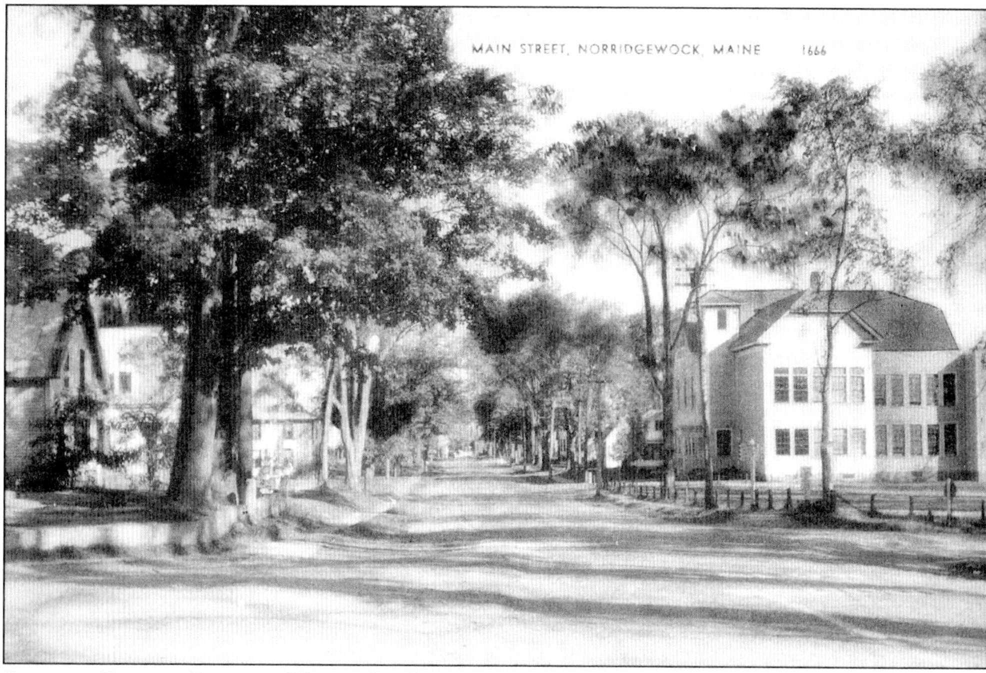

FORMER EATON SCHOOL. This school is a reminder of another man who did much for Norridgewock, Hamlin Eaton. The former Eaton School building is on the right in this postcard of Norridgewock's Main Street in the 1920s. By that time, the former school had become the Grange Hall.

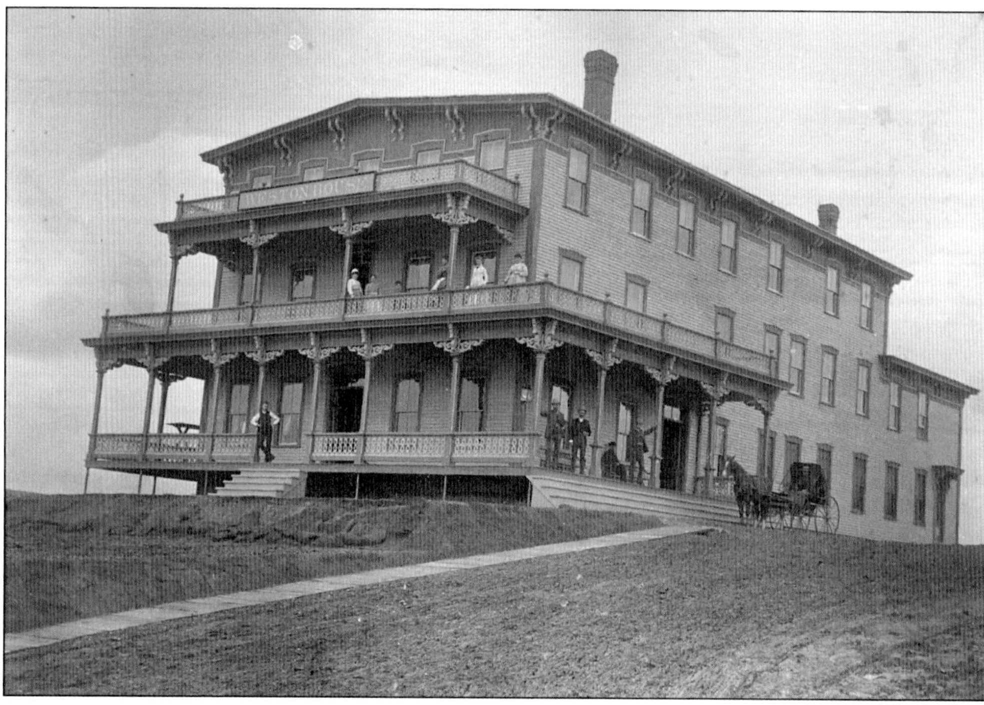

WESTON HOUSE IN MADISON, MAY 13, 1891. There are three levels of porches, with women enjoying the view on the second level.

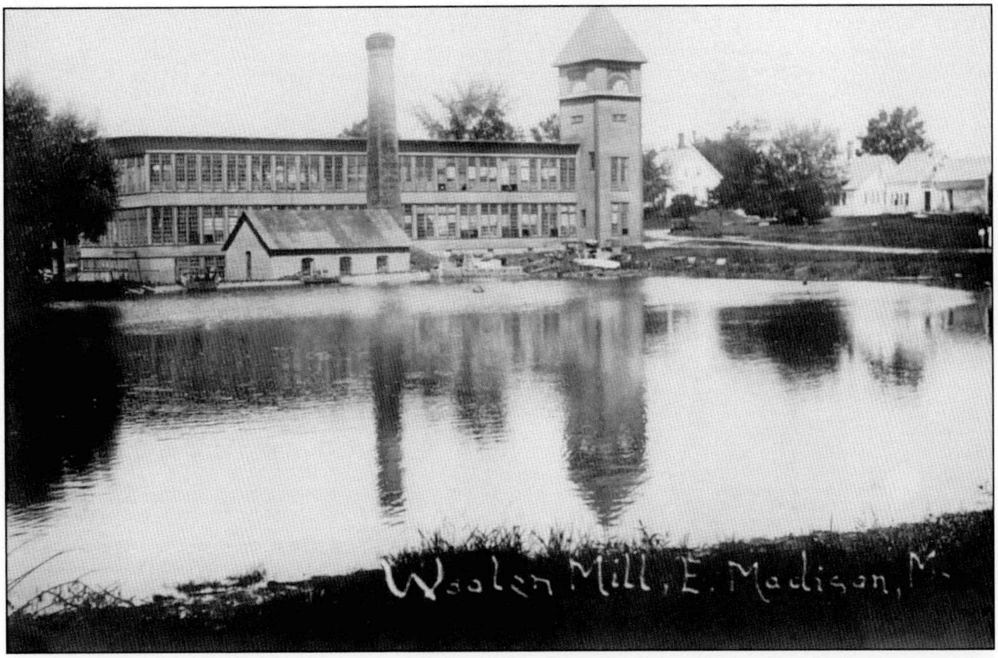

WOOLEN MILL IN EAST MADISON, C. 1900S. Manufacturing spread out from Madison into its nearby suburbs.

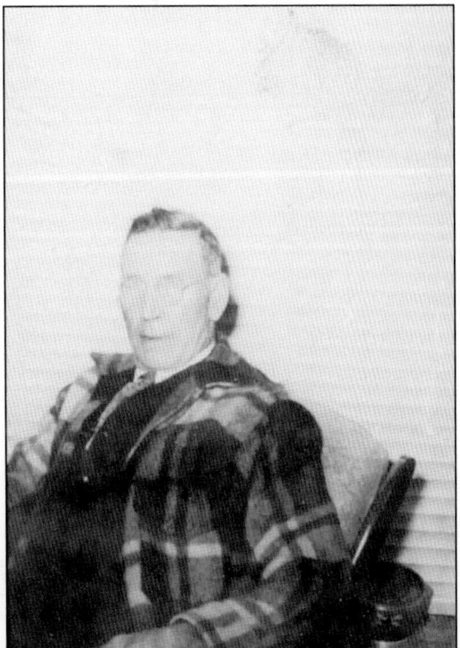

BEN EVERETT, NORRIDGEWOCK CARPENTER AND HOME BUILDER. Seen here in 1953, he built this Dutch colonial house for himself in Falmouth Foreside, Maine.

Acknowledgments

Far and away the most help on this book came from Mrs. Kay (John N.) Harris of Topsham. The idea for the project originated with her. Kay Harris supplied many of the photographs and gave me most of my leads into the three towns. I've known her for years. When I was business editor of the Portland papers, she and her husband used to drop in, usually with John's ideas on new power installations for Maine and northern New England. As it now has worked out, it looks as if John Harris was too far ahead of his time. At least some of his ideas would have helped this state greatly, especially with the shut down of Maine Yankee in Wiscasset.

In Madison, my principal sources were Irene Church, head librarian at the Madison Public Library, and Joseph Gill, chairman of the library's board of directors.

For Norridgewock, Mrs. Lucille Greer, president of a very active historical society, led me to Phyllis Barstow, the society's treasurer, and Elsie Stanley, its secretary, each of whom had treasure troves of photographs.

In Smithfield, Erla Merry led me to Bob Corson, who dug hard for some excellent photographs.

Once again, Earle Shettleworth, executive director of the Maine Historic Preservation Commission, provided a sturdy photographic foundation for this book. This included one photograph which arrived on my doorstep during part of the winter's gigantic ice storm. The image was rescued unharmed by me from its ice and snow covering.

I would also like to thank Jim McLoughlin of Brunswick, who has helped on several of my books.

As ever, in my 11th book for Arcadia Publishing, I'd like to thank the people there: Jim Burkinshaw, the executive vice president; Rebecca Heflin, my editor; and Jamie Carter, Michael Guillory, Becky Cooper, Laura Dearlove, and Caroline Wolfe.

—Frank H. Sleeper